CLANLANDS
ALMANAC

CLANLANDS ALMANAC

Seasonal Stories from Scotland

SAM HEUGHAN & GRAHAM McTAVISH

with Charlotte Reather

HODDER &
STOUGHTON

First published in Great Britain in 2021 by Hodder & Stoughton
An Hachette UK company

1

Copyright © Sam Heughan and Graham McTavish 2021

Recipes on pages 49, 109 and 199 kindly provided by Tony Singh (tonysingh.co.uk)
Clan badges drawn by Peter Liddiard (suddenimpactmedia.co.uk)
Maps drawn by Rosie Collins (rosiecollins.co.uk)
Illustration by Iain McIntosh (iainmcintosh.com)
Photographic endpaper design by David Eldridge at
Two Associates (twoassociates.co.uk)
Men In Kilts photography by Robert Wilson. *Men In Kilts* © 2020 Sony Pictures
Television Inc. All rights reserved. Artwork © Starz Entertainment, LLC.
Starz and related service marks are the property of Starz Entertainment,
LLC. All other images are care of the authors' personal collections.

A CIP catalogue record for this title is available from the British Library

Hardback ISBN 9781529372151
Trade Paperback ISBN 9781529372182
eBook ISBN 9781529372199

Typeset in Dante MT by Hewer Text UK Ltd, Edinburgh
Printed in United States of America by Lakeside Book Company

Hodder & Stoughton policy is to use papers that are natural, renewable
and recyclable products and made from wood grown in sustainable
forests. The logging and manufacturing processes are expected to
conform to the environmental regulations of the country of origin.

Hodder & Stoughton Ltd
Carmelite House
50 Victoria Embankment
London EC4Y 0DZ

www.hodder.co.uk

To you, dear reader, about to embark on this epic journey with us, through a heart-full Scottish year! I suspect we will get lost along the way, celebrate way too much, laugh, bicker yet praise the 'greatest wee country in the world' (though we are biased). Hold on to your hats, gird your loins and watch out for oversized haggis! X

– Sam

For all our families. The unbroken line of those who have overcome many hardships and offered great sacrifice to help all those who have followed. This book is for their history and for their precious gift of a future.

– Graham

PROLOGUE

GRAHAM

I love almanacs. I like their eclectic nature, the stumbling on fascinating facts and the opportunity to take meandering tangents into uncharted territory. This book is an exploration of Scotland, her history and people, interspersed with our personal reminiscences; one minute we'll be telling you about the time Sam got stood up outside a McDonald's by his date (he went to the wrong burger joint), the next we'll conjure the occasion Sam dangled me from a rope over the edge of Kilt Rock on Skye, whilst I desperately clung onto life, barely able to breathe.

Then, out of nowhere, Sam will recommend a Bevvy of the Month, as if to help get my blood up again, before I settle in to recount a bloodthirsty clan Battle of the Month, prompted by the time of year. And there's the odd recipe. Well, we couldn't do a book without food, could we? It's also a competition, charting our rivalry whilst filming *Men in Kilts*, as well as testing the limits of how much we can insult each other in writing and still remain friends.

For me, as with many Scots, the ability to give and receive insults is a true measure of both friendship and self-deprecation. By that standard, this book is a masterpiece of the sly dig, the robust rejoinder and the sharp backhand, laced with an exaggeration of the truth. So while reading it, three things should be at the forefront of your mind: every single piece of history is true, all the people and places really do exist, and everything else should be read with a substantial pinch of salt. But above all, I hope you enjoy it.

SAM
The above should be disregarded.
    Welcome to MY BIG BOOK OF SCOTLAND!

Clan Galloway
Motto: *Higher*
Lands: Galloway
Clan Chief: None, armigerous clan [*Sam: I would like
to think I'm the chief, having just found out my family name
is associated with Clan GALLOWAY! RALLY TO ME!*]

JANUARY

Auld Lang Syne
We two have paddled in the stream,
from morning sun till dine;
But seas between us broad have roared
since days of long ago.
Robert Burns , 1788

Clan Campbell
Motto: *Ne Obliviscaris* (Do not forget)
Lands: Argyll

KEY DIARY DATES

1	New Year's Day Hangover
	Loony Dook – Edinburgh New Year's Day swim
4	Graham James McTavish's Birthday (*Capricorn*)
5	Twelfth Night
11	Diana Gabaldon's Birthday
	National Hot Toddy Day
25	Burns Night
Late Jan–Early Feb:	Celtic Connections - a celebration of Celtic Music at The Glasgow Royal Concert Hall
Jan–March:	Up Helly Aa – Britain's biggest fire festival takes place on Shetland

GRAHAM

JANUARY. In some ways, the cruellest of months (except perhaps February, which we will get to in due course), unless you live in New Zealand where the sun shines bright and the days are long. But if you're a northern hemisphere baby, you are familiar with the crushing spiritual hangover that is January. December has pace and energy. The great build-up to Christmas – the lights, the shopping, the parties, the winter solstice. It all combines to give December some real punch (both literally and metaphorically). January by contrast is like the morning after the night before. You've missed the last bus / train home, you're out of money, the person you fancied at the party went home with someone else . . . (You get the idea).

January is just a bit shit.

SAM

Wow! What an upbeat way to begin our *Clanlands* meander through the year, Graham. Yes, January's an anti-climax, a bit like kissing yer auntie from Aberdeen – it's cold and miserable (not the auntie, or Aberdeen, ahem). Okay, it's completely freezing and I never want to hear the phrase 'Beast from the East' (which thwarted shooting of season six of *Outlander*, along with Covid and Graham's hotel room bill), but that's why we Scots have invented so many whisky-soaked celebrations to get us through. Starting with Hogmanay. Every year, as part of our tradition, we commence January with an almighty hangover – a real proper beastie right behind the eyes.

In Gaelic we call it a *ceann-daoraich*, which is what happens when you get blootered, minging, awa wi it, on the sauce, three sheets, steamboats, aff yer tits, reakin', trollied, and oot yer tree at Hogmanay, our Scottish New Year's Eve partaaay. And by god do we do love to party, hence the extensive vocabulary focused on imbibing.

[*Graham: May I butt in here?*]
[*Sam: Butt? Yes . . . So soon?*]

COMPETITION CORNER
GETTING TROLLIED

GRAHAM

As readers will know from our *Clanlands* and *Men in Kilt* adventures, everything is a competition to Sam and I mean EVERYTHING. And while I'll admit that Sam has an *inhuman capacity* for whisky (leaving me trailing hopelessly as the lightweight that I am), we both still only dabble in the drink. Duncan Lacroix, who plays Murtagh in *Outlander*, however, is truly a black belt master of the dark arts. The Usain Bolt of booze-hounds. The Yo-Yo Ma of whisky chasers.

Readers of *Clanlands* are familiar with our evening at my flat where he fell through my coffee table and I was forced to carry him to bed. On another occasion, Duncan (accompanied by his wingman for the night, Stephen Walters, who plays Angus MacKenzie in *Outlander*) went to his local pub and found himself getting on famously with a young lady at the bar. It came to the end of the night and Duncan seized the moment to invite her back to his for a 'nightcap'. This she did while failing to mention that she would be bringing the rest of her criminal family (a gang of beer-swilling beasts who had been sitting quietly watching their cousin get cosy with Lacroix). As far as I know, they never left his flat and may still be there.

Duncan has related a few harrowing tales of boozy debauchery to me. There was the night he got run over by a car, the morning he awoke to find his flat covered in blood, and I have a vague memory of something that happened in Cuba, no doubt with Fidel Castro.

And then there was Stephen Walters' leaving party.

Oh dear.

Stephen was the first of our motley Highland gang to leave and we gave him a great send-off at a local restaurant. The evening came to an end. Graham 'McLightweight' announced he was heading home for his bed. Likewise Stephen, Sam and even Cait (Catriona Balfe, Claire Fraser in *Outlander*), who is not a stranger to the smell of the barman's apron herself, departed – which left Duncan and Grant O'Rourke (Rupert MacKenzie in *Outlander*), who both cheerfully announced they were going for 'one more' back at Duncan's place. (Hopefully he had wiped it clean of blood.)

Cut to 5 p.m. the next day. I get a call from Grant.

They are in the pub. They have not been to bed. I can hear Duncan ordering more booze from the barmaid. He utters something I can't make out, but I definitely hear the barmaid's response, 'No! I won't be doing that!'

Duncan then grabbed the phone and proceeded to tell me he was considering murdering one of the producers at the table read and that I should have my phone on to record it.

The next day came, and the table read began. Duncan and Grant arrived.

To say they looked like 'death warmed up' is a dreadful

slur on death. It looked as if they had been buried overnight, and then dug up and brought to the studio. Their faces were the colour of old rotting pastry. When the script required them to speak, it was like listening to someone reciting their own death warrant in a foreign language. Duncan sat with his head in his hands focusing on not puking over the script. I do think Grant may have been quietly weeping.

Needless to say, Sam and I loved that table read.

SAM

Graham's right, like many other talents that elude him, I *am* good at drinking, but no one is in the same league as Duncan, who has an honorary doctorate in dipsomania. Compared to Duncan, Graham and I are total amateurs, but what sets the Grey One and I apart in this National Sport of Champions is I have a better ability to function. Well, maybe a better ability to hide the fact I am three sheets to the wind. Graham, however, after three glasses of Sauvignon Blanc is *flying*. Sometimes literally. Such as the time we were on a ferry to Lewis in the Outer Hebrides for *Men in Kilts* . . .

Graham had been entertaining everyone at the bar, guzzling the 'free' prosecco. However, when travelling by ferry I prefer to stand above deck for the entire journey – watching the landscape pass by, staring out across the blue looking for signs of sea life. I love the whole experience, because it feels like an adventure. You can see whole sea lochs and look back at the land from a different perspective. You feel as if you're exploring, forging a path into the wilderness; only to see the islands appear out of the mist, dark and foreboding. It's magic.

But Graham wasn't interested in any of that. His first port of call was the canteen for a latte (and, of course, something to munch on), then he hit the bar. A little later, he returned to the canteen for something to eat again.

When he finally emerged on the top deck, ruddy and over-refreshed, the wind suddenly took him by surprise and I have a video of him throwing himself into a gale, dressed in a grey shirt to match his grey beard, MY stolen Sassenach tartan scarf (which he never returned), an 'I Love Scotland' baseball cap and a pair of Palladium boots (his favourite 'young men's fashion' label, which he wore as a teenager back in the 1940s). He outstretched his arms dramatically as if attempting to fly, the obligatory glass of Italian fizz still clutched tightly by his long-fingered hand. Less Kate Winslet, more yob/elderly wine snob. He stayed a few minutes, then returned below deck for 'one more tiny glass of prosecco'. And a snack.

4 January 1961 - Graham James McTavish's birthday.

SAM

Moving on from Graham's ferry shenanigans, let's get to the real celebrations because the fourth of January marks the momentous occasion that is . . . Graham's birthday!! I believe this year is his hundredth and he will be receiving a letter from the Queen! Do Centenarians drink champagne? With a straw perhaps?

[*Graham: It's not so much that I am 100 years old, I just feel like it after two tours of duty with the Ginger dipsomaniac.*]

GRAHAM

January babies are a special breed, because as well as being the Sparta of months, it's also the 'Do not pass go, do not collect £200' of birthdays. I can count the number of birthdays that I have 'celebrated', probably on two hands. Given my advanced years that makes for a low percentage. I don't remember having a birthday party when I was a child. Mind you, children didn't have parties much when I was growing up. Now they seem to have a party simply for being able to make up a bowl of cereal, unaided.

The fourth of January is just not a date people want to party on. I was actually due on the first of January, but thanks to hanging around in the womb for an extra three days, I have been condemned to a lifetime of birthday indifference instead of a rollicking celebration as the clock struck midnight each and every New Year's Eve! It's not that people don't want to celebrate. They simply forget to. Or they're broke. Or they're still hungover.

I was never at school on my birthday. Basically, when it came to birthdays I was like Oliver Twist: 'Please, sir, can I have some more?' Panto (*see* DECEMBER) provided me with the only occasion when I was at work on my birthday. The cast actually bought me a whisky flask and presented it to me between performances. It was so thoughtful, and hitherto unknown, that I practically wept with joy and gratitude. I have a photo of me on my first birthday. I was in my parents' bed, surrounded by my gifts – a blue Teddy (I still mourn his loss), a plastic double-decker bus and some wooden blocks. Put it this way, there was a LOT of room on the bed for other gifts that NEVER arrived.

For my second birthday, I probably got a lump of coal and a used pencil. Come to think of it, my mother remembers her father being given a lump of coal as a Christmas present by his aunt! I'm not kidding.

[*Sam: They should have given him a latte. Even as an infant, I'm sure he would have approved. A babycino?*]

At the age of one, I was so blissfully unaware of the decades of disappointment that were to come, that I was actually smiling beatifically, looking very satisfied indeed.

[*Sam: He now claims he remembers being one year old!*]

[*Graham: Some memories cut deep.*]

Fast forward to my eighteenth birthday, which I actually celebrated in July, as I knew no one would come in January. That was a good party. Lots of people from school. My parents let me have the party while they were away. Looking back, this is extraordinary. Although, in reality it meant I was so terrified of any damage being caused that I was incapable of enjoying the party myself. Everyone else did, including the couple who locked themselves in my parents' bathroom until I managed to force open the door. All the reports were that Graham's eighteenth was a resounding success. If only I had been able to relax, I might have agreed.

Since then I have celebrated big birthdays such as my twenty-first, thirtieth, fortieth and fiftieth. [*Sam: Graham's birthday timeline: twenty-first – The Great Depression, thirtieth – Germany invades Poland, fortieth – Soviet Union detonates the*

first atomic bomb, fiftieth –Fidel Castro takes power in Cuba . . .
you see a pattern here?]

I organised the parties myself, with one honourable exception when my ex-wife arranged a great party for my forty-eighth birthday. I even went so far as to organise THREE parties for my fiftieth, one in London, one in Los Angeles and one in New Zealand. Clearly by then, my life of not having the parties that I wanted had since been replaced by my gigantic ego.

My thirtieth was a good one. I booked a Thai restaurant in Camberwell for about twenty-five friends. About half an hour into the meal, one of the Thai waiters emerged from behind the foliage of a large potted plant, with a huge video camera. (He'd been filming for some time, unbeknownst to any of us.) He then proceeded to film the whole meal. I still have it (transferred from VHS to DVD). It stands as a testament to my disastrous fashion choice for the evening – a gold velour waistcoat, cords and a puffy white shirt, teamed with a burgeoning moustache I was growing for *Twelfth Night* (the play, not the date) – and to the fact that of the twenty-five guests, I have NO idea who at least five of them were.

[*Sam: Did they pay the bill though?*]

By my reckoning, that makes a total of eight birthdays that are worth mentioning as being anything other than a quiet pint down the pub with a handful of friends. I look forward to adding to the list. At this rate, I might gain about four more such evenings if I do live to a hundred.

5 January - Twelfth Night.

SAM

I can't get the velour waistcoat, cords, puffy white shirt and moustache out of my head (and I bet the readers can't either), but it's a neat and slightly creepy link to the fifth of January, known as Twelfth Night. The twelfth day after Christmas, the night before Epiphany and the start of the carnival season (through to Mardi Gras), is a celebration of upturned worlds.

Allow me to take you back to 1997. I was cast as The Duke Orsino in a school production of *Twelfth Night*. Sporting a velvet cloak, green turban and borrowed fake moustache, a few years before I was able to grow one (McTavish the Grey will likely say I still can't). [*Graham: As if I would say that. Your moustache is the envy of countless twelve-year-old boys.*]

Orsino addressed the audience. The Duke is, or at least thinks he is, madly in love with Countess Olivia. It actually happened that I too was infatuated with a girl of the same name, she wasn't a Countess and, alas, I also never won her heart. Orsino is infatuated until he meets Viola, who's pretending to be a man and, through a series of miscommunications communication and much cross-dressing, the Duke and Viola finally get it together. Phew, thanks Shakey. It was to be my first Shakespearean production and I sucked. I felt wooden and unable to grasp the dense language or iambic pentameter.

It was, however, at this time I joined the Lyceum Youth Theatre and met some of the professional actors performing on the main stage there. Under their guidance, they encouraged me to look at another character in the play and use it for my audition piece for drama school. I applied to the Royal Conservatoire of Scotland (among others) and eventually received a place to study classical acting on a three-year course. I have recently set up a new bursary, giving two students a year the means to study and pursue their careers in the arts. I'm so proud to be able to give back. I remember struggling to afford food and basic living expenses during most of my student years, so hopefully this will help some budding thespians of the future. [*Graham: In return I have petitioned the Pope to have you declared a living saint.*]

In *Twelfth Night*, Sebastian, Viola's brother, is being pursued by Olivia (because Viola is dressed as a man, and Olivia mistook Sebastian for him/her). Confused yet? All you need to know is, whilst pretending to be Sebastian, I successfully managed to convince the drama school tutors that I could indeed act (or dress up as a woman) and the rest, as they say, is history.

Sebastian
That I am ready to distrust mine eyes
And wrangle with my reason that persuades me
To any other trust but that I am mad —
Or else the lady's mad.
Twelfth Night: Act Four, Scene Three

25 January - Burns Night.

SAM
Ah, Rabbie. We could not produce a *Clanlands* almanac
without including Burns Night – a crucial date in the Scottish
diary. So first of all we need to turn the spotlight on the Bard
of Ayrshire himself, the Ploughman Poet, Scotland's National
Poet and favourite son, Robert 'Rabbie' Burns. Born on 25
January 1759 in Alloway, Ayrshire, he was a farmer before
becoming a tax collector to make ends meet. He is still
considered a founding father of the Romantic movement and
his poetry and lyrics in the Scots language or dialect are witty,
satirical and full of passion for his subjects and Scotland.

To a Mouse
Wee, sleeket, cowran, tim'rous beastie,
O, what a panic's in thy breastie!
Thou need na start awa sae hasty,
Wi' bickerin brattle!
I wad be laith to rin an' chase thee
Wi' murd'ring pattle!
Robert Burns, November 1785

Every January as a child, I was commanded to learn and
recite what appeared to me to be a load of gibberish. The
school would hold a competition to recite the works of
Burns, with only the promise of a certificate with your name
on it as a reward. I was desperate to come first, but always
ended up with a scroll of 'merit'. Bah. I'd choose the shortest
poem from his vast anthology of songs and poetry. The only

one I really understood was 'To a Mouse', which was about a poor wee harvest mouse that had its home destroyed by the farmer's plough. The first line was my favourite, 'Wee, sleeket, cowran, tim'rous beastie'. And that's about as far as I got. The rest was way too long and after days of cramming those tongue twisters, I still didn't understand the story.

Twenty-five years later, Bruce Wayne was holding a large knife and was ready to stab a Scottish sausage. Whilst on tour with *Batman Live*, an arena tour that I played in internationally for over a year, we celebrated Burns Night. Our Edinburgh-born tour chef had supplied enough haggis to feed the whole cast and crew, and I had supplied enough whisky to drown them all. We were somewhere in Germany, or was it France, I don't recall, but it was cold and snowing outside and we were having dinner before the final performance of the day. The Joker was about to get beaten by Batman (me), Catwoman and Dick Grayson (poor old Dick), newly named 'Robin'.

I stood up and recited 'To a Haggis' (fortunately not whilst wearing Batman's mask), toasting the Scottish pudding. Everyone assembled was confused by the broad Scots, nervous to eat the sheep's stomach-filled delicacy, but elated by the fire water. And, in that moment, I finally understood what the words meant!

As with Shakespeare, the language is dense and complex but the rhyme and meter, once studied, opens up to reveal meaning. The words are beautiful, many Scottish words are onomatopoeic, incredibly descriptive and fun to get your tongue around. I read that the Scots language is one of the only dialects to use every possible sound in the mouth. The 'ch' – as in loch, can sound like you're bringing up phlegm.

It is actually the correct way to say Heughan – 'Heoo-chhan' – although I've heard many variations. [*Graham: So essentially the correct pronunciation of your name resembles the sound a drunk makes while struggling over the toilet bowl after a particularly spicy kebab . . .*] However, the best attempts are always when I visit our American friends: Hewhaw, Hugan, Heooghan and even, Huge-un. I did consider changing my name to something more international, but all I came up with was 'Sam Galloway', which sounds like a 1950s porn actor! Anyway, I digress, the Lallans (Scots) that Robert Burns uses is just brilliant:

- Blether – utter nonsense
- Bickering brattle – quick, indecisive charging around, but I always felt it refers to the noise of indignation made by the wee mouse as his home has been rudely broken
- Gang – to go; as in his 1794 song, 'A Red Red Rose': *And I will luve thee still, my dear / Till a' the seas gang dry*
- Auld Lang Syne – the good old times
- Auld Reekie – Edinburgh

SAM'S BURNS NIGHT GUIDE

Legend has it the first Burns supper was in July 1801, when nine friends sat down together at the Burns' cottage in Alloway to mark the poet's passing with a meal of haggis and sheep's head. They gave speeches in his honour, performed his work, drank copious amounts of whisky and, all in all, had such a good night, they decided to do it again on his birthday.

On Burns Night, as with any other Scottish celebration, it's important to look your best.

For a formal Burns supper, gentlemen should wear a black tie version of Traditional Highland Dress. The first thing is to get kitted out properly with a kilt and sporran – preferably in your own clan's tartan.

[Graham: The McTavish's have a range of tartans: Dress, Hunting, Modern Red]

[Sam: And so do the Galloways (my clan). Exactly the same.]

[Graham: This isn't a competition.]

[Sam: Everything is a competition.]

[Graham: You need analysing. I'll come to that later on.

If you don't have a tartan you can buy some wonderful modern creations in this patterned woven wool from Sassenach.]

Gentlemen's Highland Dress:

- Full plaid/fly plaid or a kilt, or trews. This must be 'dress tartan' or regular clan tartan (if you don't have a 'range' like the McTavishes). For those without clan bloodlines or from outside Scotland, you are welcome to wear the Sassenach tartan
- A kilt pin
- A dress shirt with shirt studs, French or barrel cuffs, and a turndown collar
- A bow tie, plain or matching tartan. I prefer a white lace jabot (think nineteenth-century judge look, a total hit with the ladies)
- A Prince Charlie Jacket – a short cut jacket with short tails in the back and silver buttons
- A Dress sporran with silver chain
- Evening dress brogues
- Garter socks: matching tartan or plain with silk flashes or garter ties [*Graham: Glow sticks perhaps?*]
- Black, silver-mounted *sgian-dubh*

Ladies' Highland Dress (not quite as exciting, I'm afraid):

- Full tartan skirt in clan tartan, universal tartan or to match your partner's kilt
- Neutral blouse
- Matching tartan sash
- Clan brooch to hold the sash in place

The Order of the Evening

The host will say a few words, everyone is seated and the Selkirk Grace is recited:

Some hae meat and canna eat,
And some wad eat that want it,
But we hae meat and we can eat,
Sae let the Lord be Thankit!

The haggis is piped in by the playing of bagpipes and as this great Caledonian delicacy is set upon the table, the host recites

Burns' 'Address to a Haggis' and the assembled party toasts the special savoury pudding. This haggis is accompanied by neeps (turnips) and tatties (potatoes) and washed down with more whisky. After dessert, the guests who can still see out of both eyes perform 'Immortal Memory', 'Toast to the Lassies' and 'Reply to the Toast', as well as other favourite poems. Then someone gives a vote of thanks, everyone stands to sing 'Auld Lang Syne' and after that the music is turned up and that's when the real drinking begins!

DRAM OF THE MONTH
MAN O'SWORD 2015, ANNANDALE DISTILLERY COMPANY

SAM
Due to the tax laws at the end of the eighteenth century, distilleries were taxed not on the volume of alcohol they produced but by the size of their stills. So, in order to get around this minor detail, the clever Lowland distilleries built shallower stills and ran them upwards of forty times a week. This did not produce great alcohol, but it did produce a superb profit. Much of the alcohol was flavoured and sold in London gin palaces, and the fiery product was aptly called 'gut-rot' and would not have been very palatable. However, they did supply over a quarter of all spirits consumed in England, at that point. So Lowland whiskies have struggled to gain a stance amongst their more established Highlands or Speyside brothers, which is a shame, as they have the potential to be extraordinary.

Owing to its close proximity to Ireland (some twelve miles away), the south-west of Scotland had a distillery that used similar techniques to smooth Irish whiskey and also had the wonderful soft Scottish water to draw upon. Bladnoch distillery was founded in 1817 and has opened and closed multiple times. I desperately want it to do well, as it is the nearest distillery to my hometown, but I have to admit, the last expression I tried was closer to the afore mentioned fire-water than smooth Irish whiskey. So my recommendation is the Annandale Distillery, one of Scotland's oldest working distilleries near the Scottish/English border. Geographically, it's the first and last distillery in Scotland. The Man O'Sword 2015 was featured in the *Whisky Bible* and was very highly rated.

BATTLE OF THE MONTH
THE BATTLE OF BENBIGRIE, JANUARY 1598

GRAHAM

Even by Scottish standards, January was a bloody month. Let us cast our attention to three battles. The Battle of Benbigrie, the Battle of the Spoiling Dyke, and the Battle of Glendale. There are a number of remarkable facts about all of these battles: firstly, they were fought in the Western Isles with two taking place on the Isle of Skye, and one on Islay. Now these islands are not exactly huge. In fact, I've cycled from one end of Skye to the other in a day. Islay is even smaller. So the idea of hundreds of bloodthirsty Highlanders rampaging across the landscape spoiling for a fight is quite a terrifying thought.

Secondly, it's January. For those who haven't had the pleasure of being in the Highlands and Islands in January – it's freezing. And dark. In fact, no sooner would a Highlander have said, 'Look Jessie, it's sunrise, time to get up!' than the island would be plunged back into darkness again. 'Time for bed, Jessie!'

Thirdly, it's JANUARY! In other words, the time available for a giant punch-up was short. But that didn't seem to deter the MacDonalds (who were present at all three January dust-ups), or indeed the MacLeods who (as we shall see), even when the battle didn't directly affect them, never let that stop them getting stuck in.

'Alasdair? Hear there might be a bloodbath happen' tomorra on the other side of the island. Fancy goin'?'

'Aye, let me grab ma axe!'

So, before we get into the details, let's set the scene. It's freezing. It's dark. It would be highly probable that wind, sleet, rain and blizzard (perhaps all four) would feature on any given day. But they still couldn't simply enjoy a day by the fire? Nope. There was killing to be done.

Welcome to the Western Isles.

Let us talk of the Battle of Benbigrie. We find ourselves looking at the MacLean clan here, along with the MacDonalds of Islay, the Camerons of Lochiel, the Mackinnons, the MacNeils, and, of course, the MacLeods (no fight is complete without them).

The wonderfully named Hector Og Maclean, Clan Chief, managed to get himself one of those obtained 'commissions of fire and sword' against the MacDonalds of Islay. As readers of our first book may remember, the commission was basically DefCon 4, 'anything goes', 'release the Kraken' option in Highland life. If you got one of those named against your clan, you might as well be facing Genghis Khan's Mongol horde, armed with nothing more than a toothbrush and some harsh words.

Our pal Hector summoned the Chiefs of the Clan Mackinnon, MacLeod of Dunvegan and MacNeil of Barra to his assistance. Not wanting to be left out, the Chief of the Camerons of Lochiel joined this force with his clan. The united clans, armed to the proverbial teeth, then proceeded to Islay. Sir James MacDonald, 9th of Dunnyveg, in anticipation of this movement gathered the entire clan of Islay and Kintyre as he thought things might get nasty. They met at a place called Benbigrie.

It is unclear whether there was even an attempt at negotiation. Perhaps one of the MacDonalds said, 'Let's all calm down and have a chat,' or Hector Maclean said, 'I don't want any trouble,' or even the Chief of the MacLeods stepped forward and said, 'You know me, I'm a lover not a fighter' . . . but all seem unlikely.

More likely was the MacDonalds uttering a stream of expletives to which Maclean, MacNeill, MacLeod, Mackinnon and Cameron shouted as one: 'I'm gonna cut your heid aff and pish doon your thrapple!'

Even if this was not actually said out loud, MacDonald made it clear to his men that they risked losing EVERYTHING if they didn't win. As a result the MacDonalds fought with 'uncontrollable fury'. Given that most Highlander's choice of default battle mode could never be described as controlled fury, this must have been eye-poppingly violent.

The battle raged until the slopes of Benbigrie were covered with dead MacDonalds. Their chief was carried off badly wounded, and the allied clans literally chased them all over Islay, killing any they encountered. It was possibly the most dangerously bloody game of hide and seek ever. After three days (yes, three) of this slaughterous rampage, every human habitation was burned to the ground. The poor surviving MacDonalds hid in caves and clefts of rocks with no food or warmth. Another Hector Maclean (of Lochbuie) had treacherously sided with the MacDonalds. His reward for this treason was to be left in chains along with his followers for six months.

The wholesale destruction and slaughter was so complete that, after Benbigrie, the MacLeans and MacDonalds were described as living 'on the happiest terms of friendship and reciprocal goodwill'.

It is truly awe-inspiring to picture Islay at the time. The land soaked with the blood of MacDonalds, the sky blackened with the smoking ruins of their homes, the survivors starving and freezing (remember IT IS JANUARY). It's like something conjured in the imagination of Hieronymus Bosch.

Next time you drink a glass of Islay malt whisky, it's worth bearing in mind that the peat cut used to smoke the whisky that gives it that distinctive flavour is literally carved from a landscape soaked with the blood of those MacDonalds . . . *Sláinte!!!*

REGION OF THE MONTH
DUMFRIES & GALLOWAY AND SOUTHERN SCOTLAND

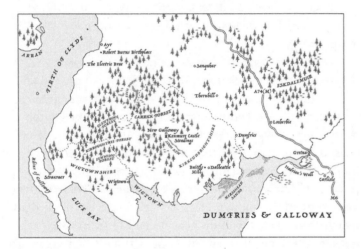

SAM

I spent my childhood growing up in New Galloway, the smallest royal borough in Scotland. We lived in a stable block called the Steadings at Kenmure Castle, a thirteenth-century ruin on the shores of Loch Ken. The walled garden, banked meadows and dense Forestry Commission woods became my playground. I realise how lucky my brother Cirdan and I were growing up, it was truly idyllic.

History was always around us with the ominous but enchanted Castle Kenmure looking down on us. I used to sneak inside to explore the ruin, imagining the ghosts of soldiers past as I mounted the spiral staircase. This is where I developed my imagination and connected with the stories of the Roman invasion – often visiting nearby Hadrian's Wall – and devouring every detail of the myths and legends emanating from these lands, such as Merlin, Excalibur and King Arthur.

As kids, Cirdan and I frequently visited Dumfries, the nearest 'metropolis' but actually a quiet, market town. We were drawn to the town for its cinema, large grocery store and the only Indian restaurant for miles around: the Shazan. My mother would treat us every so often and we would look forward to these authentic Indian dinners. They made the best fish and chips I'd ever tasted. I guess my taste buds had not quite developed enough for charcoal barbecued paneer cheese, or spicey chickpea daal quite yet, but I did like the poppadoms!

It certainly wasn't the type of food Robert Burns would have been sampling when he worked there as an excise officer in 1791. I learned recently that he had a desire to emigrate to Jamaica (probably dreaming of a rum punch on the beach), but he never raised enough money to make it a reality. Despite being one of the most prolific poets, he died penniless at the age of thirty-seven in 1796, in a first-floor flat in the 'Stinking Vennel' in Dumfries, today known as the Sanghoose of Scotland.

My mother used to take us sometimes to the thatched cottage where Burns was born in nearby Alloway, South Ayrshire. She would always take us via the Electric Brae – a gravity hill. ('Brae' is a Lowland Scots word for slope or brow of a hill.) When a vehicle stops on the Electric Brae and is put in neutral, or a horse is given a well-deserved rest and the cart is left at standstill, it will begin to roll UP the hill! Even a very large lorry or truck will start to move and gather speed. Literally rolling UPHILL! It's as though some mysterious force is at work or an invisible electric ley line. However, apparently it's an optical illusion and not some dark magic, which is hard to believe.

No, it's definitely some ancient druid spell at work . . .

And, talking of magical men with white beards, I wonder if Graham will let us take the campervan there . . . We are yet to do the lowlands together. I'd like to take him to Kenmure Castle and the tranquil waters of Loch Ken – maybe a day picnicking and kayaking. [*Graham: You had me at picnic . . . and lost me at kayaking.*] In fact, I'd like to show Graham around all of Galloway, because it's such a great place. The region is famous for cattle and cheese-making, but it also has lots of historic counties with Tolkienesque names such as Kirkcudbrightshire and Wigtownshire, which are right up Graham's street.

The name Galloway, derived from the Gaelic *i nGall Gaidhealaib* (amongst the Gall Gaidheil) translates as 'place of the foreign Gaels', referring to the mix of Scandinavian and Gaelic ethnicity found there during the Middle Ages. These west-coast southerners were viewed with the same amount of wariness and suspicion by city folk as the Highlanders. Galwegians would have spoken with a different type of dialect (Galwegian Gaelic, now extinct) and would have had allegiances to Ireland, Northern England, the Isle of Man and even Wales and Cornwall. There are many ancient Celtic links to those seafaring areas.

The Galwegians call the Highlanders 'Teuchters', a derogatory name meaning 'country bumkins' or anyone from the north, but the southern Scots were just as culturally different. Being born in Scotland but with an anglicised accent (my mother is English with French heritage), I remember locals in Galloway considering my family outsiders or Sassenachs (Anglo Saxons). That's why I refer to myself as Scot(ish) on my Instagram page and why the Sassenach name means so much to me, because deep down it's how I felt growing up. How I still feel. We are all Sassenachs in some form or another, whether you don't (or don't wish to) fit in, we are never alone, as we are surrounded by strangers who may soon become dear friends.

Writing *Clanlands* inspired and motivated me to start digging into my own family history – I really wanted to know where my ancestors had originated from. As I said, my mother's side is mostly English and Western European, but I knew far less about my father's side. After engaging the services of an ancestry sleuth, Elizabeth Cunningham, I was fascinated to be able to trace the Heughan line back to the

1600s and possibly earlier, to Kirkcudbrightshire, close to where I was born. In particular, Elizabeth pinpointed an old Mill in Buittle, which has been the residence of a branch of Heughans for hundreds of years. And that mill is only nineteen miles from my hometown!

As the story began to unfold, it would appear a direct relative of mine moved to Yorkshire, working as an affluent draper, and married a local girl in northern England. There would have been a lot of trade up and down the coast there and they would have travelled easily to their new lodgings by boat from the Solway Firth. Interestingly, there is a medieval town called Heugh in Northumberland, which would definitely make me a Sassenach! However, in Gaelic, a 'heugh' or 'heuch' means a steep ravine or precipice. Taken further, it can denote a steep bank above a river, which makes Heughan 'Man from riverbank with steep sides'.

Not exactly a sexy Native American moniker! BUT could it be that Heughan derives from the people who lived in the old Mill, on the banks of the river?

CLAN GALLOWAY

SAM

As Elizabeth did more digging, we soon discovered another incredible family link to Galloway. The name itself. Because the Heughans are part of Clan Galloway – a very ancient Pictish clan, first recorded in the area in AD 600 or 700. Not only did I discover I had a clan – my very own clan – I had discovered that my clan bears the name of an entire region and my birthplace, where I was 'hewn'.

The feeling of being an outsider or Sassenach was given another layer of meaning when I found that many Galwegians were probably descended from Englishmen, allied to the invading Norsemen. They had their own unique clan system distinctive from the Border and Highland clans and had strong ties with Ulster and the Isle of Man linked by trade, Gaelic law and the Gaelic language from the earliest time.

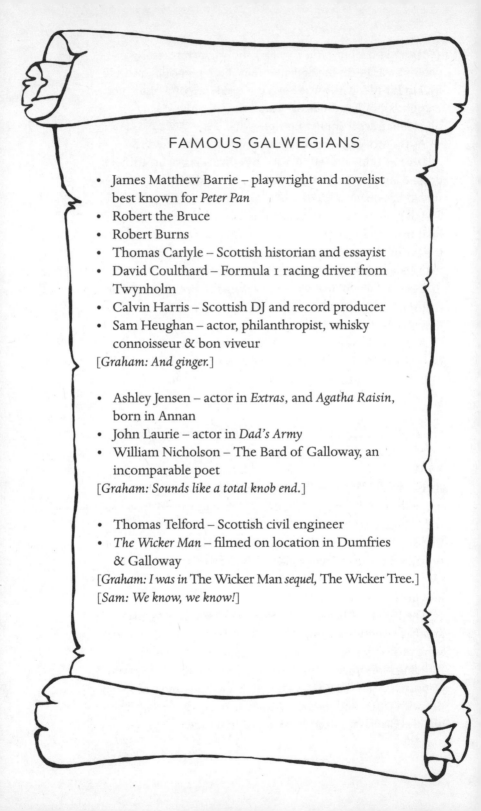

FAMOUS GALWEGIANS

- James Matthew Barrie – playwright and novelist best known for *Peter Pan*
- Robert the Bruce
- Robert Burns
- Thomas Carlyle – Scottish historian and essayist
- David Coulthard – Formula 1 racing driver from Twynholm
- Calvin Harris – Scottish DJ and record producer
- Sam Heughan – actor, philanthropist, whisky connoisseur & bon viveur

[*Graham: And ginger.*]

- Ashley Jensen – actor in *Extras*, and *Agatha Raisin*, born in Annan
- John Laurie – actor in *Dad's Army*
- William Nicholson – The Bard of Galloway, an incomparable poet

[*Graham: Sounds like a total knob end.*]

- Thomas Telford – Scottish civil engineer
- *The Wicker Man* – filmed on location in Dumfries & Galloway

[*Graham: I was in* The Wicker Man *sequel,* The Wicker Tree.]
[*Sam: We know, we know!*]

GRAHAM

I have never been to Galloway. I have nothing against it, but I've always preferred the western Highlands and Islands. Perhaps it's in the blood.

[*Sam: Graham lives in New Zealand in Hobbington, but some parts are the REPLICA of Scotland.*]

[*Graham: For someone named Samwise, you should know your people actually come from Hobbiton, not Hobbington!!!*]

Obviously if I'd known Heughan was growing up in the rural idyll he describes, I would've gone out of my way to visit .

Actually that's not true.

I was asked the other day when Sam and I first met. Officially it was August 2013 in a hot, dank studio in Soho for *Outlander*, but it's highly likely that as a teenager he may have seen me tread the boards in Scottish theatre. Perhaps it was Heughan, in fact, who gave the critical appraisal of my panto performance at the Citizens Theatre as 'pure shite' . . .

CRACKING CASTLE OF THE MONTH
DRUMLANRIG CASTLE

SAM

We were filming *Outlander* (Season 2, Episode 11) in the pink palace of Drumlanrig Castle, with its 120 rooms, seventeen turrets and four towers. Built in the 1600s and fashioned out of distinct pink sandstone, it has had a wealth of historic figures stay there, including Bonnie Prince Charlie, as he retreated in 1745. It also boasts some ornate Victorian gardens and extensive grounds that we had filmed in the night before. Our characters covertly entered the castle that night, making sure not to disturb the beautiful plant beds, on the way to surprising and capturing the Duke of Sandringham.

I had visited the castle before as a child numerous times, but usually entered through the main reception and up the magnificent staircase, rather than sneak over the battlements and in via the backdoor!

The Duke of Sandringham quivered and withdrew to the furthest corner of the room, to escape the glare and furrowed bushy eyebrows of the formidable Highlander, Murtagh. 'Keep him away from me. He's a psychopath,' the Duke, or should I say, actor Simon Callow, whispered nervously as he squeezed by me.

Simon, one of Britain's most decorated stage and screen actors, appeared in *Outlander* for five episodes, until his character literally lost his head for being a traitor to Jamie Fraser and his allies. His pitched voice and wily ways were very alluring; he was a devious, untrustworthy politician, who managed to manipulate those around him. A favourite catchphrase of ours on set was one of his lines that he'd delivered in the most delightful way: 'Oh, just GO TO BED!' It made us corpse every time.

However, this time the Duke would not be able to use his cunning or wit to get out of this sticky end. Certainly not if Murtagh had anything to do with it. Duncan Lacroix was to act out the beheading with a sharp axe and was taking the task VERY seriously. We giggled in the green room upstairs after overhearing that Simon was overtly wary of Duncan and his bristling beard.

Duncan decided that he would try to torment Simon as much as possible that day, staring silently at him with unblinking eyes between takes, or offering him a menacing frown whilst stroking his axe. I have to admit, even I was getting nervous that Duncan may go a little 'method'. The axe looked very sharp and Duncan, extremely sinister. Simon was terrified and was convinced that Duncan might really go for him.

THWACK. The Duke's head rolled onto the ground. A life-like prosthetic replica Simon's head covered in blood with a surprised expression set upon his lips lay still on the flagstone floor. Not stopping there, Duncan began to hack away at the body. It was grizzly viewing and the assistant director eventually had to call 'cut' to stop the crazed axe murderer.

'CUT, CUT, CUT!' he yelled. 'You really can stop now, Duncan,' he pleaded over the butchering.

Duncan finally stopped, reached down and picked up the severed head and slowly turned it to face Simon Callow, who by now was shaking in fear in the corner of the room. Simon let out a yelp and disappeared upstairs, never to be seen again. Duncan gave me a satisfied wink and raised one of his bushy eyebrows.

'We going again?' he said with a smile, hoping for a second take.

ADVENTURE OF THE MONTH
THE MERRICK IN THE GALLOWAY HILLS

SAM

Every New Year's Day, my family and other folk from Balmaclellan used to walk to the top of the Merrick, the highest hill in southern Scotland and at the heart of the Galloway ranges, and then return to someone's house or the town hall for a party. There is a popular ascent from Loch Trool (8.3 miles), which gets you to the top in four to five hours and is well worth the effort for beautiful views over the Galloway Forest. (On a good day, mind!) Which reminds me, my 'wicker' uncle – the weaver, who used to live on the Isle of Eigg – lives on the Solway Firth and, if blessed with kind weather, you can see across to Northern Ireland and the Isle of Man. Well, almost.

GREAT SCOT!

NOTABLE BIRTHDAYS, DEATHS AND SIGNIFICANT EVENTS

GRAHAM

Scottish history is packed to the gunwales with interesting events and fascinating characters, some of which we could write entire books about. (Don't tempt me!) So for each month we have hand-selected our favourites for the delectation of the *Clanlands'* Caledonian connoisseurs.

1 January 1600 – First recorded celebration of New Year in Scotland.

1 January 1766 – Bonnie Prince Charlie's father, James Stuart, the 'Old Pretender', died.

8 January 1940 – Rationing of sugar, butter and bacon introduced.
[SAM: Must have been a tough time for your Grey Dog, what with your appetite. How did you manage?]

16 January 1746 – The Battle of Falkirk Muir.

GRAHAM

It's time to have another look at that endless source of fascination for all lovers of Scotland: the second Jacobite Rising of 1745. Much has been written about it (not least by Samwise and myself), but there's always room for more.

The Battle of Falkirk Muir was another January occasion – on 17 January 1746 to be exact. The Highlanders had probably only just recovered from a legendary Hogmanay hangover when they decided to get stuck into 7000 Hanoverian troops led by the particularly odious general, Henry Hawley. Now, Henry was quite the character: a January baby himself, born 12 January 1685, at twenty-five he killed a fellow officer in a duel, for which he was pardoned by Queen Anne.

We don't know much about his enthusiasm for a fight before then, but given that his nickname after Culloden was 'Hangman Hawley', it's safe to assume that he probably hospitalised a fair few fellas during his teenage years, and had quite the reputation for a good punch-up in pre-school, when he wasn't nicking other kids' lunch money and torturing their pets.

He also managed to become stinking rich based on the immense amount of plunder he took at the Battle of Vigo in Spain.

He was offered command of the Government forces sent to fight in the West Indies. He sensibly turned it down and thus avoided the fate of the 9000 chaps who died of yellow fever on that expedition.

So he was a killer, a thief, and he was bloody cunning. Let's not mess around.

This was the man who met the Highland forces at Falkirk on that January day in 1746.

James Wolfe, who famously refused to follow an order of Hawley's at Culloden to shoot wounded Highlanders, said of him that 'the troops dread Hawley's severity, hate the man, and hold his military knowledge in contempt.'

Come on, James, tell us what you really think!

The January battle of 1746 was the last significant victory up here by the Jacobites.

They had reached Derby on 4 December 1745. The decision taken in a cramped bar in Derby to turn back is one of the great what-ifs of British history.

What would've happened if they'd pushed on? I mean, really gone for it.

They weren't aware, for instance, that the Welsh Jacobites had risen in support, and that those of Oxfordshire were about to follow suit. That George II and his German-speaking brood were already packed and ready to board a ship on the Thames to take them back to Deutschland.

London was in a panic.

But, instead, they turned back on 6 December.

Some have said that if they'd gone those final 129 miles, the English and French would have avoided the conflict that lasted seventy years. The English wouldn't have had to raise taxes in the colonies to pay for their wars with the French, and as a result the Americans would've had no cause to fight a war for independence.

The world would've been a very different place if that bitter argument on the evening of 4 December 1745 had gone the other way.

But instead, on a gloomy day in January, amidst heavy snowfall, Hangman Hawley met Lord George Murray and a battle ensued.

Hawley totally underestimated the Highlanders.

When a messenger warned him that the Jacobites were approaching, he simply refused to believe them.

'Er . . . Sir . . . there are eight thousand murderous Highlanders on their way to beat the shit out of your army!'

'No,' came the reply. 'I think you'll find that's not true.'

By the time he realised the truth, it was too late.

His hastily assembled army was soundly beaten with a loss of 350 dead or wounded and another 300 captured.

It's a sobering thought to imagine the Highland charge, the skirl of the pipes, and the howling war cries of the clans descending out of the swirling snowstorm onto the terrified lines of red-coated Government troops.

However, in true Highland style, they failed to take advantage of their victory. They let the enemy get back to Edinburgh and reassemble, while our kilted friends helped themselves to anything that wasn't nailed down.

It was the escape back to Edinburgh that, in some ways, allowed for Culloden to happen.

Hawley earned his nickname with his ethnic cleansing of the Highlanders and their families in the aftermath of Culloden. He lived another thirteen years. He was given a Christian burial, despite stating explicitly in his will that 'I hate priests of all professions'.

Even in death, Hawley managed to be thoroughly unpleasant. He is buried in St Mary's church in Hartley Wintney, England, if you fancy paying him a visit . . .

17 January 1795 – Duddingston Curling Society was founded.

SAM

We shot the *Clanlands* cover at Arthur's Seat, above Duddingston Loch. I lived nearby as a teenager, so I know the neighbourhood well. Check out the Sheep Heid Inn. Established in 1360, it's the oldest pub in Edinburgh, possibly even Scotland, and it has an old-fashioned skittle alley! What's not to love?

I'm strangely fascinated by curling and at the last Winter Olympics I was obsessed with watching it. We Scots are very good at it with the British women's team taking Gold at the Winter Olympics in Salt Lake City in 2002.

TEAM GB 2002
Rhona Martin
Deborah Knox
Fiona MacDonald
Janice Rankin
Margaret Morton

The sport is basically sliding stones across an ice rink towards a target area comprising four concentric circles, a wee bit like bowls. All the granite used in Olympic curling stones comes from the island of Ailsa Craig in the Outer Firth of Clyde on the West Coast.

17 January 1883 – Compton Mackenzie born, author of *Whisky Galore*.
26 January 1861 – One o'clock gun fired for the first time from Edinburgh Castle.
31 January 1788 – Charles Edward Stuart aka Bonnie Prince

Charlie died in Rome and is buried in St Peter's Basilica, Vatican City. [*Graham: He actually died on 30 January, but they changed it, because it was the same day his great-grandfather Charles I had been executed in 1649.*]

FEBRUARY

'I talk to you as I talk to my own soul,' he said,
turning me to face him. He reached up and
cupped my cheek, fingers light on my temple. 'And
Sassenach,' he whispered, 'your face is my heart.'
Diana Gabaldon, *Dragonfly in Amber*

Clan Murray
Motto: *Tout Prest* (Quite ready)
Lands: Morayshire

KEY DIARY DATES

1-2	Imbolc Gaelic Pagan Festival
14	Valentine's Day
	International Book Giving Day (Give someone the gift of *Clanlands*!)
14 Feb 2021	USA release date of *Men In Kilts*
16	Pancake Day
Feb-March	Six Nations Championship. An annual international men's rugby union competition between the teams of England, France, Ireland, Italy, Scotland and Wales. [*Sam: And one of my favourite events.*] [*Graham: Hmmmm . . .*]

SAM

We start the month of February with Imbolc, which sounds like a preparation for constipation, but is in fact a pagan festival celebrating the beginning of spring. Any excuse for a party! And there is much lighting of candles and fires representing the return of warmth and the increasing power of the sun over the coming months. However, back in Glencoe on 13 February 1692, there were very few signs of spring. In fact, it was snowing. Hard. (Typical Scottish weather.) The towering mountains of the glen, carved out 380 million years ago by volcanic eruptions, moving tectonic plates and icy glaciers, were encased in freezing snow, partially obscured by the nimbostratus clouds of a snowstorm.

Little did the MacDonalds know that night the Campbells were coming. For THEM. In fact, they were already there, guests in their houses, biding their time, waiting for the order to stab, shoot and burn their hosts . . .

BATTLE OF THE MONTH
THE GLENCOE MASSACRE, 13 FEBRUARY 1692

GRAHAM

More of an attempted genocide than a battle, for those of you who've read *Clanlands*, the Glencoe Massacre is one of the stand-out familiar stories to even non-Scots. The brutal slaying of innocent MacDonalds at the hands of the evil Campbells in the middle of the night. Now, while we have previously shown there were very few Campbells actually involved in the massacre, exactly how far did the reach of the Campbells go in the events leading up to that infamous February night?

To understand what led to it, we need to widen our view of the time in question.

The emerging kingdom of England, Ireland and Scotland didn't want a Catholic king. Unfortunately the current monarch, James II, was showing increasing signs of a fondness for burning incense and Latin. The last straw came when he insisted his son and heir go full Papal, and given that the country had literally spent generations fighting against the man in the big pointy hat in Rome, this did not go down well.

The solution? Well, invasion of course.

William of Orange (who happened to be Charles I's grandson – I hope you're keeping up), hopped across the The North Sea and took the crown. (This would be a little like Harry and Meghan launching an invasion from Hollywood to snatch the crown from the aged hands of Queen Liz).

James fled to the Continent, but crafty old William was married to James's Protestant daughter, Mary, and made her co-regent. (I know, I know, it's fiendishly complicated.) Put simply, William took the opportunity, James went into exile, and Britain remained very, very Protestant.

Meanwhile in Scotland, many were loyal to James because he was of Scottish descent. He may never have spent any time there, probably hated whisky, and couldn't speak Gaelic, but that didn't matter to the clans. 'He's one of us!' they bellowed.

Except some of the clans could see who was likely to be the winning team.

Enter John Campbell of Breadalbane. He could see that William was probably the horse worth backing, but he hedged his bets and supported James as well, hence Campbell's nickname, 'Slippery John'.

Breadalbane's plan was to prove he was more loyal than slippery by bringing the clan chiefs together to pledge allegiance to William. But it was going to take cash. Lots of it. He persuaded the government to give him £12,000 for EACH clan chief. A fortune! So Slippery John (SJ henceforth) organised a big old meet-up of the chiefs at Achallader Castle on 30 June 1691. 'Come to Achallader! I've got a proposal for youse, and I've also got stacks of cash!'

Present at the meeting was Alistair MacIain, Chief of the MacDonalds of Glencoe. To put it bluntly, MacIain was on 'the bones of his arse'. He was broke, resorting to that old Scottish pastime of stealing cattle from his neighbours.

These neighbours included John Campbell who was not happy about this. Not in the slightest. So he reminded MacIain at the meeting that he owed him money for the cattle he had stolen, far more that £12,000. You see, slippery . . .

MacIain was angry. Not only about the cash, but also the risk – if James II returned to find the clans all cosied up with his sworn enemy, what then? So, SJ proposed a second oath. If King James *did* come back, they'd tear up the oath to William.

Sounds reasonable.

But the clan chiefs weren't completely naive. They asked for a letter from James . . . giving them permission.

Meanwhile James, who was holding out for French help to mount an invasion, finally did send his permission on 12

December. With the deadline for the oath on 31 December 1691, there was plenty of time, right?

Wrong.

Anyone familiar with the postal service will know this was a risky strategy, indeed.

Enter stage right, John Dalrymple, Secretary of State for Scotland. He was a Lowlander who hated Highlanders, particularly those from the Lochaber region. James II's letter was intercepted by Dalrymple's spiesand the contents sent JD into an apoplectic rage. He resealed the letter and sent it on its way and on 21 December it arrived in Edinburgh. From there it had to reach remote areas of the Highlands, and go from chief to chief, glen to glen, in the middle of winter.

Meanwhile, Mr Dalrymple sent 400 soldiers to Fort William in anticipation of the clan chiefs failing to meet the signing deadline. It's not too difficult to imagine him literally rubbing his hands with glee.

On 30 December, Cameron of Lochiel received the letter with only twenty-four hours left to get it across Rannoch Moor and on to Glencoe, where MacIain was probably wearing out his leather shoes by furiously pacing up and down.

With the deadline literally upon MacIain, there was no way he'd get to Inveraray in time, so he opted for Fort William. However, there he was told by the garrison commander, Colonel John Hill, he couldn't accept his oath. 'You better get going to Inveraray and see Sir Colin Campbell, pal!'

So off MacIain trudged through the snow, taking three days to get to Inveraray, where he was detained by soldiers in Campbell territory. Eventually he rocked up at Campbell HQ on 2 January, no doubt panting like a racehorse, freezing his balls off and clutching the letter ready to sign.

'Och, you're looking for Sir Colin? He's out of town for three days, so if you'll just park yoursel' in that Campbell tavern, surrounded by folk who hate your guts, you can see him when he gets home.'

It must have been a tense few days and I don't imagine he

slept particularly well, his hand prized to his dirk (ie dagger).

Colin returned. 'Absolutely, MacIain! Totally understand the delay. Could've happened to anyone. Just sign here and we are all good.'

Phew, I hear you say.

The signed oaths were all sent to Edinburgh.

Colonel Hill even sent a letter to MacIain stating he was now under protection of the Fort William garrison. Happy Days!

The package arrived with the privy council in Edinburgh. But inside was a wee note from the local sheriff wondering if MacIain's signature should be counted . . . Just asking.

There were quite a few powerful Campbell lawyers on the council. They looked at the packet of oaths, looked at MacIain's, looked at the Sheriff's note and said: 'Naaaa. I don't think we can count that one.'

So five days after MacIain had signed the oath, Dalrymple received a letter saying that MacIain's name had been struck from the list 'due to a technical fault'.

More gleeful hand rubbing ensued, and the rest, as they say, is history . . . thirty MacDonalds slaughtered in the snow at Glencoe.

So, was it the Campbells? Yes, and no. Sir Colin, SJ, accepted the signature, the lawyers didn't. Who knows what other shenanigans took place along the way. There were plenty of other clans – Camerons, Glengarry – who wouldn't be sad to see MacIain of Glencoe taken out of the equation. We shall never know.

But if your name is Dalrymple . . . Just sayin'.

And the moral . . . Post your letters early in winter, and when the letter does arrive . . . run!

CLAN CAMPBELL

GRAHAM

There is a lot of competition for who was the most feared clan in Scotland. The title moved around a bit, some years it would've been the MacNeils of Barra (more on them in JULY), then there were the MacGregors, the MacDonalds, the MacLeods of course, the Keiths. (It goes on and on. No, it really does!)

The clans were a little like the present day Premiership in football, some years it was Liverpool, sometimes Manchester City, Chelsea or Arsenal, but if we want to see the equivalent of the Manchester United of the 1990s in terms of clan ferocity, it has to be the Campbells.

They really pissed off a LOT of other clans.

When you heard that top tune 'The Campbells are coming' blasting away across the heather, it was rarely a welcome visit. Rather like the worst kind of in-laws coming for Thanksgiving, who also happened to come armed with axes.

One branch of the Campbells was particularly feared: the Campbells of Breadalbane (whom you've just met) and their chief purveyor of unmitigated violence, Sir Colin Campbell, known affectionately as 'Grey Colin'. It puts you in mind of a faithful old wolfhound, curled up by the fireside. Only in his case, this one would've been gnawing on a human bone and tearing lumps out of anyone who tried to pet him.

Sir Colin held the extravagantly titled 'Power of pit and gallows'. That's something you want engraved on your business card. In fact, given my experiences with Heughan on the road, I suspect he has it on his Twitter page.

The power of the pit and gallows does what it says on the tin.

Sir Colin could look at you and go, 'I'm afraid it's the pit for you, pal.'

Or, 'It's gallows time, baby!'

It helped that the Campbells had the ear of the King. They were his right hand in Scotland. And, a very bloody hand it was too.

It was, of course, religion that got them in trouble first.

While most clans moved towards Catholicism after the decline of Paganism, the Campbells opted for the joy police of all religions, Protestant Presbyterianism. Now, no offence to Presbyterians, but they're not noted for their parties and wild times.

This put the Campbells on the wrong side during the Covenanter wars, and they suffered as a result.

But if there is one thing the Highlander excels in, it's a long and unforgiving memory.

So we find their involvement in the Glencoe massacre, their persecution of the MacGregors, MacEwens and Macnabs and many other clans to the point of extinction, as well as their particular fondness for decapitation. Even amongst a culture like that of the Highlander, the (Campbells took beheading to new heights). It was almost as if when they saw someone's head they simply couldn't be happy until it was separated from their body.

'How many did you behead today, Grey Colin?'

'I stopped counting at fifty, Tam!!'

They were also fiendishly good at acquiring land through guile, and through the manipulation of the law.

Other Highland clans are reluctant to forgive the Campbells, even though they themselves were often as bad – but hypocrisy has always found a way to be woven into the plaid of the Highlands.

Think of the signs in pubs in restaurants and bars in Glencoe stating: 'We don't serve Campbells' – they don't mean the soup.

Or how the wonderful author Compton Mackenzie has a character in one of his books, who trained his dogs to attack at the command: 'Campbells!'

If you feel you are the descendant of a clan who has suffered at the hands of the Campbells, next time you're in Inveraray (ground zero for the Campbell gang), try out this quaint ancient custom.

As you cross the ancient stone bridge that faces Inveraray Castle, extend your hand towards it, with your forefinger and little finger extended, and your middle fingers curled into your palm. You are now making the 'devil's horn', utter the Gaelic curse *buitseach* three times and spit between your fingers three times.

A Macmillan tried this a few years back, and three weeks later the roof burned off the castle.

For those who are bearers of that ancient name of Campbell, perhaps take pride in how much power your people wielded in a land well-known for its treacherous backstabbing. But also remember to not mention your surname at the next Burns supper you attend, as you will be told that it is common practice to remove the knives when one dines with a Campbell.

COMPETITION CORNER
AXE-WIELDING MAD MEN

SAM

And, speaking of knives.

And axes . . .

Our TV show *Men in Kilts* was released on Starz in the USA on 14 February 2021, Valentine's Day. Those who have watched it will know it's a celebration of the landscape, culture, food and people of Scotland, with a healthy dose of sporting events and competition thrown in for good measure. What I never expected was that Graham might actually win a few of them. Any of them. I mean he's twenty years older than me! But it's all about taking part, right?

First up was a return to Castle Leoch, seat of the MacKenzies in *Outlander*, but known in real life as Doune Castle, near Stirling. We were booked in for a spot of axe-wielding with Charlie Allan and his gang, a bunch of scary looking Scottish re-enactors, who arrived on motorbikes like Hells Angels from the 1700s. Now, if you've read *Clanlands*, you will have heard of the notorious Charlie 'Chic' Allan (spelt He emailed me after the book was published, claiming we had spelt his name wrong. I quickly blamed the publisher and only hope he doesn't get to them before this book is published. Anyway . . .).

Charlie is hewn out of stone. Even his voice is pure gravel. His handshake, vicelike. Well, if you thought he was scary, wait until you see his SON!!! At seven foot and one inch, he towers above myself, Graham and Charlie. He could barely fit on his motorbike, one that would dwarf myself or my Protein-stealing friend. I volunteered that McHungry should tackle him first. 'A sharp blow to the face (if you can reach) should earn some respect?'

We were being shown a series of blows to use with either sword or Lochaber axe. Charlie told us, 'Thrust. Cut. Up on an X, across the body and over the head.'

Graham McScary picked up the axe and, as soon as the cameras were rolling, he started to show off his mighty prowess. Thrust, cut, up, across the body and over the head. 'You're so close you can smell the breath of the man you're fighting,' Charlie explained. As the red mist descended, Graham's fearsome sound effects increased.

'Arghhh!' the bald one roared.

'The fear is what kept you alive because you fought harder,' said Charlie. Graham was now in full force, a terrifying display of unmuzzled violence, a one-man, axe-wielding threshing machine as he gave the drills 100 per cent.

For a few takes.

The effort is only there for the first few takes with Graham, lest he might do himself a mischief or break into a sweat. In performance terms, he is a sprinter (one at a pre-school sports day race) and I am a marathon man. Needless to say I aced it and it was another round to me, but annoyingly his aggression had impressed the giant warriors. This was short-lived, however. Graham quickly returned to his natural Lady McTavish state and, after an effeminate elbow bump with the hairy Alpha males, he dramatically

flung his scarf over his shoulder, turned tail and legged it!
Well, almost.

GRAHAM

Not content with meeting the bearded one on our first tour
in the campervan, we arranged for round two. This time at
Castle Leoch, otherwise known as Doune Castle. I think we
both felt that somehow we'd be meeting Charlie on our
home turf, thereby feeling more secure.

Such naive thoughts were quickly dispelled when we saw
Charlie and his posse roll up on their gigantic motorbikes.
Charlie's bike seemed to have grown visibly since our last
encounter. It looked like a motorbike on steroids with the
bowel-loosening, gravelly engine growl to match. It was as if
Charlie were astride a living thing. A thing that hated namby-
pamby actors in campervans.

[*Sam: Charlie wants me to buy a bike from him. I'm too scared
to say no* . . .]

Riding next to him appeared to be someone on a child's
bike. It was only when this individual stood up that I
realised the bike was normal size, but he was a giant. I
don't mean giant like he was a big guy. I mean a fucking
GIANT.

Seven feet one inches. This was Charlie's son Finn. Now,
I've not met Finn's mother, but I have visions of her cracking
walnuts with her bare hands and punching tree trunks for
fun.

He was huge.

The bike looked relieved when he got off it.

I almost expected him to start shouting 'Fee, Fi, Fo, Fum'
as he strode across the castle courtyard.

We were in an upstairs room. They entered, Charlie first,
and then Finn, followed by the sun being blotted out. We
exchanged the necessary emasculating handshakes. Finn's
was like that of a Kodiak bear.

I think he may have muttered, 'I fucking hate baldies,' but
maybe I imagined it. They took us through our paces with
the broadswords and Lochaber axes.

I watched Heughan out of the corner of my eye and was glad to see he was as nervous as me under the glaring eyes of Charlie and MacShrek.

We finished our weapons drills.

I was pathetically grateful that our instructors didn't double over laughing, or (God forbid) suggest a mock fight. I had visions of Finn backing me into a corner with his gigantic sword and tossing me out of the open window for shits and giggles.

Instead they merely nodded gravely at our attempts.

I think Charlie smiled, but it could've been flatulence.

Finn roared like a lion and wrestled us both to the ground . . . (actually I made that bit up, but it's what I thought he might do).

Sam mumbled something about leaving now and he and I shuffled out of the room, our frail masculinity diminished once again.

And now it's time for a little L.O.V.E..

14 February - Valentine's Day.

From my experience of life I believe my personal motto should be: 'Beware of men bearing flowers.'
Muriel Spark, author of *The Prime of Miss Jean Brodie*
(1 February 1918–13 April 2006)

SAM

I'd consider myself romantic and love to send flowers, gifts and take my date out for dinner. I would, of course, always insist on paying. Unless I'm having dinner with Graham, then I'd demand he did. Just saying, you know.

As a teenager, aged sixteen, I was deeply in love with a girl from my class at school. I was obsessed: she was Scottish, but had spent a great deal of time in Australia, and had the most beautiful freckles from the Aussie sun. Somehow, perhaps more out of pity than attraction, she agreed to go on a date with me. I was delighted and extremely nervous. She was certainly one of the cooler kids at school and I felt completely out of my depth. My belle suggested we meet in town, perhaps go for some food or do some shopping. We were to meet outside McDonalds, not a Scottish clan store (though perhaps I should have heeded the warning?), but the one with the golden arches.

This instantly proved a challenge for me as I'd never stepped foot inside one, being raised a vegetarian all my life, but hoped that she wouldn't want to eat there and it would merely be a meeting point and the beginning of the rest of our lives together. Standing outside the 'Mickey D's – the Scottish name for McDonalds – I shivered in the biting wind. I hadn't worn a jacket, as she might think me weak if I needed one. Wearing nothing but a T-shirt and jeans in the freezing cold, I think the customers inside thought I must be a homeless person, standing for what seemed like hours looking forlorn and lost.

Well, in truth it *was* hours. At first I thought she was being fashionably late. Four and a half hours later, my lips had turned blue and I smelt of fried food. I realised that, perhaps, I'd been dumped . . . it was before everyone had mobile phones (though I was to be one of the first in my class to own one, a necessity so that any potential dates didn't have to speak to my mother when calling).

I trudged back home and tried to warm up my numb face and dark mood. At school the next day, my now 'ex' had a face of thunder, even her freckles looked angry.

'Where were you? I waited for an hour,' she said, no hint of the charming Australian accent.

'So did I,' I mumbled, my face turning bright red. 'At McDonald's west-end, like we agreed.'

She looked stone-faced, 'We were supposed to meet at the east-end one,' she sighed, turned and strode off.

I had been waiting at the wrong bloody Mickey D's, only a short walk away. We had missed each other, like some bad, teenage remake of *Sliding Doors* – despite being on the same ruddy road.

Cut to 2020, some twenty-four years later and I'm dancing topless, pouring water over my bare chest, wearing a grass-flower headdress, complete with sheep skull on top to finish the fetching look. Graham and I are shooting *Men in Kilts* and have recreated the Pagan festival of Beltane, celebrating the coming of summer, fertility and blossoming relationships. Complete with fire dancers, druids, witches, a bonfire and, wait for it, a group of drummers.

ONE drummer in particular, catches my eye. Oh my god, it can't be . . . my childhood obsession and McDonald-loving bae, sporting a large African drum, sweet smile and those pretty freckles. Despite looking like an escaped sheep on steroids, I ran up and spoke to her, removing my ceremonial headdress lest she think my fashion sense hadn't got any better. We spoke and she smiled (this time it was definitely out of pity) and I was delighted when she agreed to go out for dinner . . . for a burger.

I only needed to make sure we both went to the same restaurant!

GRAHAM

I like to think of myself as romantic (well who doesn't, unless you're a complete unfeeling brute. As someone who has been on the receiving end of Black Jack Randall's romantic advances, I'm sure that Sam wouldn't see him as the red roses and Champagne sort).

[*Sam: I can vouch for that. Black Jack never picks up the cheque!*]

As a young boy I had crushes on people all the time, such as my best friend's sister, Laura Williamson, who lived almost next door. I would've been seven years, she was probably ten. Her brother, Andrew, and I were obsessed with Batman – the Adam West version, not the rather disturbing *Dark Knight* version.

At the end of an episode Andrew and I would burst from our homes dressed as Batman and Robin. I was Batman. My costume consisted of a tablecloth for a cape, and my mask was my Mother's tea cosy stuffed on top of my head. Andrew was attired in similar fashion. We then proceeded to play Batman together. I can only imagine that there were no other children in my street, hence why we were not savagely beaten for our extraordinary outfits.

But Andrew had a sister: the beautiful Laura, the 'older woman'. I remember once pretending to hurt myself, knowing she would come and check on me to see if I was okay (I wouldn't be surprised if she didn't end up being a nurse). I can recall the image so clearly. Me on my back, feigning injury, with Laura worriedly bent over me. I can see her now, silhouetted against the sun, her blonde hair shimmering, and her small crucifix dangling towards me. I can hear her asking if I was okay, making sure I was going to be alright. It's one of my most vivid childhood memories. That was love, right there.

Then I developed a pretty substantial crush on my primary school teacher in Canada (we lived in Vancouver for two years when I was eight years old). Her name was Miss MacKay. She had long red hair, and drove an MG sports car. I adored her. To the point where I decided I must declare my love to her. I composed a lengthy letter setting out my burning passion, intending to post it to her at the school the next day. However, when it came to addressing the letter I hit a snag. I only knew her as Miss MacKay. Crucially, I did not know her first name, and I had always been told that you can't send letters to people unless you at least know their initial, if not their full name. So, the letter remained unsent. Miss Mackay was thankfully spared the pre-pubescent ravings of young McTav.

Simultaneous to my heartfelt love of Miss MacKay was my burning love for Diana Rigg. What a woman! As Emma Peel in *The Avengers* she awoke some pretty powerful feelings in my young self. To this day, she is the only actress I have ever desperately wanted to meet.

[*Sam: Oh yes, I liked her too!*]

My first kiss was at nine years old. There were two sisters in my street (the ironically named Cloisters), Jennifer and Sarah Tobbitt. Jennifer would've been nine or ten. Sarah was twelve. One day Sarah came to me and told me she wanted to take me for a walk. She led me into one of the foundation ditches near where we lived. We crouched down out of sight, whereupon she told me she wanted to kiss me. At first I was utterly horrified! Kissing! What? Why? How?

I'm not sure why she was so determined to kiss me (there must've been twelve-year-old boys in her life, surely?), but she got her way.

If you've never read *Cider with Rosie* by Laurie Lee, read it now. He describes perfectly the feeling of that first kiss. I can see her freckles, and smell the soap-scent from her skin. The gentle touch of her lips on mine, and the aroma of her blonde hair. It was a truly transformative moment. We never kissed again, even though we remained friends. It was almost as if she knew this was something I needed to experience (I am pretty sure this was not Sarah Tobbitt's first kiss), but from that moment on, life became ALL about kissing girls.

At any opportunity, I would organise kissing games. I introduced the whole street to the joys of kissing, until pretty soon we were all at it. In the woods, down alleyways, parks, wherever we could. It was wonderfully innocent and playful. However, I do remember being chased by the brother of one of the girls I loved to kiss. He was brandishing a rather nasty looking stick, and he wasn't happy.

It was only in my street that I was this precocious Casanova in short trousers. At school, I was the model, shy student. I worked hard and didn't really have a girlfriend there until I was seventeen. At home, though, it was as if I underwent a personality change. Here was a place where I could feel completely relaxed and open to the joys of romance. Myself and two or three of the girls in my street used to say, 'Shall we play Monopoly?' This was code for shall we go to someone's room and mess about together. I won't mention their names but if, by any chance, you're reading this book – you know who you are!

Meanwhile, at school I had another crush. This was even more profound than the one I had for Miss MacKay. It was for my English teacher and her name was Mrs Grew. This time I knew her first name, Pamela. I loved creative writing and Mrs Grew encouraged me to write as much as possible. (She used to read out my stories to the class. Again, amazing that I wasn't the subject of regular thrashings by my fellow class-mates.)

Looking back, she was around twenty-four years old. She seemed so sophisticated and mature. I would write incessantly in my diary about her. Even though I knew she was married, I was utterly convinced, UTTERLY, that eventually she would realise she loved me and would leave her husband, making us free to be together forever. Yes, I was truly insane!

I can't remember when my crush on Mrs Grew waned. I wonder if she ever knew or suspected. She probably did, and was kind enough not to embarrass me. But, Pamela, if you didn't know then . . . you do now!

SAM

Over the years the fans have made me feel very loved and many have sent very generous and delightful gifts. A few stand-outs:

- A blanket made up of multiple pictures of myself
- Bourbon-flavoured coffee
- Various pieces of underwear (some used)
- A crate of over-ripe avocados
- Homemade peanut butter (yum)
- A crocheted 'modesty pouch' – a little on the small side

Dougal MacKenzie's 'Complete Jacobite Lovers' Guide

1. At any mention of Valentine's Day, affect complete indifference bordering on contempt. Make them believe you don't care.
2. In the month before Valentine's, start casually leaving phallic-shaped fruit and veg around the house as a hint. I find eggplant, cucumber and obviously bananas work well for this. If you're going for a 'Lacroix' style, perhaps opt for an oddly shaped zucchini. Leave them in strategic locations: hanging above the bedroom door for instance, or under a pillow, maybe even fashion some into a necklace?
3. In the week before Valentine's, eat only oysters.
4. Say the following sentence with doleful eyes: 'Does it ever stop? The wanting you? Even when I've just left ye. I want you so much my chest feels tight and my fingers ache with wanting to touch ye again.'
5. Buy a new mattress for the bed, but don't make a big THING of it!
6. Casually announce you're considering soundproofing the house. She'll love you for it!!
7. If you have pets, get rid of them. If you can't bring yourself actually to put them down (because you're pathetic!), lend them to a friend who has no chance of getting any Valentine's houghmagandy.
8. Learn the lyrics to 'Let me put my love into you' by AC/DC and sing it at every opportunity. She'll start to get the hint.
9. On the day, surprise her! Let her see your carefree spontaneity. Sweep her off her feet, literally (best done when her back is to you). When you get home, delight her with a shout of 'Brace yoursel' lass!' It's all about setting the mood.

VALENTINE'S RECIPE
TONY SINGH'S SHORTBREAD HEARTS
(As seen on *Men in Kilts*)

Ingredients
125g unsalted butter, chilled and diced
55g caster sugar, plus extra to sprinkle
200g plain flour

Method
Put the butter and sugar in a food processor and blitz until
well combined. Add the flour and pulse briefly until the
mixture resembles breadcrumbs.

Tip out the mixture onto a work surface and gently bring
it together, then knead it into a dough. Once the dough is
formed, wrap it in cling film and chill for 30 minutes.

Preheat the oven to 160°C fan / 325°F / Gas 3.

Once the dough has chilled, lightly flour your work surface
and roll out the dough to about 3mm thick. Use a 6–8cm
heart-shaped cutter to stamp out 16 biscuits, re-rolling and
cutting the trimmings.

Place the biscuits on a lined baking sheet, then use a fork
to prick a few lines of holes in the centre of each and chill for
another 10 minutes. Sprinkle the biscuits with a little caster
sugar and bake for 10–12 minutes, or until lightly golden.

Remove the biscuits from the oven and allow to cool on
the baking sheet for 10 minutes.

REGION OF THE MONTH
CAIRNGORMS NATIONAL PARK

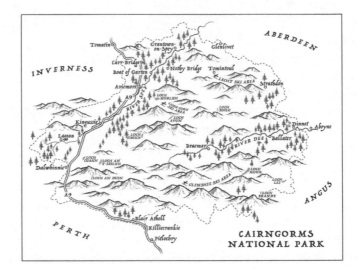

SAM

Established in 2003, Cairngorms is the largest National Park in the UK and is 1748 square miles, which is bigger than Luxembourg! It's home to one-quarter of Scotland's native forest, 55 Munros and four of the five highest mountains in the UK. However, Cairngorms National Park is not just about mountains, it's so much more – the park boasts three rivers, 60 lochs (some of the cleanest in Europe), more than half the surviving Caledonian forest, and the Cairngorm plateau has the most extensive range of arctic mountain landscape in the British Isles. It's also home to 25 per cent of Britain's endangered animal, insect, fungi and plant species, some of which can only be found in the Cairngorms, including capercaillie, snow buntings and mountain hares.

DRAM OF THE MONTH
DALWHINNIE WHISKY

SAM

Since we are talking about the Cairngorms, we need to look at Speyside whisky. Speyside whiskies are generally not peated or heavy and tend to sit at the lighter and more floral side, perfect for a Valentine's date. If your date doesn't like Scotch . . . then who are you dating?! However, it means double servings for you, plus, gently dabbed onto the neck, it can double as a Scottish fragrance! Eau de Whisky. Come here lassie, you smell like a distillery!

Speyside holds around half of all Scotland's distilleries and is named after the River Spey which was the original source of water used in whisky-making in the area. The land is ideal for growing barley and tends to get more sunshine during the summer months – I have noticed it does ALWAYS seem to rain on the west coast. Fruity and fragrant, with plenty of 'wood' notes, despite there being a vast array of famous brands and different expressions, I'd say that Speyside whiskies all have an inherent sweetness and are delicious!

For me, Dalwhinnie would be my Speyside choice. On the edge of the Cairngorms, driving up to Inverness, you can't help but notice the picturesque distillery on the side of General Wade's military road. During the winter, the snow gates may close and access to the Cairngorms is not possible. It's a remote and windswept place and the highest-elevated working distillery, however, the summer months are also reflected in this easy drinking and warming dram. As with all whisky, it conjures an emotional response upon tasting, unlike other libations. It was the first real single malt I tasted and enjoyed. Whilst living in London, I remember drinking it for the first time and feeling a little homesick, as the whisky reminded me of the rugged scenery, clear water and majestic glens of home.

I also recall sampling the majority of a bottle with my good friend Cameron McNeish, before shooting a winter hiking TV show the next day. The man has a generous hand and my hangover was only cleared by the freezing cold and snowy terrain the next day. If your date hasn't tried whisky, pour them a little of this light, heathery dram and I assure you, they'll fall in love. Hopefully with you and not the bottle!

ADVENTURE OF THE MONTH
SCHIEHALLION, PERTHSHIRE AND KINROSS

SAM

My Munro of the Month has to be the magical and perfectly diamond-shaped Schiehallion mountain that sits watch over Loch Rannoch and is situated in the shires of Perth and Kinross. We filmed the magic stone circle here, under the shadow of the mountain, and between takes I'd longingly look up at its sharp peak and yearn to climb it, even in the snow. The name roughly translated from Gaelic means 'Mountain of the Caledonians' and it was clearly a very important place. The long slopes of its back have been inhabited since the first millennium BC. It is also thought the name could mean 'Mountain of the Faeries' and it certainly does feel quite magical. Thankfully no faeries in *Outlander*, yet.

Another interesting fact is that the mountain was used in the eighteenth century to measure the 'weight/mass of the world'. The experiment took place in 1774 (while Jamie and Claire were in America, trying to avoid the American Revolution?)

The day after my thirty-fourth birthday, nursing a hangover, I managed to sneak out of the hotel and try to reach the top, before the production noticed I was gone. I jumped in a local taxi and got the friendly cabbie to drop me off at its base. It's a relatively easy hike, with a well-maintained stone path, however at the top, the mountain was still covered in snow and thick ice. Maybe a hundred metres from the summit, I reached an ice field and could go no further without crampons, for risk of sliding off the edge.

I made myself a shelter in the thick snow gathered by a boulder and looked down through the moving clouds, just making out the fake stone circle and ant-sized filming crew below. I'm sure not they would have been too happy to see me slide off and land at their feet, some three and a half thousand feet below.

Whilst up there, contemplating my now heavily reduced hangover and wishing I'd brought a dram of whisky with me, a couple appeared out of the snow and mist, who had also been turned around by the bad conditions. They unzipped their large rucksacks and brought out a Tupperware box of well-iced fruit cake, their wedding cake (do I look like I eat a lot of cake?), as they had been recently married and climbed the mountain to celebrate. Munching heartily, I wished them all the best before they disappeared into the mist again in a trail of crumbs. Clearly it's a very magical and romantic mountain, ideal for taking your newlywed partner, but check they aren't afraid of heights (or soggy cake) before tying the knot.

Sam's Tops

- 'Munro tops' must have an elevation of at least 3000ft
- 'Corbetts tops' have an elevation more than 2500ft but less than 3000ft
- 'Graham tops' must have an elevation more than 2000ft but less than 2500ft (and a rest, snack and a latte)
- 'Donald tops' must have an elevation of at least 2000ft
- 'Sam Tops' must have a large dram of Sassenach whisky (and a tepid latte for Graham) at the summit

GREAT SCOT!

NOTABLE BIRTHDAYS, DEATHS AND SIGNIFICANT EVENTS

1 February 1918 – Muriel Spark born. Author of *The Prime of Miss Jean Brodie*.

2 February 1987 – Alistair MacLean died.

[*Graham, His books included* The Guns of Navarone, Ice Station Zebra *and* Where Eagles Dare. *It was his books that inspired a teenage McTavish to dream of being a writer one day.*]

7 February 1603 – The Battle at Glen Fruin.

GRAHAM

On 7 February 1603 (ironically around the same time Shakespeare was busy writing *All's Well That Ends Well*), the MacGregors got busy slaughtering two hundred of the Colquhoun clan. It was more *Romeo and Juliet* than *All's Well* really.

A couple of MacGregors had found themselves hungry and tired on Colquhoun land. They went and asked for shelter, which was refused by the Colquhouns.

It's worth noting here that the MacGregors had a wee bit of history. After Clan Gregor had been stripped of its lands by Robert the Bruce and handed over to the Colquhouns, the Gregor boys had a habit of stealing whatever they could. This may have prompted the rather curt refusal to let the MacGregors bed down for the night

MacGregor: 'Ahhhh. Wease are lookin' for a bed for the night!'

Colquhoun: 'You're no' a MacGregor by any chance, are ye???!!!'

MacGregor: 'Er . . .'

Colquhoun: 'Cos if you were, I'd tell ye to get tae fuck!!!'

MacGregor: 'Erm . . .'

Colquhoun: 'Is that a feckin MacGregor tartan youse are wearin???'

MacGregor: 'Not sure . . . mebbe . . .?'

The door slams.

You get the picture. Cold and hungry, our MacGregor boys do what any Highlander would under such circumstances. Find a sheep, drag it bleating to a cave, cut its throat, eat it and settle down for a well-earned sleep.

Sadly, the next morning the head honcho of the Colquhouns found them, no doubt quite literally surrounded by an eviscerated sheep carcass, slathered in gore, probably holding the gnawed bones of said sheep in their hands. Our Colquhoun friend quickly put two and two together and decided it would be best for all concerned if the MacGregors were instantly executed.

Needless to say, this did not go over very well with the Clan Gregor . . .

By the time 7 February 1603 arrived, the Colquhouns were given permission by King James VI to pursue their age-old foes, and with 500 men on foot and 300 on horseback (swelled by men from Dumbarton and Cardross), they entered Glen Fruin.

The MacGregors were waiting, with 350 of their men gathered on the hillside.

At moments like this, it is useful to imagine the scene. It's a ball-freezing February day in the Highlands of Scotland. There would definitely have been snow on the ground. The sun (such as there was) had been up since 8 a.m. No doubt the MacGregors had been there some good time before that, gathering quietly in the dark, climbing the hillside, their broadswords wrapped in their plaids to minimise sound.

They would've stood, alone in their thoughts, their breath in that biting winter air being the only sign of life. And those thoughts would've been concentrated on one thing – vengeance and slaughter.

Meanwhile the Colquhouns would have been walking through the snow confident in their numbers, and their royal warrant, ready to fall upon the MacGregors.

Colquoun: 'Looking forward to murdering some MacGregors with total impunity, Tam?'

Tam: 'Aye, the snow looks nice doesn't it?'

Suddenly, erupting from the hillside would've been the war cry of the Gregorach, *Àrd-Choille!* which translates as 'High Forest', the meeting place on MacGregor lands where the clan gathered when under threat. They would then have descended upon the unsuspecting Colquhouns with the bloodcurdling, ululating yell common to all warring clans (the Confederate Rebel yell on steroids).

The only sound coming from the Colquhouns was probably the Gaelic for 'Oh, shit . . .'

The attack forced the Colquhouns to retreat straight into the path of a second force of MacGregors.

No mercy was shown. Two hundred Colquhouns were put to the sword and axe, the snow dyed red with their blood.

The response of James VI was to proscribe the Clan MacGregor, and decree that any of that name be 'rooted out and exterminated' (no room for misinterpretation there).

Clan Chief Alastair MacGregor of Glenstrae evaded capture for a year, and then made the rookie mistake of asking the Campbells to take him and his men safely to the border. He had obviously forgotten that 'Campbell' translates as 'crooked-mouth'. The Campbells duly escorted them straight into the arms of the soldiers who had been told to expect them. Those Campbells, eh?

He was taken to Edinburgh along with eleven of his men and hanged at the Mercat Cross. Because of his rank, he was hanged higher than the others, who were forced to wait and watch while their chief was taken from the Tolbooth prison, hanged, drawn and quartered in front of them.

The entrance to the Tolbooth, by the way, is now marked by the famous Heart of Midlothian placed on the High Street in Edinburgh. For any that have been to the nation's capital, you may not know the tradition of spitting on the Heart as you pass by. It is now seen as good luck, but it originated as a mark of disdain by those who knew what it commemorated. It is, perhaps, interesting to think that Alasdair MacGregor began that custom on his way to the gallows that January day in 1604.

The MacGregor name was restored in 1661 by Charles II, but banned again in 1693 by William of Orange. It was only in 1784 that the name MacGregor was allowed to be used again and once more given the rights of a citizen. The seventeenth and eighteenth centuries were DEFINITELY a hard time to be a MacGregor.

4 February 1716 – Prince James Francis Stuart, the Old Pretender, left Scotland after a stay of only three weeks, effectively bringing the first Jacobite Uprising to an end.

4 February 1941 – SS *Politician* ran aground on Eriskay in the Outer Hebrides, inspiring novelist Sir Compton Mackenzie to write *Whisky Galore.*

16 February 1746 – Government Forces attempted to capture Prince Charles Edward Stuart at Moy Hall, south of Inverness, but were thwarted by a handful of Jacobites.

23 February 1976 – *Trainspotting* actor Kelly Macdonald born in Glasgow.

23 February 1303 – The Battle of Roslin.

GRAHAM

It seems that winter was never a deterrent in Scotland when it came to piling up the corpses. Three hundred years before Glen Fruin, the Battle of Roslin happened on 23 February 1303 during the First War of Independence in Scotland. Nearly 720 years later, Roslin is almost forgotten as a battle, but it is arguably as significant in terms of Scottish history as Bannockburn and Stirling Bridge. It also holds the dubious title of the bloodiest battle ever fought on British soil.

A Scottish force of a mere 8000 men laid waste to an English army four times their size. It is estimated that 35,000 men lost their lives on that day. To put that in context, consider some of the bloodiest battles in history:

Gettysburg in 1863: 46,000 dead over 3 DAYS

Cannae in 216 BC: 60,000 dead in ONE DAY

First day of the Somme, 1 July 1916: 68,000 dead

The Battle of Leipzig, 1813: a staggering 84,000 dead

However, with the exception of the Roman battle against the Carthaginians at Cannae (clearly the Carthaginians never got tired of killing Romans THAT day!), *all* the other battles were using rifles, artillery and sometimes machine guns.

Roslin was fought with bladed weapons up close, and bows and arrows. It's a staggering thought.

It happened during a period of prolonged instability in Scotland. Edward I was known affectionately as 'The Hammer of the Scots' (also known as 'Longshanks' – you'll remember him from *Braveheart*). Well, at Roslin it was his turn to get hammered.

His army was led by Sir John Seagrave, who barely managed to escape with his life, along with only 2000 of his fellow English soldiers, out of an army of 32,000.

Seagrave would come to have the last laugh, however, as he saw to it that it was he who oversaw the hanging, drawing and quartering of William Wallace on a scaffold in Smithfield, London, two years later on 23 August 1305.

28 February 1638 – The National Covenant was signed in Greyfriars' Kirkyard, Edinburgh. It set out to defend the nation's religion from liturgical reform and English governance as decreed by Charles I. So emotive was the covenant, some signatories signed in their own blood.

MARCH

Spring Song
The air was full of sun and birds,
The fresh air sparkled clearly.
Remembrance wakened in my heart
And I knew I loved her dearly.
Robert Louis Stevenson, 1918

Clan Fraser of Lovat
Motto: *Je Suis Prest* (I am ready)
Clan Lands: East Lothian, Aberdeenshire

KEY DIARY DATES

Meteorological start of SPRING: 1 March–31 May

1   Start of Spring
    Early March: Braemar Mountain Festival
6   Vernal Equinox & Ostara
    World Storytelling Day
27 World Theatre Day
    International Whisk(e)y Day

Throughout March: Glasgow International Comedy Festival

REGION OF THE MONTH
PERTHSHIRE, KINROSS, ANGUS, FIFE

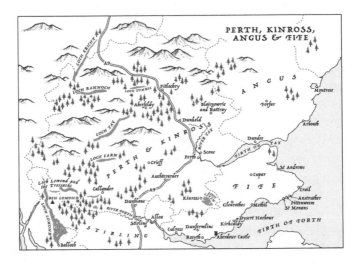

SAM

It's spring and a great time to visit the Kingdom of Fife. This area fascinates me, perhaps because it always seems to get more sunshine than any other part of Scotland! It's the

'Costa del Scot'. Even the place names are different due to the large Norse/Viking influence. I'm sure our bearded Scandinavian neighbours, after making the rough crossing across the freezing North Sea, would have found this part of the world very appealing. Ideal for settling, the land perfect for grazing animals, and the ocean and shoreline abundant with sea life, it must have felt like a Scottish holiday resort.

Outlander has used the area multiple times to shoot in its various scenic locations. The ancient town of Culross is almost a complete example of a seventeenth/eighteenth-century Burgh. We filmed in Culross Palace with its original painted woodwork and replica seventeenth-century interiors. In Season One, Episode Three, we shot outside at the Mercat Cross, where Jamie helps a young lad who has had his ear nailed to the cross for thievery. It looked like the film crew had stepped back in time, or travelled through the magic stones that day, as the whole town centre was converted to eighteenth-century Scotland.

Except that is, for ONE house. Right in the centre of the street, the owner had refused to allow production to pay to change his windows to more 'historical' window panes. Despite offering to replace the windows and then convert them back, the owner stood fast, probably thinking this film crew was rather a nuisance. And who's to blame them? Hundreds of crew, extras, horses, dirt and noise, arriving on your doorstep at 5 a.m. every day? I'd shut them out too. So we shot around the middle house and tried not to make too much noise.

I half suspect Graham was the owner and sat inside the living room, cursing me, as I tried to free the young lad of his seventeenth-century earring.

Another location we shot at was Aberdour Castle, in the town of the same name. It's a stunning location and featured as an abbey for Season One of *Outlander*. Jamie is convalescing from his injuries sustained by Black Jack Randall. Claire and her Highland Gang eventually rescue Jamie on the back of a cart and take him to safety. It is one of two of Scotland's oldest standing castles, parts of it built in the 1100s, and has seen the likes of Mary Queen of Scots and Robert the Bruce.

On this particular day I brought my family along to watch. My character was suffering from extreme torture and violence and I was hoping I'd impress my mother with some 'serious' acting. However, after introducing her to the other cast and producers and 'getting into character', I didn't see her again. Some hours later, after Jamie had finally been retrieved and taken to safety, the back scars had been removed by the make-up team and I had 'given my all', I went to look for my guests.

Apparently they were nowhere near the main crew nor had seen me perform, as my mum had been fascinated by the prop department and was currently studying the various pots, pans and general paraphernalia that adorn the *Outlander* set. She was very impressed by the castle though . . . and by the extras dressed as monks. 'Very authentic'.

As I mentioned, this area of Scotland is coastal and is a seafaring region with many small and picturesque ports and fishing towns. The incredible Dysart harbour, a Gaelic-named port meaning 'heritage or religious retreat', was a main trading hub for salt between the Netherlands and Baltic countries, earning it monikers such as 'Salt Burgh' and 'Little Holland'. Due to its Dutch influence, they even have buildings that could be straight out of from Amsterdam complete with imported Dutch roof tiles.

The harbour has incredibly high stone walls to one side, carved out of the natural rock, which make an impressive and formidable defence against the elements.

We were shooting the beginning of *Outlander* Season Two Jamie and Claire had arrived in a French port and sailed on a small boat from the UK. The real boat was called *The Reaper*, renamed *Crystabel*, and was a restored herring drifter. For most of the nineteenth and twentieth centuries it was the most popular type of fishing vessel on the east coast. That day, I remember a loyal group of fans, the Outlandish Bakers, had somehow found us yet again and supplied my favourite peanut butter cookies (and gluten-free cupcakes for Caitriona) to the set. It felt like a fitting way to start the season: sugar, salt and Sassenachs!

On *MIK* we visited Pittenweem, an active port north of Dysart, with a bustling fish market. Ninety-five per cent of the catch landed there is exported, which is a shame, because we really do have some of the best 'fruits of the sea' on the planet. We need to eat more of our seafood here in Scotland, so Graham and I decided 'to do our bit' by jumping aboard a jolly fishing boat called the *Karisma*, to harvest some fresh shellfish for our dinner.

Dressed in the whole deep-sea fisherman's kit with waterproof overalls and thick gloves, 'Captain Kirk' Doig didn't really know what to make of the pair of us. I kept cracking *Star Trek* jokes, while Graham shook his head in embarrassment, now fully immersed in the role of 'wily seadog': call me Captain McTavish. The real captain told us he loved his job because of the freedom and the thrill and that no two days are ever the same, which Graham told him was exactly like being an actor. Who knew?! Except that Captain Kirk has to brave the North Atlantic and Captain McTavish, the next five-star hotel.

The crew hoisted aboard a vast net, bursting at the seams with langoustines. The net spilled its contents into a chamber – and it was plain to see that, yes, there was probably just enough for Lavish McTavish's supper. As we sifted through the haul, small lobsters and fish were returned to the sea (to keep the fishing sustainable). Graham and I felt rather sorry for our captive crustaceans and tried subtly to release as many as possible, dropping them overboard when Captain Kirk wasn't looking, lest he zap us with his ray gun.

It wasn't until afterwards, we realised that most of the fugitive prawns we dropped over the side had fallen straight into the jaws of a rather docile and well-fed grey seal, who happened to be waiting below.

Whilst surreptitiously aiding a small lobster to his safety, I suddenly spied something as bald and as pink as Graham's head, with a strange orifice and an ugly texture. Graham and I both looked at it in horror – what *was* it? I waved it in Graham's face before chucking it over into the icy blue. It was TRULY disgusting.

However, perhaps I can solve the mystery here today, as I know many viewers of *MIK* were also curious and slightly disturbed by it. After many hours of research (on Google), I have concluded that what we saw that day was . . . Sea Pork. Yep, you read that right: SEA PORK. A truly disgusting phrase. I mean certain words just aren't meant to be combined, are they? Like . . . [*Graham: Like Sam and Graham?*] Part of a family of tunicates – rubbery sea creatures with 'sac-like bodies' – they filter the seawater to feed on plankton. Also known as sea squirts, they come in a variety of colours from pink, red, green and black. Some are good guys, some are invasive species catching rides on the hulls of boats.

Case closed!

[*Graham: Thank you for that most enlightening passage about sea pork.*]

[*Sam: You can't beat a good sea pork tangent.*]

GRAHAM

Our day at sea with Captain Kirk was a real highlight of our entire adventure. I loved seeing our food's journey from the ocean, to the boat, to the hands of Tony Singh, and then straight down my throat, all in one day. I also loved seeing Sam wearing a pair of tiny gloves.

I genuinely appreciate watching people who are really, really good at their jobs. Whether it's a fisherman, a chef, a shepherd, or a historian. When you're an actor, however good you may THINK you are or not, you always struggle with the fact that you spend your life pretending to be other people. We even talk about it in the show. We pretend to be better horse riders than we are, among other things. I've been a policeman, a doctor, a mercenary, a Highland war chief, a Dwarf, a cowboy from Hell, a seaman on an oil tanker, a priest (twice!), a psychiatrist, a vampire, a Russian gangster and a Roman general (and that's only in the past few years).

But I've pretended to be all of them. Which is fine, that's my job, but it means I have a real admiration for the real thing (vampires excluded).

The hardest part of the sea voyage wasn't Sam revealing his sea pork, or the moment when he asked the baffled captain to 'make it so', no, it was going up and down the ladder on the harbour wall.

I've always hated ladders. Some people can scramble up and down them like monkeys (Sam), but I ascend and descend a ladder more like a hippopotamus. By the time I'd finally got up the ladder from the *Starship Enterprise* (God, even I'm doing it!!), Sam had clearly whipped together a charcoal stove, and was living it large with the fabulous Tony Singh.

I was given the job of mashing up ingredients to make a seaweed butter (sounds disgusting, tastes DELICIOUS), while Tony went about making cooking look easy.

When I cook, I need complete silence and concentration. I am never more than six inches away from the recipe, which I follow religiously. Sam, of course, spoiled my culinary fun (as he spoils many sacred moments in life) by pouring in the ground coriander from his mortar, which then blew into my face and all over my sweater, meaning that I was weeping from coriander-stung eyeballs while Tony waxed lyrical.

Tony was able to be entertaining, informative, nimble and merciless in his treatment of the various crustacea we had brought back.

Our lobsters and langoustines arrived ashore very much alive. They relaxed on the rocks, probably exchanging stories from their time in the ocean together, asking after each other's families, and generally being very convivial.

Right up until the moment when Tony decided to grill the langoustines alive, and dismember the lobsters before our very eyes.

Like all the best executioners, Tony barely gave any warning. A jovial reference to Valhalla and the next moment Bill the lobster and his langoustine companions were being subjected to the crustacean equivalent of hanging, drawing and quartering.

I say 'before our very eyes', but Sam and I both turned away, unable to witness the casual brutality that Tony was meting out to our oceanic buddies (after all, I felt like we'd been through something together on the ship, and I DID play King Atlan in *Aquaman*).

Sam and I tried our best to talk over the sound of shells being torn open, and the sizzling of live langoustine calling for their shrimpy parents as they took a last look at the ocean. But shortly afterwards, Sam and I were eating them.

And they were delicious.

Truly.

Fabulous.

Even as I write this, my mouth is watering.

What Tony did that day on the rocks of Pittenweem harbour was akin to a religious experience for me. The delicious Indian spices mingling with the salty tang of the sea.

Bill and the langoustines' last moments on Earth were transmuted by the magic of Tony Singh into a sacred culinary moment for me and Sam.

Do I feel guilty?

No! I feel hungry.

SAM

I'm obsessed with cooking shows. Food Porn I like to call them. I used to wake early every Saturday and watch hours of them, from *Saturday Kitchen*, Nigella Lawson, *Chef's Table*, Rick Stein, Anthony Bourdain, and the one that inspired all the bad boy chefs: Keith Floyd. One of my favourite guests on the UK shows was a brilliant Scottish chef called Tony Singh, OBE. Originally from my home town of Edinburgh, he's a fourth-generation Sikh and knows a thing or two about spices. When we discussed who to bring on to the show for *Men in Kilts*, I knew Tony was our man, and he didn't disappoint.

To soak up our daily hangover, Tony decided to cook the lobster with chilli, garlic and seaweed butter. Langoustines were toasted on an impromptu beachside grill and new potatoes boiled in fresh seawater and seaweed. It's honestly the best thing I've ever tasted, due to the surroundings, subtle spicing, fresh seafood, sunshine, garlic, chilli and perhaps even the company. I still salivate now when I think about that meal.

Tony was an excellent host, and not only did he provide lunch for the whole crew when we recently went to his house to film some promotional material (chicken curry, pâté, soup, cheese and crackers), he also provided a late-night barbecue with homemade burgers to soak up the Sassenach whisky we consumed during the shoot. Unfortunately, Graham couldn't be there . . . so I ate (and drank) his share!

TONY SINGH'S SEAWEED BUTTER
(As seen on *Men in Kilts*)

Ingredients
250g of unsalted butter, softened
30g of seaweed, an equal mixture of sea lettuce and purple
    dulse, fresh if possible. If not fresh, rehydrate, finely chopped
2 tsp toasted and crushed coriander seeds
5g washed and spin-dried fresh coriander, finely chopped
1 red chilli deseeded and finely chopped
1 lime, juiced

Method
Toast the seaweed in a hot dry pan until aromatic.

Grind the toasted coriander seeds to a powder using a spice or coffee grinder/pestle and mortar then stir through the softened butter, with the other ingredients (chilli, fresh coriander and lime juice). Check for seasoning.

Wipe a work surface with a damp cloth and place a smooth sheet of clingfilm on top of it. Wipe the clingfilm with the cloth to smooth out any creases, then place another sheet of clingfilm on top and wipe again.

Spoon the butter out onto the centre of the cling film and form into a neat log.

Tightly wrap it up and secure with a knot at each end.

Chill and cut and use as needed on top of BBQ langoustines.

TONY SINGH'S BBQ LANGOUSTINES
(As seen on *Men in Kilts*)
Typically six per person

Start by getting your barbecue nice and hot.

When the coals are hot, place the langoustines on the grill. Cook them for about 3 minutes each side. (A light charring on the langoustines is a good thing!)

When the langoustines are cooked, take them off the grill and give them a squeeze of the lime juice.

Whack the seaweed butter all over them.

Peel the tails and get stuck into that juicy meat and remember to keep dipping them in the melted seaweed butter.

DRAM OF THE MONTH
AQUA VITAE, LINDORES
ABBEY DISTILLERY

In whisky terms, this is a difficult area as it falls into the Lowlands catchment and there are quite a few established and mighty distilleries to celebrate. However, that's not to say that Fife in particular is not without its history or partial to a strong drink or twelve. Quite the opposite, it's a very holy area in close proximity to St Andrews and the path that pilgrims would take to get there. One such site is Lindores Abbey. A friend of mine told me a few years ago that he had invested in a distillery there. As whisky takes some time to create and age, the Lindores Abbey Distillery had decided to follow the past inhabitants of the abbey and create a traditional *Aqua Vitae*.

Scottish people love monks, or at least the fortified wines that they produce. 'Buckfast' is hugely popular 'bevvy', originally made by a group of masterful monks in England, who resided in at Buckfast Abbey, Devon. Due to its controversial strength and caffeine content, the tonic (not 'Toxic') wine is popular in Glasgow where some locals drink it to get 'made wi it' because it's essentially rocket fuel!

Lindores Abbey makes a much more mellow and refined which can be traced back to this area in the late 1400s. The precursor to whisky, it was more of a flavoured fruit spirit (the abbey had terrific orchards and fruit groves, tended by said alcoholic monks). By this time, drinking was becoming more of the national sport it is today and the Crown wanted to supply their army with good drink, to fuel them as they tried to overcome the vicious seafaring warriors of the Western Isles.

My friend sent me a beautiful bottle of the liquor and it was my first taste of the potent stuff, with flavours of lemon, spice, cloves and honey. The only other time I recall drinking *Aqua Vitae* (*akvavit* or *aquavit*) was in Copenhagen with a rowdy bunch of Viking-like Danes who were gambling on a dice game that had barely any rules. By the end of the night and multiple '*Skol!*' later, I was singing fluent Norse and ready to raid a monastery or two!

Lindores Abbey is also distilling a terrific whisky which my Viking buddies and I can't wait to try!

Eden Mill is definitely worth a mention as well. More famous for their Gin, they now supply a large amount of their product to other brands and were the first combined distillery and brewery. Perhaps don't mix them both, unless you wish to be singing like a Viking too!

SKOL!!

ADVENTURE OF THE MONTH
FIFE COASTAL PATH

SAM

And after the food and whisky, we'll be needin' a walk. Not a Munro, but a spectacular 117-mile walk along the Fife Coastal Path is not to be missed, though perhaps don't try it all in one go. From the north banks of the Firth of Forth, past Kincardine, North Queensferry and the spectacular Forth Rail Bridge and newly constructed Road Bridge (for a quick walk across the water, you can walk the old road bridge from north to south Queensferry; it holds wonderful views of the rail bridge and a dizzying height down to the water below), be sure to stop off in South Queensferry, a cobbled fishing town, for a drink or bite to eat.

It was nearby, in Hopetoun House, we stayed a few times whilst shooting *Outlander*. It doubled for the Duke of Sandringham's house, among other locations, in Seasons One to Three. Over the years, we watched the new Road Bridge being built and I remember seeing the day both sides of the bridge met and were connected. Jamie was serving as a captive groomsman at Helwater estate. The duke had long been dispatched by Murtagh at this point.

The coastal path passes Culross, an eighteenth-century village, first taken over by our crew in Season One (Caitriona and I stopped off for a beer one day after work, still in our costumes, so you could say Jamie and Clare drank in the Red Lion Inn). If you haven't imbibed too much, you can continue along Dalgety Bay and Burntisland, the castle that doubled as a monastery where Jamie recuperated at the end of Season One. Following the coastline you pass Dysart, the harbour where we set sail for France. Then nearby Pittenweem, where Graham and I fished for local prawns and barbecued lobster on the beach. (There's a brilliant fish and chip shop where we treated the whole *Men in Kilts* crew to breadcrumb battered fish and chips and I introduced my friend and business partner, Alex Norouzi to pickled onions. He was horrified!)

Rounding Fife Ness, the lighthouse protecting ships from the rocky coastline, you eventually head towards St Andrews and the Home of Golf (more on that in a moment . . .). After teeing off on the Old Course and avoiding the bunkers and natural sand dunes, you will finally arrive in Dundee and the shores of the silvery Tay – where both Graham and I have played at Dundee Rep Theatre, many years ago. The locals still haven't forgotten.

SAM

Golf. A sport I've never really been interested in or wanted to play. However, as soon as I can't do something, I have to be good at it. And I was determined to be good at golf when we visited the hallowed grounds of St Andrew's Links for *MIK*. I was so sure I would prevail, I made a bet with McTavish – the loser of our golfing challenge would swim NAKED in the North Atlantic. He grumpily agreed, but his hackles were up and although I admit to being extremely competitive, McTavish is equally zealous.

As we walked out onto the first tee at St Andrew's Old Course, I made sure I looked the part – I was channelling Tiger Woods, while Graham went for the more 'traditional' approach: Santa in a sweater. It was my first time holding a golf bat, or whatever they're called, but I knew I had to hit the ball. And hard. Graham had played before and could tell the difference between a birdie, eagle and a sparrow. I was up first and my hands were trembling. I had to win, but I knew I had only one swing.

What if I missed? What if old McTee-off beat me and I had to fulfil the debt of an ice-cold skinny dip in the North Atlantic? I took a breath and tried to look like one of those guys on TV during the Masters, or is that Crufts? I raised my baton and hoped to the great golf ball in the sky that it would sail way over that miniature bridge and land somewhere near

the attractive-looking pub at the far end of the pitch. *Ker-Ping.*
My wee ball didn't get much air, but it bounced over the
green some 300 yards into the setting sun. Well, at least I
made first base, I thought.

Next up was the old Jedi Master himself. The enthusiastic
and rather biased caddie next to me provided a running
commentary. I wondered if he worked as a sports reporter on
the side. *Ping!* McTavish swung his festive, majestic frame and
his golden ball soared then bounced into the sunlight. I
instantly felt sick. The chill of the North Atlantic felt ever
closer. Our bubbly caddie didn't stop for a breath to break his
torrent of superlatives, as he admired Graham's handiwork. I
began to feel I'd been stitched up by the old dog and
suspicious he'd been out at dawn, practising his slam dunk.

Graham had beaten me by some four or five yards or so,
the caddie informed me, as he beamed cheerfully. Graham
went on to beat me at some 'putting', something akin to
snooker, but played standing up, where one doesn't hit the
ball hard (what's the point?) and tries to sink it in a small
mouse hole.

A few days later, the crew and I visited a driving range,
armed with a large bottle of whisky. By the end of the bottle,
I was smashing the ball well out of sight. If only I'd had a
drink first in St Andrews. Or perhaps some practice.

Unable to lose, I suggested to Graham that this was the
start of a series of sporting activities. He eyeballed me
steadily. 'Hmmm. Okay,' he said. At that moment, I knew
there would be only one person swimming in the freezing
Scottish waters and win or lose, it wasn't going to be
Graham.

GRAHAM

One of the great joys of writing this book, like our first
literary tome, is the opportunity to enjoy different
perspectives on the same event. I like to call it the difference
between fact and fiction. Samwise has treated us to fiction,
(and thoroughly entertaining it is too), now it's the turn of
that notorious killjoy – fact.

Sam's competitive streak precedes him. When I mentioned to Caitriona Balfe that Sam and I might compete in some sports, she warned me, 'Be careful, he doesn't like to lose.'

Now, in fairness I don't like to lose either, I like to win. On this point Sam is spot on in his description of events. After this point, however, Sam is definitely 'in the rough' (to borrow a golfing term), vainly looking for truth but finding only the meanderings of his fevered imagination. At some point Sam suggested we have a bet on the golf. I was nervous. The ONLY reason that he would offer such a bet was his cast-iron confidence in thrashing me on the fairway of St Andrews Old Course.

I hesitated.

'What happens if I lose?'

'You go skinny dipping in the North Atlantic,' he responded cheerfully.

I think the only reason I agreed was that my mind simply could not imagine how cold that would be, plus it was about three weeks away (he'd forget, forgive, feel pity, or all three and I would escape my ball-freezing bath). Also I knew I couldn't say no. To do so would invite endless accusations of cowardice and give him bragging rights for the rest of the shoot, possibly for eternity.

'Okay,' I murmured.

'Prepare to get wet, McTavish!' he barked.

It was at this point that I asked if he'd played golf before.

'Have you?' he enquired

'Twice,' I replied. 'In 1992. I hated it both times. What about you?'

'Couple of times,' he said evasively.

'When?' I persisted.

'I don't know. Couple of years back maybe.'

It was then that he couldn't resist telling me the truth.

'Actually I beat a semi-professional golfer. They couldn't believe it!' he crowed, while I felt sick.

He's beaten A SEMI-PROFESSIONAL GOLFER!!!

I knew I was doomed. I was already feeling decidedly cold.

The day came.

I tried to put on a brave face, but I knew it was pointless.

The caddie, Dave, was relentlessly cheerful (reminiscent of how an executioner probably behaved on the gallows in the Middle Ages).

He took us through the most basic of lessons and Sam elected to go first.

I looked on with that feeling I used to have at school. You know the one, when you look at the captain of the team scoring yet another goal and being mobbed by his teammates, while you stand freezing at some far-flung corner of the pitch watching your legs turn blue with the cold.

He swung the club in a glittering arc and the unmistakable sound of a golf ball being soundly hit echoed across the fairway. It sailed into the distance among appreciative murmurs from Caddie Dave (aka Fraser Riddler). I think some onlookers may even have applauded, the sun glinting off the white speck as it disappeared from view up the fairway.

He'd smashed it.

It was straight, true, and a long way away.

I attempted a smile, which in reality probably could've been mistaken for indigestion mixed with a man about to shit himself. Good job I'd chosen the brown tweeds.

I took my tee and strolled up to take position, attempting nonchalance, but knowing I was moments away from the sound of Heughan saying, 'Oh, bad luck mate! We'll look for your ball when the tide brings it back in.'

It was at that moment I realised there was no point worrying.

I was going to lose.

I was going swimming.

Naked.

That's all there was to it.

And in that realisation, I suddenly felt unburdened.

I relaxed.

I looked at the ball.

And the ball looked back at me (a little like Nietzsche's abyss).

I looked down the fairway and took the club in my hands, ready to swing.

At that moment, I became aware of Sam's running commentary: 'Don't miss it mate! Remember which direction to hit it . . .' and other such encouragement.

I hit it . . .

With my eyesight, I had no hope of following its trajectory. It was only Caddie Dave's 'Ohhhh' that alerted me to the prospect it might not have been a complete disaster.

Then I turned to look at Heughan.

There was no mistaking it. His chest had visibly deflated. His jaw was hanging slightly open, his eyes were glassy and filled with foreboding.

We walked to where our balls landed.

Even at a distance, I could see what had happened.

This is where Sam's version falls further from the land of truth. As Dave said (on camera), my ball had landed fifteen yards ahead of Sam's, straight up the middle. It was still ahead even when Sam kicked his ball in an attempt to reach mine. Fifteen yards ahead, which by my rudimentary understanding of mathematics is about three times the distance of five yards.

Now, I'm not proud of this fact but, yes, I did talk AT LENGTH about how far my ball was in front of Sam's. I will also admit that when he insisted on a putting game to even the score, I may have gone into a lengthy and flamboyant happy dance when I beat him at that too. And, yes, okay, I may have talked about it A LOT for the rest of the day, possibly the week.

As I say, not proud. Childish, yes. Disproportionate, definitely. But at that moment it was as if years of being one of the last picked for football had finally found its response!

I had won.

I think I may have kept both golf balls.

I may have written the number 1 on mine, and number 2 on Sam's. I can't remember.

But I do remember being sure to look up the definition of *schadenfreude* that evening.

I will allow Wikipedia to explain:

Schadenfreude is the experience of pleasure, joy, or self-satisfaction that comes from learning of or witnessing the troubles, failures, or humiliation of another. *Schadenfreude* is a complex emotion where, rather than feeling sympathy, one takes pleasure from watching someone's misfortune . . .

I may even have argued that this should have been the name of that episode of *Men in Kilts*. But that would be going too far – fifteen yards too far.

[*Sam: I'm never going to hear the end of this.*]

DRAM OF THE MONTH
ATHOLL BROSE WHISKY LIQUEUR

SAM

One of the stories of how Atholl Brose came to be is the tale of Dougal (MacKenzie?) and Graham, the Giant of Atholl. A very long time ago this giant, who was six feet four inches (an inch taller than me), terrorised the region of Atholl (the top of Perthshire) raiding the land for food to feed his insatiable appetite. He would steal grain from the grain stores, lattes, macchiatos, protein bars (sound familiar?) and cattle, but his tummy would still grumble. Even a family-sized packet of biscuits didn't hit the spot and soon the people of Atholl began to starve.

Dougal, a local hunter, was boiling with fury at Graham the Giant's constant raids for sustenance and plotted to rid the Atholl lands of this hungry hulk. So one night he went to the giant's glen and hid himself amongst his stash of whisky and various nibbles including nuts, oats, honey, protein bars and biscuits. He took a handful of oats and put them into the giant's drinking vessel, adding honey, a pint of whisky and stirred well. He then arranged some salted nuts and pretzels by the giant's favourite armchair and waited.

When Graham saw the drink and snacks laid out, his eyes lit up with excitement and his stomach purred – yes, he preferred Sauvignon Blanc, but that was hard to come by back then, so he had learnt to appreciate whisky (far more than Our Graham today). He ate the nuts and pretzels and drank his fill of Dougal's whisky liqueur, eventually falling asleep, mouth open, snoring like a bush pig, as he does.

Dougal laughed as he slit Graham's throat from ear to ear (you like the violent bits, Grey Dog) and, being a man with an equally large appetite, stole all the whisky and snacks for himself. Dougal returned home a hero and his recipe of Atholl Brose whisky liqueur was passed down the generations.

Here's a traditional recipe the way the current Duke of Atholl makes it: [*Graham: A friend of yours?*] [*Sam: Naturally.*]

Ingredients
Scotch whisky (not too peaty)
3 tbsp of steel-cut oatmeal
2 tbsp of honey

Method
Soak the oats in water for a few hours until thickened (or for a more boozy taste, soak the oats in the whisky!). Put the oats into muslin or a pair of clean tights (Graham will have plenty of pantyhose lying around his house) and squeeze out the excess liquid. Discard the oats and the tights (or you could reuse to polish your Palladian boots or store your onions, but that's a whole different tip entirely).

Pour the creamy oatmeal into a silver cocktail shaker and add two silver tablespoons of honey, four double measures of whisky and shake well. Serve in coupe glasses.

GRAHAM

Marvellous! A seamless alcoholic link to the Atholl
Murrays . . . It's almost like we have a structure to these
ramblings. The Murrays – an ancient clan, this one. Mind
you, none of them have been what you would call recent.

The Murray clan motto is *Furth, Fortune, and Fill the Fetters*,
which basically translates as 'Go forth against your enemies,
steal everything that isn't nailed down, and bring home lots
of captives.' It's the kind of motto that Genghis Khan
probably had embroidered on the saddlecloth of his Mongol
pony as he rode his merry way across Asia.

They are descended from a Flemish nobleman whose name
(and I'm not making this up), is Freskin. Fortunate not to have
an 'o' in his name and be teased relentlessly at school, he rowed
over from Flanders with a lot of other fellas who, I imagine,
had equally awkward names, at the behest of the Scottish King
in the twelfth century. Freskin's surname was de Moravia,
which got bludgeoned by the Scottish tongue into 'Murray',
probably because the Scots couldn't be arsed to pronounce it
correctly. I'd guess he promptly dropped his first name too.

From then, however, there was lots of historic glory and
significance for the spawn of Freskin. They fought with
conspicuous valour in the wars of independence. Their Chief,
Andrew Murray, was killed at the Battle of Stirling Bridge in
1297. His son went on to marry the sister of Robert the Bruce.

In 1490, the clan had one of those Highland battles that we
have come to know and love. This one was the Battle of
Knockmary between the Murrays and the Drummonds. All
seemed to be going well for the Murrays, until it wasn't.
Driven from the battlefield by the Drummonds, who had
been reinforced by some mates (probably from the local pub),
the Murrays decided to take refuge in a small church near
Crieff.

Smart move, I hear you say.

The Drummonds couldn't find them, but then one of the
Murrays (possibly one of the more mentally challenged

members of the clan) decided to fire an arrow at one of the Drummonds, thereby drawing the entire clan to the door of the church.

At which point, with the Murrays reluctant to come out for an uncivilised chat, the Drummonds heaped gigantic piles of combustible wood around the church and burnt it to the ground.

In all, 160 Murrays perished in the holocaust inside. Only one was spared by a sentimental Drummond, who recognised him as a relation. 'Awww, it's you Tam, come on oot!'

Let's hope it wasn't the guy who fired the arrow.

In the sixteenth century, the Clan Chief, Murray of Tullibardine, had a staggeringly impressive number of sons. Seventeen in total. This arguably makes the Clan Chief of Murray the most fertile man in Scotland. I wonder why he stopped at seventeen? Exhaustion on the part of his poor wife, I imagine. Murray was probably game to go for a round twenty!

You'd think at twelve sons he would've called it a day, but, no, he wanted the full rugby team plus substitutes. Or perhaps he simply lost count. Could he even count beyond ten? Who knows. All we can be sure of is that his wife was pregnant for at least seventeen years.

Could he even remember all their names? Or did he just use numbers? No doubt they had to keep building a new dining table every year to accommodate the Murray brood for family gatherings. I imagine Tullibardine having to shout to one of his many sons at the other end of the table to pass the salt.

'Pass the salt, son!'

'What was that da'?'

'The salt!!!'

'The what???'

'The bastard SALT, whatever your bloody name is!!!'

Still, one of this flourishing brood ended up 'smashing in the face' of the Earl of Argyll with the hilt of his sword. For anyone that has held a basket-hilted broadsword, you do not want to be hit in the face with the hilt of one. It would definitely chafe. Unfortunately, son number 14 did this in front of the king himself. As a result, the son was promptly banished from the kingdom.

However, all was not over for the banished son, Will Murray. In his absence, people started stealing the king's mails, stealing and slaughtering his cows, and generally not giving a damn about anything. The king became so desperate that he was heard to cry out, 'If only Will Murray was here!!!' To which someone (perhaps son number 12) replied: 'Will would be happy to come back, if you promise not to kill him.'

The King duly promised, Will Murray returned and promptly set to work making sure all the mails were returned along with the missing cattle. No doubt his basket-hilted broadsword got involved in this. As a reward, the king immediately made Will 'Lord Comptroller' (whatever that is!).

The moral of this story: 'If you're going to smash in someone's face with the hilt of your sword in front of the king, make sure you're good at rescuing stolen cows.'

By 1594, the Murrays were fighting alongside the Campbells of Argyll (yes, Argyll, he of the smashed face). This is all too common in clan history. Your enemy one day becomes your friend the next. Your blood relation one day becomes the guy you try to burn to death in a church the next. On this occasion. it was an all-star gathering at the Battle of Glenlivet and no, they weren't drinking Glenlivet whisky on the day. Heughan would've been there flogging 'Sassenach' if he could go through those stones, no doubt.

On one team were 1000 Murrays, Campbells, Forbes, and Mackintoshes. On the other side were 200 made up of Clan Comyn, Gordon and Clan Cameron. No prizes for the team who won that day.

Jump to 1644 and the Clan Chief, James Murray, welcomed the Royalist leader James Graham of Montrose to Blair Castle. However, it wasn't long afterwards that Murray led 1800 of his men AGAINST Montrose at the Battle of Tippermuir. Such are the fickle ways of Highland alliances.

Possibly their most famous clan member, after actor Bill Murray of course, was Lord George Murray, Bonnie Prince Charlie's second-in-command at Culloden.

After that pivotal defeat, Murray fled and died in Europe. While there, he tried to visit the similarly exiled Prince, but was denied an audience with the Young Pretender.

To this day, the Murray clan claim the unique honour of having the only private army in Europe, the Atholl Highlanders (try saying that after too many whiskies). Queen Victoria bestowed this privilege in 1845 and they've enjoyed it ever since – along with, I suspect, Mons Bolin at Finlarig (see *Clanlands* for more on Mons).

All in all it will definitely make watching Bill Murray a different experience in future . . .

SAM

If we disregard Jenny and Ian Murray, Jamie Fraser's fictional sister and brother-in-law, the most famous Murray that springs to mind is Andy Murray, Scotland's greatest tennis player – which has informed the slang of 'going for a Murray' (curry). Mine's a chicken korma, but I can also tell you that Andy Murray is a true Scottish Legend, known not only for his brilliant tennis playing but also his distinctly deadpan, droll Scottish humour. Watching Andrew give an interview is a lesson in 'less is more'. He and his brother Jamie play doubles sometimes and I know I wouldn't have a chance returning a single serve. Perhaps McTavish and I could take them on!? Now knighted by the Queen for his services to sport, Sir Andrew Barron Murray OBE has been ranked World No. 1, has won three Grand Slam singles titles (including two at Wimbledon) and reached eleven major finals.

I watched him win Wimbledon from the Arctic Circle in Norway, in the summer of 2016. The WiFi was so bad, every shot would be followed by a five or six second delay. By the time I knew he had won the championship, the rest of Scotland (and the UK) were already celebrating. We went for a sub-zero dip in the Arctic Ocean the next morning to mark his victory.

NATURE NOTES
HUMPBACK WHALE MIGRATION

SAM

January to March is the annual migration of North Atlantic humpback whales, when they leave their winter feeding grounds in Arctic waters, and travel across the ocean to mating and breeding grounds in the tropical waters of the Caribbean. And who can blame them! The annual return trip can exceed 15,000 kilometres (9320 miles) and is one of the longest migratory journeys of any mammal on Earth.

So for those of you who want to brave the east coast off Fife, January to March might be the best time to get a glimpse of them, or indeed sometimes around the west coast islands.

NORTH ATLANTIC HUMPBACK WHALE FACT BOX

- A species of baleen whale
- They can live up to 70 years of age
- They can grow up to 12–16m in length and around 25–30 tons
- Diet: small fish and krill
- North Atlantic humpbacks sing a different song to the whales in the North Pacific
- Numbers: 12,000 in the North Atlantic; 80,000 worldwide – a concerted effort to protect them saved the humpback from near extinction, but the work continues
- Megaptera Novaeangliae means 'Big-winged New Englander, (as so many were seen off the New England coast in America)

Humpbacks used to be a common sight off the coast of Scotland; I remember seeing one on the crossing to the Isle of Eigg, as a boy. Now sightings of dolphins are more common as they tend to follow the ferry, 'catching a wave' and generally acting like the hooligans of the North Sea. I love their joy and sense of play. I think I'd be a dolphin in a different life. You can guess who'd be a slow, grumpy whale . . .

After centuries of whaling and recent entanglements in crab and lobster creels, numbers of humpbacks of the coast of Scotland sharply declined. HOWEVER, the great news is that since 2017, humpbacks have started to return to the Firth of Forth off the coast of Edinburgh, apparently using it like a motorway service station and grabbing a quick coffee (latte) and a sandwich (or twelve, and stealing my protein bar) before hitting the pelagic highway again.

The last time I got close to a whale was in the Arctic, off the coast of Norway.

[*Graham: Was it a Sperm Whale?*]

[*Sam: Dear God.*]

I was shooting an independent movie called *The Heart of Lightness*, based on Ibsen's *The Lady from the Sea*, directed by a charismatic Norwegian celebrity chef. Arriving in Oslo, eight actors boarded a train, then a ferry or two, finally making our way to the Arctic Circle. But before you think of snow and ice and Shackleton [*Graham: Wrong continent*], it was summer. So therefore, instead of the Arctic tundra, we were greeted by constant sunshine (24 hours a day), fjords, wildlife, strong drink and the occasional whale.

Jan Vardoen owned several restaurants in Norway and had shipped a CONTAINER of fine wine, meats, cheeses, condiments, chocolate and cigars (oh, AND his head chef!) to our base camp, an old school house on the main island, near to, well . . . nowhere, in the Norwegian wilderness. Yet, despite the abundance of delicious gastronomy, one of the first meals we were offered was . . . whale. A steak, of whale.

I was horrified and sad that this was still a local delicacy. So for the duration, I decided to become a vegan. For days we ate like (plant-based) Vikings, drank the local Ole and Bassard beer (source of great amusement) and waited to film the movie. Each morning we would run from our lodging, naked, scaring off the local wildlife, into the Arctic Ocean. The challenge was to stay in the water the longest. I think the record was two minutes, the winner – proud to be the victor was colder than Graham in a freezer without his precious thermals.

One day, we needed to shoot on a ship so commandeered one and took it out onto the vast ocean. Took one out into the vast ocean. No sooner had we left port, than a large humpback whale rose beside us, taking air. Gunnar, the captain, let us listen to the sonar. The whales sang as they went down, then would go silent for about twenty minutes. They would dive and then resurface, breaking the water like an organic submarine. Beautiful and majestic, we pulled alongside our new friend, the 50-foot humpback, as he took a breath. I reached my hand out to touch him, and with one enormous pulse of his tail he shot off and slipped under the icey water again. We returned to our school house base camp that night, and the director/restaurateur vowed to never eat whale again.

As I mentioned, I met my Scandinavian whale friend, I had seen a few before on the ferry to the Isle of Eigg. As a child, I would go there in the summer to visit my uncle, who lived and worked on the magical island. A tiny isle, with a single road and a handful of islanders, it was a remote and mystical place with rock pools full of crabs, golden beaches, sea eagles and grey dolphins to accompany you on your arrival.

Across the 'singing sands', a golden beach that squeaks as you walk, towards the notorious 'massacre cave' of the MacDonalds (and possible hiding place of Bonnie Prince Charlie), you would be greeted by an awful stench and a cacophony of bird. A long, white, exposed carcass once lay on the beach. Like join sentences a dinosaur skeleton in the museum, or ancient structure left by a deceased civilisation, the birds landed on the whale carcass and screamed as you went past. Pieces of festering blubber fascinated me as a child. This giant of the sea had found its final resting place and I felt sad that it wasn't out in the deep grey ocean, or filling its lungs with fresh Scottish air, before diving down again into the endless Sea of the Hebrides and the warmer Gulf Stream beyond.

GREAT SCOT!

NOTABLE BIRTHDAYS, DEATHS AND SIGNIFICANT EVENTS

3 March 1847 – Alexander Graham Bell, inventor of the telephone, was born in Edinburgh.

4 March 1890 – The Forth Bridge opened. A cantilever railway bridge across the Firth of Forth in the east of Scotland, 9 miles (14 kilometres) west of central Edinburgh.

5 March 1790 – Flora MacDonald died. Described in the *Skye Boat Song*, she helped the Bonnie Prince escape the Government troops and led him to safety via the Isle of Skye. She later supported the Union and spoke as a celebrity for the Government and retracted her actions and support of the Jacobites. She died in the same bed that the Bonnie Prince slept in during his escape at Kingsburgh, Skye.

6 March 1708 – Prince James Stuart, 'The Pretender', sailed from Dunkirk for Scotland with 5000 troops and a French fleet ready to lead a Jacobite uprising against Queen Anne.

7 March 1744 – The Honourable Company of Edinburgh Golfers was founded.

SAM

The oldest golf club in the world, The Honourable Company of Edinburgh Golfers was where the Twelve Rules of Golf were drawn up for the very first competition, in which the winner received a Silver Club (there, I now know what it's called now. I looked it up). One of the early recipients of this golfing trophy was a man named John Rattay. Not only was John a brilliant golfer, he was also the Surgeon General to the Jacobite army and personal physician to Prince Charles Edward Stuart. After the defeat at Culloden, John was rounded up like other Jacobite soldiers and taken to Inverness prison, where he was condemned to execution. UNTIL . . . his golfing connections quite literally saved his life.

Duncan Forbes, President of the Council, one of Scotland's most senior judges and John's regular golfing partner at Leith Links, intervened to save his neck! Thanks to Duncan, John lived to play another five holes again (that was the extent of the course back then) and in 1751 he won the coveted Silver Club, whilst continuing to practice as a surgeon in Edinburgh. You see, 'It's not what you know, it's who you know.'

[*Graham: In that case, I'm doomed.*]

8 March 1859 - Kenneth Grahame was born in Edinburgh.

GRAHAM
Kenneth Grahame was the author of the wonderful children's classic *The Wind in the Willows*, the book I have read more than any other. I must have read it about ten times now, including to both of my children. I first knew of it when my mother chose it as a bedtime story when I was about five years old. From its opening description of Mole's spring cleaning to the climactic battle with the weasels at Toad Hall, it is a joy to read.

The characters of Mole, Ratty, Badger and Toad were so real to me as a child. Their adventures, but most of all their friendship, have stayed with me as I have grown older. Even now, as I write this, I am reminded of the chapter 'Piper at the Gates of Dawn', which is as perfect an evocation of nature as you will ever read.

I so wanted to live in their world, the calm reassurance of the river, and the other-worldliness of the Wild Wood. Badger's house in the Wild Wood is the epitome of safety in an otherwise dangerous world.

I was lucky enough to be in Terry Jones's film of the book in 1995, playing a drunken weasel. I was doing *Richard III* at the time in London. Terry wanted me in the movie, but I had a gap of only a couple of days in which to do it.

I was fitted with my weasel teeth and given a mechanical tail and had the pleasure of legendary Shakespearean actor,

Nicol Williamson, who played Badger, drop a barrier on my head.

That night after filming, Nicol invited me to his trailer for a drink. I expected a can of beer, but when I walked in, he literally had a whole barrel of beer set up in his trailer from which he proceeded to pour us frothing pints.

He was old school!

And it was such a Badger thing to do! of course, he was Scottish!!!

10 March 1916 – Birth of James Herriot (aka James Alfred Wight), author of *All Creatures Great and Small*. [*Sam: I loved this series of books as a child and have always wanted to play James Herriot. Graham has a good story about finding his arm stuck inside a cow's behind (truth!), perhaps he too would like to play a veterinarian?*]

13 March 1873 – Scottish Football Association founded.

16 March 1995 – Death of Simon 'Shimi' Fraser, 15th Lord Lovat. Instrumental in developing a Commando fighting force in the British army, he received a DSO (Distinguished Service Order) at the Dieppe Raid in 1942 and led the 1st Special Service Brigade at the Normandy Landings (D-Day) in 1944 (with Piper Bill Millin. See JUNE) He was awarded the Military Cross and the Légion d'honneur and the Croix de Guerre by the French.

17 March 1984 – Scotland won the rugby Grand Slam at Murrayfield for the first time in 59 years.

20 March 1814 – Birth of Dr John Goodsir in Anstruther, Fife. In 1842 he proved that bacteria, a cause of disease, could be destroyed by selected poisons, eighteen years before Louis Pasteur, who is credited with the discovery.

21 March 1925 – Edinburgh's Murrayfield Stadium opened. Scotland defeated England 14–11 in the first match and won their first Grand Slam, repeated only in 1984 and 1990. Yazzz.

23 March 1848 – First Scottish settlers arrived in Dunedin, New Zealand. [*Sam: Including Sir Graham McTavish*].

27 March 1871 – First Scotland v England rugby international (20 a side!) played at Raeburn Place. Scotland won, of course. Yazzz again!!

28 March 1642 – The Scots Guards Regiment was formed by Archibald Campbell, the 1st Marquess of Argyll, Chief of Clan Campbell. Initially called the Marquis of Argyll's Royal Regiment, the foot guards' motto is: 'No one assails me with impunity'. When on public duty, they can be seen as sentries outside Buckingham Palace, dressed in distinctive scarlet tunics and bearskin caps.

31 March 1950 – Actor Robbie Coltrane was born (Anthony Robert McMillan) in Rutherglen. [*Sam: A graduate of the Glasgow School of Art, he plays a very fine Hagrid in the Harry Potter movies. His daughter, Alice McMillan, was in Season Two of* Outlander *as Molly Cockburn.*]

31 March 1971 – Actor Ewan McGregor born in Perth.

SAM

Trainspotting is one of my favourite Scottish movies and I'm a huge fan of Ewan McGregor and am excited to announce that I will be starring opposite him and Mark Strong in Everest next year! I loved Ewan and Charley Boorman's *Long Way Round/Up* television series. They have ridden the length and breadth of the world on motorbikes, which gives me an idea for our next motorbike and side-car adventure . . . Graham?

Graham: Sadly Sam, I shall be busy stabbing needles in my eyes instead.

APRIL

Clan MacTavish
Motto: *Non Oblitus* (Not forgetful)
[*Sam: A memory like a bloody elephant!*]
Lands: Dunardry, Argyll

KEY DIARY DATES

1 'The Glorious 1st'. The Haggis Shooting
Season Begins

EASTER

22 Earth Day
23 William Shakespeare's Birthday
30 Sam Roland Heughan's Official Birthday
(*Taurus*, 1980)

End of April: Spirit of Speyside Whisky Festival

THE GLORIOUS 1ST APRIL

GRAHAM

We touched on the subject of haggis in *Men in Kilts*. The First of April marks the official beginning of the haggis shooting season. It wasn't always the case. Once, haggis were so plentiful that they could be hunted almost any time of the year, except the mating season: December–March, when hunters respected the lengthy mating ritual of the haggis. This period is also when the plumage of the haggis is at its most vibrant. Greens, yellows and scarlet tones creating a riot of colour over the snow-covered glens.

[*Sam: Unless you're talking about the lesser-spotted haggis? The males are very hairy.*]

Now, however, their rarity has meant the haggis shooting season is a short one. Twenty-one days to be exact, unless it's a leap year. April is definitely NOT a month to be a haggis.

The stalking and finding of haggis is a specialist job, with a proud history going back hundreds of years. It is a job passed from father to son. The MacHaggis clan were, not surprisingly, famous for their stalking abilities. Nowadays, haggis ghillies head into the hills wearing only the stitched-together pelts of haggi (the plural of haggis) and imitating the bark-like call of the haggis. Some younger ghillies prefer to use the haggis 'trumpet' that imitates the sound, but the older, more traditional, stalker still produces the sound in his own throat (for those that have not heard it, the call resembles the hacking cough of a sixty-a-day smoker mixed with the sound of an engine backfiring).

[Sam: I do a very good impression of a lowland haggis, less guttural and more, perhaps, musical.]

If you have never seen one up close (sadly, I haven't), the haggis is like a marmot mixed with a badger, possessing the agility of a very small deer.

[Sam: I'd say more like a hedgehog, with three legs, the ones I've seen.]

Its powerful hind legs (longer than its forelegs) give the haggis the ability to spring unexpectedly from cover. This is particularly dangerous when they are cornered. Many an inexperienced hunter has lived to regret startling a wild haggis, watching in horror as it springs towards his groin.

I say 'wild' haggis, because some have been tamed in the past. In the seventeenth century, it became the height of style to adorn your castle with a trained haggis.

[Sam: Or indeed wear them, on the front of your kilt, where the traditional 'sporran' originated. Just make sure they are well fed and asleep first, before attaching to the belt, or you may suffer the same fate as many unfortunate Scotsmen who don their kilt and haggis, before realising it is feeding time. Very unfortunate injuries have been the result. Scarred for life.]

Haggi were occasionally even employed as 'guard dogs'. Donald MacDonald of Sleat was famously reputed to have several haggi that he would walk around the grounds of his castle.

But it wasn't all fun and games: Among the more grisly punishments meted out to unfortunate prisoners was the practice of 'Death by Haggis'. Here, the prisoner was allowed a 30-second head start before a bladder of haggi (their collective noun) was unleashed. Able to cover a distance of 100 yards in a little over eight seconds, the prisoner stood no chance.

Their teeth are particularly vicious. For an animal that is a vegetarian, they possess freakish incisors. Rather like a very small, furry, sabre-toothed tiger.

[*Sam: They also used to throw haggis at the Highland Games, before the shot put was favoured, due to the tossed haggis escaping and terrorising the gathered crowd. Sometimes it burrowed into the long jump sand pit and built its own sandcastle lair, where it would collect various knick-knacks and discarded snacks, building a nest out of stolen kilt material and biting the hapless long-jumping athlete.*]

As Sam pointed out in the show, thankfully the giant haggis is long extinct. Roaming the Highlands freely in the Pleistocene era, they grew up to ten feet when standing on their hind legs. The skeleton of one found in a peat bog in Skye sits in the National Museum of Scotland.

[*Sam: I believe they found it perfectly preserved, with a broad smile and legs crossed as if it was buried whilst reclining in the sunshine?*]

Nowadays we all enjoy the taste of a haggis, but their habitat is getting smaller every year. Limited to the area north of Ullapool between Lochinver and Scourie, with a few bladders scattered on the smaller, more remote Hebridean islands. This is my favourite species of haggis – smaller, and less prone to vicious leaping, it has been known for a human to be able to approach and pet them. They were particularly valued as live sporrans, being generally more docile. However, a notorious fight between the haggis sporran of Iain MacDubh and Ruaridh MacLeod at a Highland gathering was particularly unfortunate.

[*Sam: Oh yes. That one was bad. People still talk about that, in private.*]

In conclusion, by all means, look for the haggis, but if you see one treat it with respect and be thankful to have caught a glimpse of this rare Scottish creature – shy, handsome and elusive – rather like a furry version of Duncan Lacroix.

For those interested to learn more, I recommend these books:

The Haggis and the Wolf: The Wild Days of the Highlands, Alasdair Meallta, 1982.

My Life Among the Wild Haggis of Rhum, Peter Amadan, 1936.
  (Peter was lucky enough to live with a bladder of haggis
  for 18 months, until they ate him one Christmas Eve,
  perhaps realising he wasn't actually an overgrown
  haggis.)
The Role of the Wild Haggis in the Jacobite Rebellion, Michael
  Ku'sfesack. (Surprisingly good this one. Trained haggis
  were used to attack the Government troops, thus giving
  the name to a 'Haggis Run'.)

BATTLE OF THE MONTH
THE BATTLE OF CULLODEN, 16 APRIL 1746

GRAHAM

The fascinating thing about history is that there is always
something new to discover. History reveals itself slowly,
almost teasingly, gradually adding more pieces to the puzzle.
Sometimes this makes the picture clearer, but other times it
makes it frustratingly more difficult to get a clear image.

Nothing exemplifies this more than the Battle of Culloden.
It's like that 1000 piece puzzle that you're close to finishing,
only to discover another 1000 pieces lurking at the bottom of
the box!

In many ways, Culloden has been used deliberately to
misrepresent what really went on, for political purposes. A
somewhat popular view is that the Jacobites were a gang of
kilted primitives up against the ordered machine of the
Government troops. The fact is that by attempting to restore
the Stuart monarchy, the Jacobites represented a huge threat
to the Hanoverians and a single centralised Britain.

The Battle of Culloden also signifies the start of a national
narrative about reconciling England with its 'less developed'
peripheries. This would be used to justify the expansion of

the British Empire and the absorption of native cultures into the warm bosom of Mother England.

There is a famous painting showing the death of General James Wolfe at Quebec. We see the man (who had been a lieutenant at Culloden) looking definitely a bit peaky, his expression reminiscent of my own after a night out with Lacroix or a day being driven by Sam.

In the painting, we see a concerned Native American crouched in front of him (he looks vaguely bored to be honest!), with Simon Fraser, Chief of Clan Fraser, looking downcast and thoroughly depressed. Simon Fraser was not at Quebec, but he had sided against Wolfe at Culloden. The other remarkable fact is that Sam is not in the painting dressed as Jamie.

The message though is clear: Fraser and the Native American have both been integrated into the Empire and are very happy to be there, and very, very sad to see Wolfe perish. It would be a little like a painting of a dying Lord Vader surrounded by a concerned Ewok with Han Solo shedding a tear in the background.

The popular political message of Culloden is a bunch of badly armed savages sacrificing themselves for some prancing Italian ponce, while nobly defending an ancient way of life.

In fact, Culloden represents an attempt to restore James II to a multi-kingdom monarchy more aligned with Europe instead of colonial expansion.

The image of the Highlander at Culloden paints a picture of an outmoded army up against a modern killing machine. In reality, the Highlanders were drilled according to French conventions and indeed fought alongside French and Irish allies. They didn't take their orders in Gaelic, but in English. They not only had artillery, but actually fired more cannonballs per man than the Government forces.

What they did lack, however, was cavalry. They had, at most, two hundred horses. The Government had four times that number. Once the Highland charge failed, it was the cavalry that decided things. Swooping in from the wings and forcing the collapse of the Highlanders.

The other major factor was numbers. The Jacobites had about 5000 men, several thousand less than the Government, and a third of the strength they possessed during the rest of the rebellion. And remember, about a 1000 of the Jacobites slept through the battle from sheer exhaustion!!

It was the combination of these factors that really decided the battle that day. If they'd had more cavalry and more men, it would've been a close-run thing!

The other pervading myth is that the Jacobite adjutant-general John O'Sullivan chose the wrong battlefield. While it's true he vetoed several other suggestions from others, his own preferred site was one kilometre east of where the battle took place. The only problem was that it was very visible to the Royal Navy anchored in the Moray Firth. This delayed the Jacobites' night attack on 15 April and in the confusion that followed, they ended up one kilometre west of where they wanted to be.

So the whole 'primitive' view of the Jacobites and the story of the battle is very different from what really happened. It was the final battle in a civil war, and the defeat of the Jacobites represented the end to a Scottish alternative to a British state.

The poignant irony is that a federal kind of Britain under a single crown, as had existed in Scotland between 1603 and 1707 and was basically what the Jacobites wanted, is more of a reality today than they could ever have imagined.

I wonder what those clansmen would make of today's Scottish parliament with its devolved powers? I suspect they would have smiled and, to some extent, understood, 'Well, we got there in the end . . .'

SAM

Graham was all aquiver when we met Alistair Moffat – the historian and author of *The Highland Clans and Scotland: A History from Earliest Times*. He had collected all of Alistair's books, perhaps hoping for an autograph and was sitting there like a schoolboy, front row, trying to impress our teacher. To be honest it's hard not to be caught up in Alistair's storytelling and charisma and I too found myself wanting to impress our scholarly friend.

What annoyed Graham is that Alistair and I had so much in common academically, both being connected to the University of Stirling, from which I received my honorary doctorate degree for services to acting and charity, and where Alistair served as Chancellor's Assessor on Stirling's University Court (2009–2011).

Graham: This is akin to saying that Usain Bolt and I have so much in common athletically because, like him, I can run for 100 metres without stopping.

Sam: I have video evidence you can't.

Graham: In fact, Mr Bolt and I do have more in common than Alistair and Samwise, given that the latter's only academic achievement at Stirling University was working out where to park his car before going in to collect his honorary scroll.

COMPETITION CORNER
THE CULLODEN RUN

[Sam: Well, more of a light jog . . .]

GRAHAM
While filming dear old *Men in Kilts*, we knew we had to devote a sizable amount of time to the Battle of Culloden, that pivotal moment in Scottish history.

Sometimes, however, the reciting of its history, clans, casualties, etc., can be a little dry. I remember describing what the charge by the Highlanders must've felt like to my two young children, when they were complaining about a hike we were on.

Typical Dad stuff: 'If you think this is hard, imagine charging through exploding cannonballs and being raked by platoon volley-fire from trained Govermnent troops, watching your friends exploding, being covered in their brain matter and viscera!' (All very character forming. My children may have even wept.)

So I suggested to Sam and the crew that we should re-enact the run. Originally we considered doing it on the battlefield itself but, wisely, rejected the idea out of respect for the sacredness of that location.

Instead we found a bloody great field near Castle Fraser and did it there.

We measured it out – 300 yards.

The crew assembled. John Duncan, our wizard drone operator, would record from above and we'd have the cameras rolling at a distance as we did our run, in honour of those brave Highlanders who charged on that freezing April day in 1746.

All sounds pretty straightforward, doesn't it?

The only thing we failed to factor in was that Heughan would inevitably turn it into some kind of competition.

We were suitably dressed in our great kilts and billowy white shirts. I think we may have cheated a wee bit on the footwear. I don't think Adidas featured very big at Culloden, but we looked suitably 'Highlanderish' as we prepared to set off.

We did a warm-up. Well, I definitely did. The last thing I wanted in my tender years was my hamstring exploding or my calf seizing up. I spent a good ten minutes stretching. I suspect Sam simply stood watching with contempt. His own warm-up had probably been having his legs oiled and massaged by his German 'business partner', while downing several large whiskies.

We were ready.

We gripped the hilts of our broadswords and took a firm hold of our targes or shields.

3–2–1 and . . .

Go!!'

We set off at a gentle jog. Being the poncey actors we are, we'd had the ground carefully examined for potholes. (This doesn't mean that Heughan might not have been out digging new ones in the night for where I would run.)

As we got our rhythm, we began to move faster.

We were running side by side. I was strangely grateful that Sam was holding back so we could complete the run together.

And then it happened.

He began to lengthen his stride.

'Is he trying to beat me?' I thought, and I watched him begin to windmill his arms like a billowy shirted version of the aforementioned Usain Bolt.

He *is* trying to beat me.

With about 100 yards to run, Sam threw away all pretence of us trying to do this together.

He basically broke into a full-on sprint.

I watched as the gap opened up between us and I was treated, yet again, to a view of Sam's arse as he moved away from me.

I won't say I was surprised. After all, it's a little like the parable of the scorpion and the frog, it is in Sam's nature to attempt to beat people at everything.

The run now resembled a particularly angry type of dog being pursued by someone doing an impersonation of a Lipizzaner horse doing a slow dressage.

I gave up trying to catch him.

I never would.

Instead I watched his kilted form bounding into the distance as he passed the 300 yard mark and waited while I jogged to join him.

Bastard!

I wasn't happy. What followed was, I am prepared to admit, somewhat petty. I told the director we needed to do it again. This time with us both crossing the line together. I managed to convince myself this was to make the shot look better, and keep more in the spirit of Culloden. (In reality, of course, I'm sure there were lots of sixty-year-olds on the day of the battle struggling to keep up with their younger, faster comrades, but I wasn't going to admit THAT to Sam!)

No, I wanted us to run it again because I couldn't bear him beating me.

There!

I've said it. My bruised ego couldn't permit this.

I'm not proud of it. I literally reverted to the school playground, admittedly a place where Sam spends almost every waking moment, but still!

So, we did it again.

This time side by side right to the very end, until our egos crossed the line as one!

SAM

Although your admission of playground pettiness is welcome, I'm afraid you have left far too much detail out of this 'Culloden dash'. Allow me to fill in the gaps . . . first of all, Graham was complaining (so unlike him) about the ground. Had I checked the ground? Was it flat enough? Were there any potholes? Was it safe? Did we have insurance? He basically wanted a full risk assessment.

Me: Graham, we're just going to run across this grass. Let's just do it.

Graham: This is madness – does anyone know if it's safe?

He was busy creating a plethora of problems before we'd even started running. So I said were either going to do it or were not. FINALLY he agreed to do it, but only if he could have all my weapons (the only equipment we had) to look more fearsome. He wanted my targe and my dirk and I could keep my broadsword. I handed my weapons over to the grey one and it was agreed that we would run together at a steady pace until about halfway and then we'd both go for it, because that's what the clans would have done, right? They'd have run as fast as they could.

So that's what I did.

I ran to the end as fast as I could and stopped to look back at Graham, who was still very far away, huffing and puffing at a steady care-home pace for another five minutes, until he finally arrived.

We then walked all the way back to the crew in total

silence. Graham was extremely grumpy, muttering to himself under his grey whiskers. Suddenly as we neared the crew, he started shouting at the director.

Graham: KEVIN! KEVIN! No, no! I think we need to do it again. No!

I didn't say anything, but I could see Kevin and the crew were saying . . . it's fine, we don't need to do it again. It was great.

'No, no. We need to do it again,' insisted Graham. It was the first and only time I've ever seen Graham demand another take.

So I had to run with him for the second take. This time we agreed we'd wait until the last 100 yards and then go for it. He's not a runner, bless him. He's said that himself. He likes to take things steady and slow – he'd rather walk, admire the view on the way, consult his guidebook and stop for tea and biccies halfway. He was now even complaining about some nettles halfway.

Graham: We can't possibly run that way because the nettles are everywhere.

Sam: Just run!

We did the shot and once again I left him for dust. And once again he was rather upset about it. He's a two-take man. We've all known that for years. We can only do two takes, because that's Graham's limit. After two takes, Graham needed a biscuit, blanket and lie down. George, his driver, fanned his face and offered to take McTavish back to his nine-star hotel, but it was time for the Grey Dog to man-up, because we had a date at Beaufort Castle, seat of the Frasers.

CRACKING CASTLE OF THE MONTH
BEAUFORT CASTLE

Seat of the Frasers, Beaufort Castle (formerly known as Dounie) is a baronial-style mansion situated in 800 acres on the banks of the Beauly Firth, thirteen miles west of Inverness. There's been a castle on the site for 700 years. One of which was razed to the ground by Butcher Cumberland in the wake of Culloden in 1746, the estate was confiscated by the Hanoverian Crown, but eventually returned in 1774

In the early 1800s the Frasers built a stronger and better castle, which still houses Bonnie Prince Charlie's pistols and canteen to this day. However, it is no longer owned by the Frasers, who were forced to sell Beaufort and the 19,500 acre estate in order to pay inheritance taxes in 1994.

CLAN FRASER

SAM

Our *Men in Kilts* guest, Lady Sarah Fraser was waiting for us under the trees in the grounds of Beaufort Castle, as it had started to rain. Graham is very enamoured by aristocratic women and any woman who is well-educated in historical matters – remember Lady Cawdor?! So he was off like a shot offering her an umbrella and making great efforts to impress her. 'Graham McTavish,' he said, bowing. She smiled at him and he was away, puffing his chest out. 'I've just run the whole of Culloden!'

I imagined the lines running through his head at that moment: 'So, Lady Sarah, do you want to come back to my castle? Oh yes, I have a castle. Possibly the oldest in Scotland. Yes. Castle Sween. You must come over . . . I'll ask Tony

Singh to cook for us. Great friend of mine. Oh, Sam, no he won't be able to make it. Busy work schedule.'

(Graham really does have a castle . . . but we'll come to that next month!)

Sarah Fraser is worth all of Graham's fawning, because she is charismatic, charming and so well-versed in history, and has written some truly great books, including *The Prince Who Would Be King* and *The Last Highlander*, about her Jacobite ancestor (and Jamie's grandfather) the Old Fox, Simon Fraser, Lord Lovat. As she tells us more about the great Fraser clan, I'm expecting Graham to throw in a few scholarly comments to impress Sarah, but instead he stands there like a simpering fool, mesmerised by her knowledge and her beauty. In fact, we both yet again fell under the spell of our amazing guest, or perhaps it was that we both needed a nap after our wee run.

I added my own nuggets to the proceedings. 'I believe the Fraser name comes from the French for strawberry, *fraise*.' Sarah was impressed. 'Yes, possibly.' I always tried to pronounce 'Frisael' in the first few seasons of *Outlander*, leaning into the Gaelic and closer to the French pronunciation. It is generally believed that the name Fraser originated in the French provinces of Anjou and Normandy; as I said, the French word for strawberry is *fraise*, and strawberry plants are called, wait for it . . . *fraisiers*. The Fraser arms are silver strawberry flowers in a field of blue, and the wild strawberry became the choice of the clan for their plant badge. It is said that the clan originally based their home near a large patch of wild Scottish strawberries.

Sarah told us the Frasers had been in Britain for over 900 years, arriving with William the Conqueror. 'They came up to Scotland, married, made alliances and got into an argy-bargy with the clans, competing for territory and influence. The primary virtue of clanship was protection and defence from a predatory neighbour, whilst in a symbolic sense building up the clan identity of Clan Fraser.'

I've been playing Jamie Fraser for nearly a decade and over the years my understanding of the character and the world of

Outlander has changed greatly. We started in Jacobite Uprisings and later I found myself in the American War of Independence. This is what's great about the show: every episode is different and is always supplying a new historical challenge.

I am hoping one day to become an honorary Fraser. Sarah said it was possible for me to become a *Bollo Mio* Fraser if I 'swear eternal allegiance and in return for a fee'! [*Graham: Turns out a* bollo *means a 'little muffin' (or perhaps 'stud muffin')* *in Spanish so it would appear Lady Fraser had other plans!*] I am still awaiting the the invitation to the initiation ceremony. And the invoice. Perhaps posthumously, for services to the clan by way of popularising it through the TV show? Jamie was a MacKenzie on his mother's side – that's where he got the ginger hair and height from. Both of which I lack, as a six-foot three-inch blond.

GRAHAM

It's time for a tiny intervention here. A little like when you see a good friend repeatedly doing something that is plain wrong, at some point you have to say something.

And that something is:

YOU ARE NOT JAMIE FRASER!!!!!

[*Sam: Wait. What?*]

He's fictional

Made-up

Make believe

Imaginary

Pretend

The opposite of real.

Like an invisible friend you might've had at school to make you feel like you had a pal.

You have a pal, Sam . . . me!! . . . Well, sometimes me.

Sam Heughan is enough. You don't need to be like bloody Jamie Fraser, perfect at everything except whistling and blinking. You're REALLY GOOD at blinking Sam!!

Be proud of Sam.

Forget being the 'King of Men'. Be happy to be someone

who might know someone who once saw in the very far distance a king of men.

This has been creeping up for a while now. I first noticed it when Sam took particular interest in what happened to the Fraser clan at Culloden. Nodding sagely as our guide described their bravery.

He probably laid a wreath at the Fraser cairn on the battlefield, wiping away a silent tear for people to whom he has precisely ZERO connection.

It happened again when we were interviewing Sarah Fraser. He looked at the castle like it was home. Admittedly my family home turned out to be a broken-down ruin next to a trailer park (see MAY), but that's not the point!!

Be proud of the Heughan that flows through your veins. Admittedly they were hundreds of miles from Culloden, but I bet they were doing something REALLY interesting on 16 April 1746.

I mean, they were probably really keen to go to Culloden. Something came up, that's all. A local rock-lifting competition perhaps?

[*Sam: Very likely winning it too.*]

If your clan had been there I'm sure they would have . . . been there.

I, for one, am proud to count a Heughan as my friend, and if you had a pal like the entirely fictional Jamie Fraser, you would definitely be the King of Men's really, really good friend.

REGION OF THE MONTH
INVERNESS AND INVERNESS-SHIRE

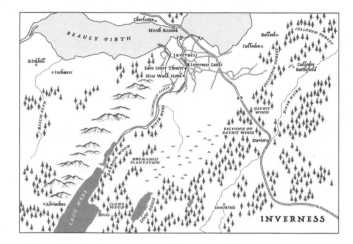

SAM

Clan Fraser of Lovat mainly controlled territory to the west and the south of Inverness, beyond Loch Ness. I love the area and the city of Inverness, which historically was considered the capital of the north. Even back in Jamie Fraser's time, it would have been the one place where there were probably lights on in the whole darkness of the Highlands. When we were filming there for *Men In Kilts*, Graham and I stayed at the Ness Walk Hotel, right on the river, which I can highly recommend. One evening I went for a wander down by the River Ness, whilse Graham sat down to another five-course dinner. There are stunning bridges along the route and I soon found myself crossing the river near the Eden Court Theatre, where I played in *Outlying Islands* and did my first 'fan-meet' with the Heughligans, shortly after I'd been cast in *Outlander*.

ADVENTURE OF THE MONTH
BEN WYVIS (GLAS LEATHAD MOR)

SAM

The same year I landed the role of Jamie in *Outlander* in 2013, I planned a climb up Ben Wyviss, a brooding Munro near Dingwall in Easter Ross, before visiting the famed battlefield of Culloden nearby, for research into the character and show. With only my hiking boots, semi-waterproof jacket, and a rucksack with water and a larger flask of whisky, I set out. As I gained height, a climber in full gear passed me and told me it was a bit blowy at the top – I may want to think twice. This warning would have been heeded immediately had I been with my cautious *Clanlands* friend, but I wasn't, so I pressed on in the vague knowledge that even Sir Hugh Thomas Munro, 4th Baronet and mountaineer (16 October 1856–19 March 1919) himself hadn't made it to the top of Wyvis.

By now I could see a dark storm approaching as I picked my way through the changing landscape, covered with snow and ice. Nearing the 1046-metre summit, the wind picked up and gusted with ferocity, forcing me to turn back. I knew it was time to descend. I took a moment to admire the view of the Culloden battlefield, the dark storm clouds moodily gathering over it, the River Ness far off in the distance. I vowed to return to conquer the Munro one day, with better equipment and in warmer weather.

APRIL BIRTHDAYS

Sam: First of all, I think it's interesting to note that William Shakespeare and I share the same birthday month and star sign. [*Graham: One was a prolific genius, the other is a prolific* ▓▓▓▓]

Graham: Let's have a quick Google to see who else was

born in April. Ah, yes, as I suspected. It says here that 'the majority of psychopaths have a Taurus star sign'. Yep. And thirty-eight psychopaths were born in the month of April and that's not counting Adolf Hitler. I think, dear reader, you're getting the general idea of who we're dealing with here.

Sam: And how many nutjobs in January?

Graham: Oh dear god. There are fifty-six.

Sam: Ha! Ha! Yes, the high-maintenance, hypoglycaemic Capricorns lose their shit far faster than the gentle, slow-to-anger Taureans!

Graham: But another compelling fact about this month according to the very reliable interweb is that most alcoholics are born in April – which given Sam's 'day whisky' stashed in the glove compartment on both the *Clanlands* and *MIK* trips is a little concerning . . .

Sam: Interestingly, my uncle's birthday is 26 April and my brother Cirdan's is on the 28th, so April is a popular month for birthdays in my family, plus my driver Davie is on the 24th.

Graham: I wonder what the collective noun for so many familial Tauruses is? A hyperactivity of Tauruses, a mad competition, a determination, a charge, maybe a trampling of Tauruses. Are your brother and uncle like you? Forces of nature, muscular Springer Spaniels that never stop. It seems a good comparison given your uncle was a gamekeeper.

Sam: Not really a gamekeeper, a musician and basket weaver. You must have been napping when I explained. Again.

SAM

I don't think you've ever celebrated my birthday with me, have you, Graham? I'm looking forward to your belated sixtieth birthday bash in Borthwick Castle! Will we all have to bring a bottle? And our own food? And cash for the pay bar? OR WILL YOU BE PAYING?!?!

[*Graham: I suspect I'll be paying in many ways . . .*]

On my thirty-fourth birthday, the day before Jamie's 293rd birthday, we were filming the first season of *Outlander*. Jamie

Fraser had been forced into a marriage with a rather strange English woman, a Sassenach, by his follicly challenged and rather devious uncle Dougal (played by my current travelling companion, Mr McTavish). In Episode Eight, as newlyweds, Jamie takes his new wife for a romantic picnic, which is pretty forward-thinking for an eighteenth-century Scottish Highlander.

We were packed off that morning from the unit base with a basket of cheese, bread, meat and berries (alas, no whisky). The producers had picked a beautiful mountain top over looking Loch Rannoch, Rannoch Moor and out towards the rolling peaks of Glencoe. Jamie was fully prepared, apart from one essential item, an umbrella. We arrived at the mountain top to find we could barely see more than ten feet ahead of us, as a heavy fog was hanging over the vantage point, hiding the beautiful scenery below. Never deterred by 'a little bad weather', we set up the picnic and began to shoot the scene.

At the same time as Anna Foerster, the talented German-born director, called 'Action!', heaven took this as a cue to open up its rain clouds and empty their contents on the two already damp actors. We continued to shoot regardless, as the cheese began to swim backstroke in a pool of water, whilst the bread gave up and disintegrated to touch. My kilt, normally brilliant at keeping out the rain, was waterlogged and became twice the weight it once was. I distinctly remember being unable to speak my lines at times, as the rain was coming in sideways and would fill my mouth with water whenever I tried to speak.

Looking back at the photos, you can see the crew were dressed in complete wet-weather gear, waterproof trousers, wellies, hats, jackets and gloves, but yet they were also struggling to remain upright as the wind and rain battered them from every angle.

During the scene, Jamie and Claire are approached by an old friend of Jamie's, Hugh Munro. Clad in rags and trinkets, Hugh is a mute beggar, who had his tongue cut out by the Turks whilst at sea. We had created a form of sign language by which Jamie and Hugh communicate, that was helpful in the driving rain. When it came to my close-up, Simon Meacock, playing Hugh, gave me a wry smile and held something behind his back. The director called for action and as we started the scene, the once-mute Hugh Munro burst into song. 'Happy Birthday to yooooou, happy birthday TO YOU!!'

At first I was confused, had he lost his mind? How was he singing without a tongue? Then Simon presented me with a rather soggy but delicious-looking iced birthday cake (the candles had long been extinguished by the incessant rain). Maybe not as romantic as Jamie had hoped for, but it was certainly memorable. I'd suggest if your 'Jamie Fraser' ever suggests a romantic picnic, don't forget to pack a brolly or two.

And, rather than take a cake for 'afters', why not whip up my favourite pudding, Tony Singh's Honey and Whisky Fool? It can't get soggy and is laced with booze – what's not to love?

SAM'S BIRTHDAY RECIPE
TONY SINGH'S HONEY AND WHISKY FOOL

Ingredients
5 egg yolks
2 tbsp of Scottish heather honey
140ml of Sassenach whisky
400ml of double cream
1 large lemon (zested and juiced)
4 strawberries for garnish
4 large mint leaves for garnish

Method
Place the egg yolks, honey and 100ml of the whisky and lemon zest in a heatproof bowl suspended over a saucepan of barely simmering water and whisk with an electric whisk / hand whisk until the mixture is pale and thick to ribbon stage (Google this if you need to!).

Leave to cool to body temperature.

Whisk the double cream and the remaining whisky until stiff, then fold the cream into the egg and honey mixture.

Divide the mixture between martini glasses and pop them in the fridge to set for at least 2 hours.

Serve with shortbread and a diced strawberry on top as garnish.

DRAM OF THE MONTH
ATHOLL BROSE WHISKY LIQUEUR

SAM

The region around Inverness and Speyside has a vast array of whisky distilleries and a fine distilling heritage. Inverness whisky is typically light and sweet, often with a fruity flavour, and is made with water from the River Spey. It's hard to choose one: from the shores of Loch Ness (Loch Ness Spirits - makes absinthe, no whisky yet), the infamous Macallan twelve-year-old with a Sherry oak finish or Tomatin (Alex Norouzi, my business partner, loves this single malt and bought us a bottle when we were on our whisky travels looking for the perfect dram), there are countless great tipples to sample in their area. I'm surprised the locals of Ness aren't sozzled all the time!

But if I had to choose a special dram for my birthday month (that's not The Sassenach 'Spirit of Home' - almost impossible!) then I'd choose a whisky which doesn't exist. The Ben Wyvis Distillery kindly made us feel at home and showed us their amazing, fully sustainable premises. High on the mountainside, wind, solar and biomass energy help produce their spirit, and they are part-owned by the community in turn reinvesting in the local area with several scholarships to aid education and work opportunities for local youngsters to work at the distillery. They haven't bottled their whisky, yet. It's still ageing but their new 'make spirit' is sublime (reminds me of Oban in its crispness) so I'm rather hoping they'll send me a barrel or twelve... for my next birthday!! SLAINTE.

NATURE NOTES
BLUEBELLS

SAM

You might not have taken me for a gardening type, but I am a keen amateur horticulturist. I even bought a book! In fact, several books. Haven't read them yet though . . . [*Graham: Well, that's a first!*]

As my canny readers will know, common dandelion (*Taraxacum officinale*), white dead nettle (*Lamium album*) and stinging nettle (*Urtica dioica*) appear in Scotland this month as well as my personal favourite: bluebells (*Hyacinthoides non-scripta*). I LOVE bluebells. Seriously. They always bring hope, one of the first flowers to appear after winter they are nature's clue that spring is well on its way. As a child, the grounds of Kenmure Castle were covered in vast fields of bluebells. They're so pretty. As they grow naturally and in abundance, I must remember to give Graham some, thus saving on further expense. In *Outlander*, Claire sees bluebells growing on the side of the road near Cocknammon Rock (*Cross Stitch*, Chapter 3).

April is also the month for Bitter Vetch or Heath Pea. Jamie soothed a horse's damaged hoof by applying a poultice of vetch leaves and honey (*Dragonfly in Amber*, Chapter 36). A plant favoured by travellers, the roots have an aniseed taste and can act as a stimulant and hunger suppressant. It was also used to flavour whisky and could be taken as a hangover cure.

[*Graham: Sam is currently hard at work doing medical trials on himself. So selfless.*]

On *Men in Kilts*, Claire Marcello, herbalist and advisor to *Outlander* on traditional forms of medicine, told us the juice of the onion can treat hair loss. Onion sales have inexplicably soared in New Zealand since Graham returned.

[*Graham: And bog myrtle apparently deters noxious midges – except around Heughan, who is so artificially sweetened, women and midges plague him. It must be his brand of hair dye. Or Sun In to cover the ginger?*]

GREAT SCOT!

NOTABLE BIRTHDAYS, DEATHS AND SIGNIFICANT EVENTS

1 April – Hunt the Gowk, the Scottish equivalent of April Fool's Day (a gowk is a cuckoo).

6 April 1320 – Declaration of Arbroath: 'For we fight not for glory nor for riches nor for honour, but only and alone for freedom, which no good man surrenders but with his life.'

6 April 1998 – Celebration of Tartan Day, recognition of the monumental achievements and invaluable contributions made by Scottish Americans.

SAM
Both Graham and I have been Grand Marshals.

GRAHAM
But I pipped him to the post and was one FIRST.

9 April 1747 – Lord Lovat beheaded on Tower Hill for high treason. He was the last person to be beheaded in Britain.

14 April 1961 – Actor Robert Carlysle OBE born in Glasgow.

SAM
I grew up watching Robert Carlysle in Hamish McBeth, *filmed in the beautiful Plockton, then he went on to play Begbie in* Trainspotting! *Scary stuff. He kindly came to my drama school whilst I was green and in my first year, to give us advice on being a professional actor. He banished the tutors from the room and then answered ANY questions we had, no matter how dark and confidential. It's something I've been able to do recently with some current students at the Conservatoire, although I may not have revealed quite as much classified information as Mr Carlysle.*

18 April 1971 – Actor David John Tennant born in Bathgate.

21 April 1838 – John Muir, born pioneering conservationist and founder of the USA National Parks movement.

21 April 1979 – Actor James McAvoy born in Glasgow.

SAM

James McAvoy was my mentor at drama school and good friends with a lot of other Scottish actor pals. We share the same brilliant agent Ruth Young in the UK and Theresa Peters in the US. It would be great to work with him one day, although does that mean our agents get paid only once, a sort of a two-for-one bargain deal?

30 April 1891 – *An Comunn Gaidhealach* was founded to secure the preservation and development of the Gaelic language.

MAY

Love makes the world go round? Not at all.
Whisky makes it go round twice as fast.
Compton Mackenzie

Family of Bruce
Motto: *Fuimus* (We Have Been)
Lands: Annandale, Clackmannan, and Elgin

KEY DIARY DATES

1-31	Whisky Month
1	BELTANE (May Day)
1	James Alexander Malcolm MacKenzie Fraser's Birthday (JAMMF), born 1721
9-17	Orkney Nature Festival
9 May 2021	UK Release date of *Men in Kilts*
29	Dougal MacKenzie's Birthday, born 1694
	Last Saturday in May: The Edinburgh Marathon

THE EDINBURGH MARATHON

SAM

As part of My Peak Challenge, two years ago, I decided to challenge myself and run two marathons in a month – and also beat my personal best. The Stirling Marathon around the impressive castle and the Wallace monument came first, and after twelve weeks of training and a sizable amount of 'carb-loading' (eating as much pasta, bruschetta and maybe a little red wine), I felt strong and 'healthy'.

The night before the marathon, I met a jovial chap in the hotel bar (I was doing some last minute 'fuelling' – club sandwich, French fries and a large glass of the aforesaid red wine full of antioxidants, my body is a temple, ahem), who had come up from London. He was nervous, as was I, but his naivety strangely put me more at ease. Before a race, your mind plays tricks with you. Will I be able to run that far? What if I get sick or injured? That night, I began to regret the Vin Rouge and opted for a large pint of water instead. I awoke to a chilly but bright morning, and despite being relative strangers, we agreed to walk to the start line together, after a hearty bowl of porridge, several lukewarm coffees and a bruised banana.

As the starter pistol went off, the surge of energy and excitement charged my body, and my training really kicked in. I yelled goodbye to my chatty friend and set off, sustaining a good 7.15-minute mile pace for the whole 26.2 miles, finishing in three hours and twelve minutes. Painful, but the carbs had paid off. And the red wine . . .

There was no sight of my buddy at the finish line, but he emailed me hours later, having finished happily in sub-four hours and made enough time to make it back to the airport, stopping only for a swift sandwich and then home to London. That evening, I went to my co-star Caitriona's house. My legs were jelly, but thankfully my arms were fine to lift a hefty celebratory beer or two. Cait had made tacos and the brilliant Sophie Skelton (who plays my daughter Brianna) had brought a cake to celebrate my birthday the day before. I felt no guilt, tucking into a second helping of spicy tortilla and chocolate cake (not at the same time), as I calculated I'd burnt well over 2000 calories that day . . . Well, that was my excuse.

Four weeks flew past, I was busy at work, and suddenly the Edinburgh Marathon was due. My legs were still a little sore and work had been hectic, so I'd not had time to run much in-between. In Edinburgh, the day was very different, no chatty London friend at the start line, only rain and the infamous east-coast wind cut through my thin ultra-tech shorts.

Starting in the old town, down the Mound, past the iconic Castle to the left and Scott Monument on the right, the race passed many landmarks I'd frequented as a teenager, the memories and the sights of bonny Edinburgh (Old Reekie) kept me from noticing the cold. It's famously a fast route, with a long downhill at the start that levels out towards the coast, the beach and golden sands of Portobello, which signal the welcome finish line. I kept glancing at my Garmin running watch.

[*Graham: How much are they paying you?*]

My legs felt heavy and I didn't have the thrill or reserves of energy I'd felt four weeks before in Stirling. I dug deep and felt buoyed by the shouts from the gathered crowd (and delusional thoughts of a large sandwich, with possibly an all-bread filling, washed down with a pint of liquid carbohydrate), crossing the finish line and beating my previous PB by one minute!! Phew. I was relieved. The local radio station pounced on me just after I crossed the finish line, which may have been the hardest part of the day, as I fumbled and tried to speak coherently after three hours of running, wishing they'd just hand me something delicious and stodgy to eat. Perhaps I'd have run faster if there was a margarita and a large piece of cake waiting for me at the end.

[*Graham: Reading this I actually began to feel cramps in my legs, and I may have been a bit sick in my mouth.*]

29 May 1694 - Dougal MacKenzie's birthday.

GRAHAM

An auspicious day. I can't help imagining Dougal was born with his beard already fully grown. As a child he probably challenged other infants to drinking games and fights, beginning with open brawling against the neighbours' kids at the age of twelve months, while shamelessly chatting up any girl that came within crawling distance.

I like to think he was born at dawn, with a chorus of birdsong. The sun shining through the window of the birthing chamber. His poor mother looked aghast as Dougal came into the world, no doubt bellowing 'Tulach Ard' from his baby lungs, while his father smiled at the new bald, bearded war chief.

Coincidentally, my own youngest daughter's birthday was on 29 May.

There was a double rainbow that day . . .

Just saying.

1 May 1721 - James Alexander Malcolm MacKenzie Fraser's Birthday (JAMMF).

SAM

Wait, WHAT?! Why are we talking about that wailing, petulant infant Dougal, when the saviour of men was born on 1 May? JAMMF was born on Beltane, when the Earth was bursting full of potent fertility and sexual energy. The word 'Beltane' originates from the Celtic God Bel, meaning 'the bright one' and the Gaelic word *teine* meaning 'fire'. Together they make 'Bright Fire', or 'Goodly Fire', and traditionally bonfires were lit to honour the Sun. Perhaps this is reflected in the bright red/ginger hair of Jamie Fraser, or his 'burning energy' and fiery nature.

I must mention (again) that my birthday is also on the eve of Beltane, 30 April, and therefore there would have been a great number of rainbows, fires, bright stars shining, earthquakes, dragons, hobbits and primal celebrations at the coming of the King of Men! Not Jamie, Me. I'm one inch shorter and one day off Jamie's birthday – ties in pretty neatly, doesn't it?

[*Graham: Please see me for an increase to your medication.*]

Another rather fabulous tradition would be that couples, young and old (though maybe not McTavish, he'd rather go to bed early) spent the night in the woods and fields, made love and brought back armfuls of the first May or hawthorn blossoms to decorate their homes and barns. However, hawthorn was never brought into the home except at Beltane – at other times it was considered unlucky. Young women gathered the morning dew to wash their faces, made Flower Crowns and May Baskets to give as gifts, then that night their future spouse would come to them in a dream or premonition.

I wonder if McTavish would dream of us, tearing along in our campervan, in a rather twisted premonition?

Beltane – the ending of winter and coming of summer, and if I'm having a particularly good time, it's still my birthday! I remember growing up watching the celebrations of the whirling white witches, painted faces and deer-antlered druids, spinning around the large bonfire on top of Carlton Hill in Edinburgh. It felt tribal and primeval. The drums would beat faster and faster and the hair would rise on the back of my neck.

When we filmed the Beltane sequence on *MIK* (where I

bumped into my drummer girl), we'd all secretly been drinking tequila that looked conveniently like whisky. I wanted to get Graham pissed, because he's way more fun half-cut. I went to Mexico in 2019 and found this amazing Reposado, aged tequila made by this brilliant third generation Master Distiller. Tequila is more of an upper, it gives you a buzz and I wanted to get everyone into the spirit of things. I'm actually fascinated by the artisan distillers and history of the Jimador – farmers that harvest the blue agave. The Mexican-Highland culture has many similarities to my Scottish roots. Their storytelling, myth and legend of the gods, love of family and community. I made a good many friends there and would love to go back!

We were supposed to go mad and crazy, but Graham kept trying to look cool, which in reality was the opposite. His familiar dance moves are the exact ones he does at conventions when he absolutely insists he goes out dancing with the fans and hits the dance floor, thrusting his sporran and gyrating his hips in some creepy uncle moves. I'm not sure if the tequila improved his dancing, but the evening certainly got stranger as we found ourselves dressed in headpieces with flowers and skulls sourced by our wonderful stylist, Laura Strong.

The party carried on back at the Wormiston House and Graham, in the midst of the madness – ever the opportunist – took the moment to ingratiate himself with the Lord of the Manor and wangle a stay in the master suite, with the resident chef delivering a five-course dinner on a silver platter and bottle of Montrachet up to his room.

Graham: Was that before or after you and your business partner had tried to set up an outlet store for Sassenach whisky in the castle grounds? (When they weren't casually trying to get a bottle of their blend prominently displayed in shot, they wore matching baseball caps branded with 'Sassenach'. I wouldn't be surprised if Sam wore this to bed.)

Sam: How did you know? With my extra-large Sassenach underpants!

GRAHAM

Let's jump to the important bit . . . MAY IS MACTAVISH
MONTH. Where we explore the Inner Hebrides and all
things Clan MacTavish, including my very own castle . . .

Sam: Yes, but there is something more important about May . . .

Graham: More important than MY castle?

Sam: Yep. It's WHISKY MONTH!

Graham: Please tell me this month isn't going to be one
long advert for your grog in an oversized aftershave bottle . . .
because if it is, I'm off to June. Fast.

Sam: Nooooo. As if I would shamelessly plug my own
multi-award-winning whisky brand, Sassenach, in the middle
of a book . . .

DRAM OF THE MONTH
SASSENACH

Not one to blow my own trumpet [*Graham: cough*] my award-
winning Sassenach whisky claimed *double gold* at the 2020
AND 2021 San Francisco World Spirits Competition, which
made me feel very proud, because this is the realisation of an
ichorous dream. [*Graham: Icarus, more like! Look it up. It's an
Ancient Greek myth about flying too close to the sun, which was
written especially for Sam Heughan.*] PLUS, a gold in the Spirit
awards, double gold for design and I know you'll all be
excited to know, we just won gold in the Spirits Business
Masters. I hope you're keeping count of all the GOLD!

Distilled in Central Scotland, the whisky is inspired by the
Highland landscape: the ancient peaks, hidden glens, rising
morning mist, fresh water and firm oak run deep in its veins.
However, a Sassenach is a nonconformist, an outsider and an
homage to Jamie's sobriquet for Claire in *Outlander*.

We mature it in Madeira casks, so the underlying fruit-rich
character is at the forefront of the blend. The nose is packed

with citrus fruits, butterscotch and cinnamon, the mouthfeel of syrupy honey, almonds, raisins and vanilla fudge gently caresses the tongue, crescendos and surrenders to the triumphant notes of nutmeg, caramel and orange blossom.

The logo is the unicorn – Scotland's national animal, the strongest of all animals. The unicorn is the only beast that can defeat the lion and be tamed by a virgin [*Graham: We need a virgin to tame you, Samwise.*] and it captures my pride and passion for Scotland.

The bottle has a ribbed glass design [*Graham: No comment.*] with a sleek black label and matching stopper, and comes in a gold embossed black box.

[*Graham: I would like to make the following brief statement: Sassenach whisky is really lovely stuff. It really is. The people of San Francisco really, really like it and so do I. Yes! It's great!! On the one occasion that I tasted it, my tongue felt like it had been kidnapped by a host of angels, and then held hostage by a pod of extra-lively dolphins. Through my teary eyes I thought for that brief moment I had glimpsed heaven. Even though the bottle does sometimes remind me of something I would find clutched in Black Jack Randall's fist during one of his particularly long 'party' nights, it's always a pleasure to say the word 'Sassenach' as I pass out on the floor.*]

SAM
A few of Graham's favourite cocktails . . . ahem:

The McTavish Moan – all of his peeves, ground-up in a glass, perhaps grind the glass and swallow.

The Grey Gentleman – normally Earl Grey tea, but swap for a latte, dash of protein bar, sprinkle of map shavings and a solitary grey beard hair used for decoration.

Pornstar McTini – all kilt and no pants, to be taken in small bursts late at night, usually as a shot, once all the other shots have been taken.

Bellendini – Bellini with a large bell.

Old OLD Fashioned – cardigan gin, scarfed down and not shared with any young whippersnappers.

Corpse Reviver – after McT has had a night out with Lacroix, force into the mouth, swill around whilst shouting Gaelic war cries into the ear. Filter through the heart of a dead actor.

GRAHAM
I like this game:

The Angry McTav – whisky, hot sauce, corn syrup, with salt around the rim.

The Frothing 'Latte' – double espresso topped with absinthe and an Alka-Seltzer tablet.

The Tulach Ard – gin, vodka, Drambuie, Crème de Menthe, with sprinkled ground-up Viagra – two tablets for those extra-long nights.

The 'JAMMF' – two parts stiff whisky, one part brown ale, mixed with the laxative of your choice.

Murtagh's Howler – absinthe mixed with lighter fuel, deck sealant and a soupçon of wasabi.

The Black Jack Depth Charge – Kahlúa, cream, melted chocolate, a sprinkle of ground-up lavender, two floating balls of whole ginger, with the rim of the glass coated in superglue.

The Bigamist's Choice – gin, whisky, grated ginger, half a teaspoon of gunpowder, a tablespoon of salty tears, topped by a sprig of heather.

SAM'S WHISKY FACTS
- 42 bottles of Scotch whisky are shipped from Scotland to 175 countries around the world every second.
- 22 million casks of whisky are currently maturing waiting to be tasted.
- In October 2020, a bottle of the Macallan Fine and Rare 60-Year-Old from 1926 became the most expensive wine or spirit ever sold, fetching $1.9 million at auction.
- IS IT WHISKY OR WHISKEY? Whisky is from Scotland; Whiskey is from Ireland. In the late 1800s, Irish distillers wanted to set their product apart, so they rebranded it Whiskey as a marketing ploy.
- Scotch whisky is the BEST, always has been and always will be and The Sassenach proves it!(www.sassenachwhisky.com).

REGION OF THE MONTH
THE INNER HEBRIDES

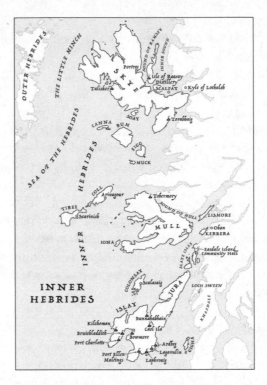

SAM

As you've probably realised by now, I am obsessed with whisky. I truly love it and it excites me like no other spirit. Firstly you savour the nose or aroma of the whisky, rolling it around in your glass to warm the burnished golden liquid, then you take a sip and note the mouth feel. I actually have my own brand of whisky. [*Graham: Yes, we know, get on with it!*]

The west coast of Scotland became a popular place for making whisky centuries ago, because of the shipping access to Ireland and North America. So for *Men in Kilts* I made sure it was on the schedule. We headed to Islay, an island on the Inner Hebrides that boasts ten distilleries. Sadly, we didn't have time to visit all ten distilleries; however, Graham and I did manage to tick off Laphroaig. But it's worth noting that I enjoy many brands including: Lagavulin, Bruichladdich, Bunnahabhain and Kilchoman. AND there are many more 'peat monsters' still to try!

Renowned for its unique smoky taste, Islay whisky draws its flavour from the environment: peat. The whole south of the island is a peat bog, so this was their natural resource. And the peat is still dug by hand today. John Campbell, the distillery manager at Laphroaig, took us to help cut some peat.

I'd arranged for us to be kitted out by Barbour, in some fetching wellies, gilet and jackets. It's an iconic British brand I regard highly. I even had my own Barbour collection several years ago. [*Graham: God. Kill me now! Actually he probably will, one way or the other.*] [*Sam: Don't be like that, Graham.*] I went to the Barbour archive and looked back at clothes from the 1940s to around the time of the Falklands, and taking inspiration from that, I helped to create my own line in 2018 and 2019. I loved working with them, but sadly couldn't continue because of my other work commitments.

[*Graham: You turned work down? You? Good God. Maybe you've been listening after all . . . It's all about balance, my ginger friend. It's okay to be in third gear from time to time, although you're built more like a child's toy car with only ON and FORWARDS buttons!*]

[*Sam: Graham loved his new Barbour Wellington boots. Let's not be ungrateful now, Beg Man. And they certainly made a welcome change from your little blue training shoes. More on those later.*]

We were filmed cutting the peat with John's special spade, the horn handle moulded to his hand. Graham was jumpy about touching another man's horn handle, but he got on with it and cut a piece of the ancient peat, which would become part of a future whisky. Back at the maltings, with John's permission I dived into the barley. The barley is dried at the top of the maltings and the peat burnt below, the smoke giving the grain that peaty aroma. It's then ventilated with cool air from the sea giving this humble cereal a taste of Islay.

The other largest islands in the Inner Hebrides are Skye, Mull and Jura, but there are actually thirty-six inhabited islands in the archipelago with many Gaelic speakers and an economy built on fishing, farming, tourism and, of course, whisky distilling – which is why Graham and I came along in the first place.

[*Graham: And, of course, to see my twelfth-century family castle . . .*]

SAM

Oh yes. That. It was like a pilgrimage for Graham to visit his family castle located in Knapdale, south of Achnamara on the west coast of Argyll. Graham smiled at me, almost sneering regally, as he conjured in his mind a magnificent castle reminiscent of Inveraray, with fairy-tale turrets. '*Caistéal Suibhne*,' he mouthed the Gaelic name for his stronghold over and over, as the seaplane slowly descended to land on the still waters of Loch Sween. The Grey Dog was almost bursting with excitement and pride to see HIS castle, HIS ancestral home . . . which stood majestically . . . in ruins by the side of the loch.

It was the first blow, but Graham took it on the chin, preferring a ruin to a fully functioning castle because 'it attracts fewer people'. Suddenly, as the plane passed the castle, an array of worn-out and rather dour-looking caravans came into view. Castle Sween was a massive caravan park!!!!! The driving rain gave the whole area a rather dreich and sober look.

I immediately pissed myself watching at the mortally punctured Graham, slowly deflating in the seat next to me. Perfect, I thought, all his glitzy glamour and high-end hotel shenanigans and Chief McTavish actually comes from a caravan park. Now don't get me wrong, I enjoy camping and the outdoors, but to see the Thane of Mobile Homes looking so disappointed and economised brought me great joy. (Is this *schadenfreude*, Graham?!) 'And to think you hate camping so much! You have your own caravan park. I mean Inveraray, Cawdor, they don't have them – but your tiny wee castle does!!!'

[*Graham: It's one of the oldest, if not the oldest castles in Scotland. At least the McTavishes have a castle! I'm not sure the Heughans' and Galloways' hovels, or possibly caves, are still in existence.*]

[*Sam: Hmmm.*]

At this point I noticed a solitary figure, sheltering from the rain, underneath what may have been the castle spa or five-star lodging, now just a pile of bricks.

'Are you a McTavish?' I called out. Graham's drooping ears perked up, perhaps a long-lost relative, or similar brother-in-arms.

'No,' shouted the miserly figure. 'I'm a Campbell.'

[*Graham: She never said she was a Campbell!!!*]

She did. We just didn't keep it in the edit.

CLAN MACTAVISH

GRAHAM

The MacTavish clan originated in Donegal in Ireland. The name comes from the Pictish Gaelic, *Taviss*, and the Donegal Pictish tribe of *Cenél nDuach*. That hardy group found their way across the small body of water separating the north of Ireland from Argyll and married with the people of Dalriada (the so-called Scots).

Fast forward to one of this gang marrying Subine Rudah of Sween and we find ourselves at Castle Sween.

She and her husband had two sons, Taviss and Ivor, and they became the progenitors of what we now know as the two clans MacTavish and MacIver (literally meaning 'Sons of Thomas and Ivor').

(Interestingly I recently discovered that 'Heughan' is from a marriage between a well-known genetically stunted man from County Kerry and a part-time bingo caller from Dumfries. The name translates from the ancient language of Gallowese into the English: 'He who is childishly competitive'. It's amazing what you discover.

But back to the caravan park, I MEAN CASTLE!!

Taviss and Ivor were apparently noted warriors of their day and were particularly good at taking land from Clan Lamont.

Apparently Kilmartin graveyard (which I discovered in 1988) accidentally after stumbling out of the pub opposite, has the two graves of Taviss and Ivor. You can still see them, the figures of two warriors carved into stone with their broadswords. It's well worth a visit! (But then I would say that.)

Their first lands were in a place called Scannish. We have no idea where Scannish was, as it has vanished into the mists of time, rather like Brigadoon.

But we do know that they have held Dunardry (their clan seat) since AD 893. They are one of the clans known as 'Children of Colla', which translates as 'children of mist'.

The MacTavishes fought at Flodden against the English. And in the build-up to Culloden, Dugald MacTavish was sending letters to Sir James Campbell of Achnabreck supporting the Jacobite cause (both men were Jacobite sympathisers). Unbeknownst to them, the Earl of Argyll (notorious backstabbing, double-dealing, wee guttersnipe that he was) had installed a spy in Sir James's household. The letters were sent to the King and Dugald was promptly imprisoned in Dumbarton Castle. On the one hand this meant that the only MacTavish clansmen at the battle were there 'unofficially', but it also meant that because the MacTavish battle standard was not on the battlefield, the clan were spared having their lands seized.

This didn't stop the Earl of Argyll demanding payment from his cousin Sir James Campbell for the cost of fielding an army in support of the Hanoverians.

It was a bill Argyll knew that Campbell couldn't pay. Sir James's lands went straight to the Earl of Argyll and the Campbells of Achnabreck ceased to be.

Classic Campbell move. Conquer your enemy through bankruptcy.

After Culloden, many MacTs (or McTs) became Thompsons to avoid the stigma of Gaelic names, but my lot didn't. Alexander McTavish came from the lands of Dunardry in about 1830 to Edinburgh, bringing his skill as a basket weaver with him (he could've been a great tennis player as well, but we will never know). He married a Lowlander and had George, who had Alexander, who had George, who had my dad (duly named with a startling lack of originality – Alexander!).

So I am Graham, son of Alexander, son of George, son of Alexander, son of George, son of Alexander. At least it makes it easy to remember. Needless to say my eldest brother is named – yes, you guessed it – Alexander.

Many of the clan left for the New World, one of whom did rather well in the Hudson Bay Company in Canada, basically creating the province of what is now Manitoba and helping to confederate Canada with the help of the country's first Prime Minister in 1867.

So if you're Canadian, next time you celebrate Canada Day on 1 July, take a moment to thank a McTavish.

CRACKING CASTLE OF THE MONTH
DUNVEGAN CASTLE

GRAHAM

Dunvegan Castle – seat of the MacLeods. Let us take a moment or two to consider the MacLeods. We spoke about them in *Clanlands*, but one could devote an entire book to this clan. Maybe it's just me, but I love the MacLeods. They're spectacularly violent, even by Highland standards. The fact that most of the carnage occurred on the comparatively small island of Skye merely adds to their legendary 'heidbanger' status.

Take the names of some of their clan chiefs for instance.

Iain Ciar MacLeod, the 4th Chief. He and his wife seemed to get out of the wrong side of the bed EVERY day of their lives. This infamous couple were described at the time as 'a tyrannical and bloodthirsty couple', who were hated as much by their own clan as by their enemies.

George R.R. Martin took much inspiration from the stories of Highland clans. In this case the Mother buried two of her daughters ALIVE, because the young girls expressed a desire to leave the clan . . .

'Mother, I've met a lovely fella from the neighbouring clan. We are to be wed.'

'IAIN!!!! FETCH ME THE SHOVEL!!!!'

You'd think the second daughter would have learned from the fate of her sibling, but apparently not. Or perhaps Mum simply buried them both alive at the same time.

'Mu-ummmmm. What yer doing?' Fun times!

Then there were these wonderful, Pythonesque names for the chiefs that followed:

John the Turbulent (1392–1448).

William Long Sword (1415–1480), no doubt known as Long Sword Willy by his pals.

Roderick the Witty (1633–1664) Perhaps ironic? We shall never know.

John the Speckled (1637–1693).

Norman the Wicked Man, who delighted in embarking on daily sprees of violence. I wonder what brave soul first called him that.

'Och, here comes Norman – the Wicked Man!' One hopes he said it quietly.

Did Norman KNOW he was known as Wicked? Perhaps he coined the name himself.

'My name is Norman, but my friends call me "Wicked".'

But my favourite is perhaps Alasdair Crotach the Humpback. He got the hump (so to speak) after being savagely mutilated at the Battle of Bloody Bay in Mull. But despite being a violent, bloodthirsty nut job, he was also celebrated as a poet, dancer and musician. He founded the piping college in Skye, and died a monk. He would've been great company at dinner.

Perhaps one of the most endearing stories about the clan involves the Fairy Flag. This is their most sacred relic, and it sits in Dunvegan Castle to this day. Legend has it that a fairy princess fell in love with a MacLeod. The fairy father agreed to their marriage on condition that she leave him after a year and a day and return to the fairy realm. This she did, but not before giving birth to an infant.

The story goes that before she left, the child's nursemaid saw a beautiful young woman wrapping the infant in a silk cloth and talking softly to the boy. Years later, the boy repeated her words to his father, saying the flag could be unfurled three times only in moments of crisis for the clan. It was raised during the Battle of the Spoiling Dyke against the MacDonalds, and during a time of a devastating cattle plague.

It has yet to be unfurled a third time . . .

SAM

I see what Graham is doing here. He's using history (again) to distract us from his rubbish caravan park stronghold, whilst also trying to throw me off writing about literally the best part of our island trip, in fact, the whole of the *Men in Kilts* adventure. When Lady McTavish almost died, again, abseiling at Kilt Rock, Skye.

COMPETITION CORNER
ABSEILING AT KILT ROCK ON SKYE

SAM

Given his point-blank refusal to go kayaking on our *Clanlands* adventure and his near-death experience in a coffin on wheels (a motorcycle sidecar, attached to my motorbike when he almost did a 'Isadora Duncan'), imagine my surprise (and joy) at Graham agreeing to go abseiling at a *MIK* pre-production meeting back in May 2020. Perhaps it was the excitement of having our own show commissioned by Starz, or it was because the director and several big LA producers were on the call, but Graham was saying yes to pretty much everything and anything. Or maybe he was drunk on Sauvignon.

I honestly don't believe Graham gave abseiling another thought until the day dawned for him to do it.

Located on Skye's Trotternish Peninsula on the north-eastern coast of the island, Kilt Rock is a 180-foot-high sea cliff with a striking resemblance to the pleat of a kilt. Graham was talkative and full of the joys of spring on our way over in the car. His appetite was still 'normal' and he was surrounded by the usual number of wrappers as we arrived at our destination. I still don't think it had hit Graham that he was about to abseil down a cliff, even as we made our way across the boggy grassland towards the edge.

And then suddenly he wanted something. It was urgent. He was flapping and jogging on the spot. Ah, there it was. The fear had set in. I approached him ready to allay his fears (okay, crank them up), but instead of a panicked pensioner, I was met by a belligerent request to 'urgently fetch his wellies'. No one had warned him! Why hadn't anyone warned him? He couldn't take another step, not in THESE CONDITIONS! His little blue trainers were getting dirty!

A crime against trainers and fashion, his blue running shoes were utterly hideous and an affront not only to my eyes, but to his own feet and his French girlfriend's sensibilities. Every member of his family, friends and colleagues wanted something bad to happen to those hideous loafers. I disliked everything about them – the shape, the colour – however, Graham was very proud of his little blue shoes.

I returned to the car to retrieve his ladyship's wellies. Upon my return, a member of the crew and I had to hold him up so he could carefully change out of his blue daps into his wellies. And all for a 100-yard walk to a cliff edge!

Whereupon he wanted to take his wellies off and put back on his little blue shoes!

And, he has the temerity to call ME a child?!

His feet safely re-encased in his blue shoes, Graham suddenly became aware of the cliff edge, our instructor (Matt Barratt) AND what he was about to do all in the same moment. We shook hands with Matt and before Graham had barely said his own name, he was garbling the words, 'I genuinely have a fear of heights. I really do.'

My ears pricked up. Oh this IS going to be fun.

Matt was understanding, but still intent on making the Grey Dog go over the edge (as was I). Graham stepped into his harness and Matt did up his helmet. I smiled at my quivvering friend and told him to be careful – he was very near the edge. He told me he'd like it if I didn't go anywhere near him. I laughed, having still not fully registered his increasing panic. Besides, surely he was invincible in his little Dorothy shoes.

I asked him if he had any last words.

Graham: Shut up. I shall have it on my tomb – Shut up, Heughan.

Sam: I'll do a nice eulogy.

Graham: I am changing my will so you don't have anything to do with it. You can't even attend.

Matt gave the first instructions: 'Abseiling is just descending a cliff. You only need to do two things. Descend backwards and hold onto the rope at all times.'

The blood from Graham's face had drained away. Irritated, he wanted more information, *detailed* instructions.

Graham: But what do I need to *do*?

Matt: Descend backwards and hold onto the rope at all times.

Graham: What *else*?

Matt: That's it.

Graham became more infuriated and the closer he moved towards the cliff edge, the wider his eyes became with sheer terror – a bit like my expression when I first saw his terrible blue shoes! It was actually a little shocking to witness the panic rising within him . . . slowly emerging like a mushroom cloud. So . . . I tried to comfort him.

'Are you okay?'

'No, I'm not okay!' snarled the Grey Dog, like he was about to meet the vet for the last time.

As the instructor inched him backwards, I couldn't resist one more quip.

'How's the view?'

But Graham was by now speaking tongues, in the vice-like grip of fear.

'Oh God. Oh, Jesus Christ. Fuck!'

Now, many will say I was still pissing myself with laughter at this juncture, but perhaps my sniggers were the involuntary noise of thinking maybe I had gone too far and knowing I HAD TO GO NEXT. Because I'm game for a lot of things, but 180 feet is a hell of a long way down and it was a pretty cold and windy day. Not the weather for a spot of abseiling.

Graham continued to descend millimetre by millimetre, until Matt told him that he was simply bending his legs and squatting down, he hadn't actually gone anywhere. Our Antique Action hero straightened his legs and began to inch down the rock, one blue-fashion-crime sneaker at a time, until he reached a ledge about forty feet down. Now, what I hadn't told Graham was that upon reaching that ledge, he would need to UNCLIP from the main rope and, tied only to one safety rope, then have to clamber his way back up the cliff, literally pulling himself up with his own arms.

The ledge was about half a foot wide, so you had to stand on your tippy toes with a 140-foot sheer drop to the rocks below. As the wind gusted harder, perhaps trying to upset the Mountain Man further, Graham started to unclip, which was truly scary because basically you're forcing yourself to go against every instinct that is screaming 'NO!!!!!' and *begging* you not to unclip!

My heart was in my mouth as Graham tried to unclip himself . . . and began to freak out.

I thought, 'Oh shit, he really might not make it. We may

have to rescue him from the edge of a cliff. What will I do if he falls to his death? Who can I replace him with at such short notice? Did he pay his bar bill last night?'

Graham took a deep breath – 'smell the flowers, blow out the candle'. He exhaled, unclipped and scrambled up the cliff face like an aged Spiderman. *He had done it!* The entire crew and I gave him a round of applause. I was very proud of him; it took great bravery to face his fears and overcome them. It made for a really memorable moment in the show and we all felt happy that he had achieved something so challenging.

What's great is that on our next *Men in Kilts* adventure, Graham has said he'd like to do more things out of his comfort zone and I feel honoured to be the one to help him achieve these milestones. I'm only pushing him to the limit for his own good! Facing death can give oneself a new perspective in life. Maybe he'll turn over a new leaf? Perhaps lose the blue shoes forever, seeing the folly of his ways?

Then it was my turn. The gods were smiling on Graham that day, as the team asked me to do the descent TWICE, leaving me on the ledge for ten minutes whilst they got the drone footage.

[*Graham: And that my friend is called karma.*]

GRAHAM

Ah yes, the abseiling. Or as our American friends like to call it, 'rappelling'. Or as I like to call it, 'brown trouser time'.

I need to start this fond reminiscence by first stating that I have long had a fear of heights. I'm not sure when it began, maybe I knew someone like Sam when I was a child, (some ginger-topped spawn of Satan who delighted in stranding me up trees?).

I suppose we can never fully explain our phobias, mine is heights, Sam's is being beaten at sport. (I also now have a fear of people named Sam.)

I had actually abseiled once before, in New Zealand, at my eldest daughter's school camp. It was about an 80-foot descent and I loved it, so I approached the abseiling day feeling positively jaunty with anticipation.

This would be fun, I thought.

This turned out to be rather like a cow developing a fondness for abattoirs.

It was a long walk to Kilt Rock over boggy ground, so yes, I changed my footwear. Sam probably has someone from Barbour, or Hunter (or some other brand that he is prostituting himself for) on hand at all times with changes of footwear at the ready. I suspect he had a separate room back at the hotel just for his free branded goods.

The walk was relatively flat which lulled me into believing all would be well.

Then we approached the Rock.

To say it was high would be like saying Sam Heughan occasionally talks about his own whisky brand. It was so high that the air felt appreciably thinner.

For a moment I thought I heard screaming, and then realised it was only the screaming voice in my head shouting, 'LEAVE NOW!!!'

I can't be sure, but I suspect Heughan had already scouted this location to be sure of its maximum 'brown trouser' effect.

There was a man waiting for us wearing a helmet and surrounded by rope. Reminiscent of a hangman.

Sam has already claimed that he was called Matt 'something'. I have no idea. I couldn't make out his name over the sounds of my stomach tying itself in knots and the probable build-up of volcanic flatulence in my drawers as I edged closer to the place of execution.

I became aware of the sound of the wind whistling through Sam's enormous grin.

Matt was a man of few words. Looking back, I'd convinced myself this was because he had never done this before. That he was, in fact, a paid stooge employed by the evil grinning Ginger to PRETEND to be professionally qualified.

We shook hands.

Did he actually say 'Any last words?', or did I imagine that bit?

I immediately confessed my chronic fear of heights. I

imagine I was hoping that he would nod understandingly and say, 'In that case, perhaps you should just watch.'

Instead he merely smiled (the kind of smile that doesn't reach the eyes. The kind that Heinrich Himmler had), and said quietly, 'Ah, I see, don't worry.'

Now, to me that translates as, 'I heard what you just said but I don't give a shit.'

I became aware that Sam was talking. I have no idea what he said, something annoyingly jovial. Or perhaps he managed somehow to connect abseiling with his Sassenach whisky.

I stood to one side. I may have appeared to be there, but in my head I was anywhere else.

Matt the 'instructor' said to remember two things: 'Walk backwards and don't let go of the rope.'

Again, this could have been translated as, 'Walk slowly to your doom in reverse, and if you let go of the rope, your face will spread like jam against a sheer rock face.'

I volunteered to go first. INSANE!!

In retrospect, I felt I couldn't bear to watch the ginger Bear Grylls bounding backwards over the cliff edge while my bowels turned to water.

I began walking backwards. I think Sam may have even been bouncing up and down with sadistic anticipation.

Matt's sonorous tones kept saying, 'Keep going.' My brain kept replying, 'Why????'

I rewatched the clumps of heather edging the cliff edge and that's when the full-blown panic kicked in. I thought I'd been afraid up to this point, but this was a whole new level of terror.

The heather made it impossible to be sure where the edge was, so as I inched backwards, Matt began to urge me to lean back. This felt akin to strapping myself into the electric chair with one hand and turning on the current with the other.

Now was the moment I seriously thought of shouting out, 'Are you crazy!!! I'm not doing this!'

I truly believe the only two things that kept me going were my ego and the fact I would rather die than see Sam look pityingly at me as I gave up.

I leant back and now I was descending.

Sam is right. It was probably only forty feet, but when the drop below you is about 140 feet . . . well, you get the idea.

I looked at the cliff face swearing like a trooper all the way down.

[*Sam: I've never heard such a creative use of the English language.*]

I don't know how long it took. It could've been less than a minute, but it felt more like watching Episode Sixteen, Season One of *Outlander* on a loop.

I finally reached what Matt laughingly described as a ledge. (More like a bump in the rock slightly different from the rest of that sheer rock face.)

I was so relieved.

It was over.

They could pull me up. It's finished.

But no!!

Instead, Matt instructs me to unclip the rope, step over it and climb back up.

I have never rock-climbed in my life. Now I am expected to grip on to a sheer cliff face with my hands and feet and drag myself up perched precariously 140 feet above the rocks below.

I was appalled.

I think I may have hurled a torrent of expletives up at both him and Sam.

In the end, the only reason I did climb up was the horrifying alternative of being trapped on a postage stamp until night fell. As it was, my bowel-loosening terror meant that my grip was so intense that I did manage to haul myself back up and over the edge.

The crew may have applauded. Sam may have hugged me (while pretending to push me over the edge – oh, how I laughed!), but all I can really remember is the feeling of gigantic relief that it was over.

I've never felt more glad to be on solid ground.

But I should definitely have worn the brown trousers.

The Skye Boat Song
by Sir Harold Boulton and Annie MacLeod, 1884

Speed, bonnie boat, like a bird on the wing,
Onward, the sailors cry.
Carry the lad that's born to be king
Over the sea to Skye.

Loud the winds howl, loud the waves roar
Thunderclaps rend the air,
Baffled, our foes stand by the shore,
Follow they will not dare.

SAM

Most of us will be familiar with 'The Skye Boat Song', which was used over the opening credits of *Outlander*. The original song is a nineteenth-century retelling of the story of heroine Flora MacDonald, who bravely helped Bonnie Prince Charlie escape to the Isle of Skye after the Jacobite defeat at Culloden in 1746. It is a well-known song in Scotland and when we were told that this was to be the show's theme tune, I was initially dubious. I thought the song was far too romanticised and over-used in the tourist centres of Scotland. However, the theme tune was appreciated by our fans and very quickly became the 'calling card' of the show.

In San Diego at the Comic Con, I awoke at 5 a.m., jetlagged and excited to partake in our first live panel. Thousands of fans had bought tickets to our first large-scale public promotion. Looking out of the twenty-storey hotel, I could see a group of Highlanders, dressed in kilts and 1980s headbands and organised by the publicity team, chanting, 'Out-lan-der, Out-lan-der!' At the head of the procession, two female pipers, who now regularly play for us at public events, performed 'The Skye Boat Song', with the pipes' evocative and lamenting wail reaching me on the eighteenth floor.

Later that day, I was amused to see our Highlanders have an impromptu cèilidh in the street with a large group of Great White Sharks, who were promoting the horror movie

Sharknado. There was no sign of Bonnie Prince Charlie, though. Unless he was wearing a Shark hat.

By the time the Bonnie Prince escaped to Skye, he had a £30,000 bounty on his head and was being hunted across the Highlands and Islands, so Flora disguised him as her maidservant, Betty Burke, by dressing him in a calico gown, quilted petticoat and large hood (Graham, do you fancy it?). She then rowed him in a small boat from the island of Benbecula in the Outer Hebrides on 27 June 1746, 'across the sea to Skye'.

Now I've checked on Google Earth and Benbecula to Kilmuir is roughly 32 MILES!!! With wind speeds and tides, it would have been an epic. Have you ever rowed a wee boat at sea?! Even in calm waters it takes great strength and stamina. I had to row Graham across Loch Ness once and let me tell you, there wasn't much help.

It's not as if Charlie Boy was gonna be a great one to lend a hand either. (1) He's a prince and (2) although he was five feet ten inches, he was a very slight man. I've seen his waistcoat at the Cameron Museum in Achnacarry and I think he had a 26-inch waist, which is about the size of Dougal MacKenzie's thigh. So Flora was not only hugely courageous, she was as tough as old boots. What a woman, she'd definitely make a good travel companion, and probably complain less, too.

After safely landing on Skye at Kilmuir, now known as 'Rudha Phrionnsa' (Prince's Point), Charlie lay low in the islands for a few more weeks before escaping on a ship to France. Flora never saw the prince again and soon she was imprisoned in the Tower of London for her part in the Young Pretender's escape. However, she was released in 1747 and went on to become a society figure, whose likeness was captured by many great artists, including Allan Ramsay (1713–84). In 2015, one painting of Flora by Ramsay sold in America for over $250,000.

Flora ended up in America herself when she married Allan MacDonald of Kingsburgh. In 1774 they emigrated to North Carolina, where Allan became a Brigadier General on the royalist side in the American War of Independence. (Fighting for a Hanoverian king after rescuing a Stuart one! Yep. It's never clear cut, is it?!)

Eventually Flora returned to Allan's ancestral home at Kingsburgh, on Skye. She died on 5 March 1790 and her grave in Kilmuir Cemetery is not far from the place where she first landed with 'the lad that's born to be king'.

BATTLE OF THE MONTH
THE BATTLE OF CARINISH, 1601

GRAHAM

In 1601, a gang of the usual suspects from Harris sailed to a wee spot called Sidinish. Probably very picturesque, no doubt a destination for Hebridean holidaymakers these days, but this lot weren't there for the ice cream.

Led by their Chieftain, Domhnall Glas, he was the worst of a right bunch of bastards who beached their boats that day in Uist. There were forty of them and they set off on a long hike to the town of Carinish. When they reached Trinity Temple, a former nunnery that was now a church, the local townsfolk ran away.

Well, you would, wouldn't you? There you are enjoying the equivalent of a cappuccino and a croissant, and up rocks forty murderous thugs led by a man whose last name was Glas!!!

These poor folk – they're always poor folk in these stories aren't they, never the Elon Musk of Carinish, or the Jeff Bezos of Uist. No, just dirt poor and terrified – had put all their belongings in the church believing they would be safe there.

But nope!

As the gang of robbing cutthroats drew nearer, the local women began to panic and cry. Yet unbeknownst to them, help was at hand. The local John Rambo had walked all the way from Eriskay, through South Uist and Benbecula, over the tidal crossing and up to Carinish, where at that moment he was hiding in the Trinity Temple.

Not a short walk.

His name was MacIain 'Ic Sheumais, which by a strange coincidence is in fact Gaelic for John Rambo . . . well, maybe not.

Dastardly Domhnall had ordered a local peasant boy to bring a pitcher and pour him a special dram into his quaich (a wide-lipped ceremonial drinking vessel. Sam probably has several engraved with the name Sassenach on his wall).

Once the boy had finished pouring the whisky, and just as Domhnall of the dirty deeds was about to take a sip, a quiet voice was heard saying, 'You poured it. But you'll never drink it!'

(I think you'll definitely agree, very Rambo!!!!)

From nowhere appeared an arrow. (Didn't I tell you!!!! You can practically hear Jerry Goldsmith's theme tune in the background!!) The arrow buried itself in Domhnall's throat.

As he literally choked on his own blood, he heard these parting words.

'Between Carinish and in the North and Ludag in the South, there is only one man who is responsible for this – Mac Iain 'Ic Sheumais!!'

Wow!!!

'Ic Sheumais probably had the biggest balls in the Hebrides and a voice like distant thunder, and the local women would become instantly pregnant simply by being in his vicinity.

As soon as these words were spoken, out came the MacDonalds from where they'd been hiding and proceeded to beat seven shades of crap out of the remaining thirty-nine boatmen. There was A LOT of killing, even by MacDonald standards. One suspects Mac Rambo did more than his fair share of the aforementioned butchery, no doubt with some gigantic knife that he'd hand-crafted in his remote croft while knitting a headband from the flayed flesh of his enemies.

To this day, there is a spot called 'The Ditch of Blood' in

Carinish. Probably a very popular romantic spot with the locals.

'Morag, fancy a wee stroll to the Ditch of Blood?'

'Oh, Iain, you're such a tease!!!!'

MacIain was apparently tended to by a local woman, as he had been wounded. He most likely sewed his own leg back on while she composed a song about it. And that, my friends, is the story of the Battle of Carinish.

ADVENTURE OF THE MONTH
THE TWELVE PEAKS OF THE BLACK CUILLIN ON SKYE

SAM

Possibly the most remote Munro, *An Teallach* – the Maiden – is one of seven Munros that dominate this area. I'd like to say it's near somewhere, but it's not. If arriving by ferry into Ullapool, on the west coast of Scotland, you may catch a glimpse of the Maiden's neighbouring family. The most intrepid madman (explorer), upon scrambling its southern side, may come across a huge hidden waterfall, and will see the water disappearing into a vast black chasm below.

A peak for the most brave (crazy) and daring explorers.

[*Graham: I have a question. Is there an espresso bar nearby?*]

GREAT SCOT!

NOTABLE BIRTHDAYS, DEATHS AND SIGNIFICANT EVENTS

1 May 1707 – Act of Union of English and Scottish parliaments proclaimed.

2 May 1933 – The story of the Loch Ness Monster first appeared in the press.

8 May 1945 – Victory-in-Europe (VE) Day, end of the Second World War in Europe.

12 May 1725 – The Black Watch regiment was commissioned under General Wade to police the Highlands.

14 May 1754 – St Andrew's Society of Golfers constituted. In 1834 it became the Royal and Ancient Golf Club.

22 May 1859 – Sir Arthur Conan Doyle, author of Sherlock Holmes, born in Edinburgh.

JUNE

There are two seasons in Scotland – June and winter.
Billy Connolly

Clan MacNeil of Barra
Motto: *Buaidhi no bas* (To conquer or die)
Lands: Barra

KEY DIARY DATES

Meteorological start of SUMMER: 1 June–31 August

1	Start of Summer
21	Summer Solstice and Litha (Midsummer's Day), astrological start of summer
Mid-June:	Royal Highland Show
Mid-June:	Moray Walking Festival

COMPETITION CORNER
SCOTTISH SWORD DANCE

SAM

Another sporting challenge on *Men in Kilts*, the 'Dance of the Swords', was originally a way of soldiers getting fit before going into battle. Highland dancer Cerys Jones had the unfortunate job to teach Lady McTavish and me some dirk dancing, which was no mean feat!

There are many different sword dances, but the basic rule of thumb is that you cross two swords on the ground in an X and dance in the quarters. Many of the dances are now lost in the mists of time, but there were apparently a variety of Highland weaponry jigs using dirks, targes, broadswords, Lochaber axes and even flails, a heavy spiked weapon on the end of a rope or chain that you swung like a mad man at someone's heid. (Sounds right up your street, Grey Dog! Got a collection of flails in New Zealand? Come on, tell us about your flail collection . . .! The man is obsessed with sharp pointy things.)

As Graham and I attempted to copy the highly skilled yet diminutive Cerys's quick steps, dressed in formal Highland Dress, the Big Beg Man started off well and had a very balletic way of placing his feet. I've noticed it when he's putting on his shoes (yes, his prized little blue ones). Even when he puts his wellies on – he points his toes and angles his foot down like he's trained at the Bolshoi, or in his case the Bullshitshoi.

I was feeling mildly confident, because I'd done it for *Outlander*, but the perfect placing of the Lady's feet was putting me off. I needn't have worried. Very soon he was struggling to keep up (as usual) and in dire need of a biscuit (as usual), a piece of Highland shortbread denied to him by me and leaping around in my pocket. I started to get the hang of it and the quicker I mastered the steps, the faster Graham's performance went into decline, quickly unravelling from a sprightly out-of-time jig to an iffy impression of a man with both legs down one trouser hole trying to jump sideways whilst simultaneously gripped by a panic attack.

As we continued to dance (becoming increasingly jaded), Cerys told us that if the warriors danced well and didn't come into contact with the swords, they would win in battle. That would be ME. If they touched the sword they'd be injured – definitely Graham. And if they kicked the weapons, they were going to die. At that very moment Graham kicked the swords apart and laughed in horror, like the ground had opened up in front of him and a horned Beelzebub was standing there beckoning him in.

I told him to be thankful he had only kicked a sword and not an actual bucket! He jumped about some more and CLANG, he kicked the sword again and again, his sugar levels plummeting to a dangerous new low.

Sword dancing points to me.

GRAHAM

What can I say about sword dancing that Sam hasn't already mentioned. Well, I suppose I could try . . . the truth.

It is true I kicked the swords, probably out of sheer frustration, or being overly enthusiastic. I suspect that Sam only avoided kicking his own swords by pretending they were bottles of Sassenach whisky. (I'm pretty sure I heard him offer our instructor, Cerys, a bottle at half price at the end).

My dancing has come in for a lot of comments from my muscular companion. I do remember unleashing my dance style in front of him at a fan convention in Rome. He was horrified.

All I can say is that I've never seen Sam dance, apart from the stomping at the cèilidh and his version of sword prancing. Perhaps he is a wow on the dance floor, the John Travolta of Galloway, the Nureyev of Cumbernauld, but we shall never know. He chooses to keep his dance pumps well hidden. Hopefully I shall one day witness him in complete abandonment on the dance floor. If I do, I shall make sure I press 'record'.

Cerys was astonishing. As I showed all too clearly, what she was doing so effortlessly was not easy. You need thighs like pistons to be able to keep this up! It is definitely a matter of great shame for me that the dance I struggled with so comprehensively is designed for six-year-olds.

Highland dancing follows rules and strict form, whereas my dancing has always tended toward the more 'freeform', spontaneous and unrestrained. Basically like an escaped, drunken Orangutan, who has consumed about eight black coffees. Mine always involves plenty of hip movement, like a testosterone-fuelled hula dancer. Definitely not for everyone.

I danced with Lacroix on a few occasions. His style is probably one favoured by violent ex-offenders out on probation. He throws himself around like a pinball, clearing a space around him with dance steps that constitute an act of war.

But, it is true that at the end of my vain attempts at Highland dancing, Heughan had avoided battering the swords with his feet and so, grudgingly, I concede that this round was his. (If you could hear me now, you would the sound of me grinding my teeth in rage.)

BATTLE OF THE MONTH
THE BATTLE OF BANNOCKBURN, 23–24 JUNE 1314

GRAHAM

If there is one thing that every Scotsman knows, it's Bannockburn. A fairly understated town south of Stirling, it is named after a stream that flows through the town into the River Forth: Bannock Burn. An English relative who met my grandmother in Glasgow for the first time was greeted with the charming, welcoming words, 'We beat you at Bannockburn.' As I've said many times before, the Scots have LONG memories.

To greet a guest you are meeting for the first time stating victory at a battle that happened over 700 years ago is the definition of 'bearing a grudge'.

But it was by no means a guaranteed victory at the time.

Robert the Bruce had successfully enraged Edward II by making all sorts of demands involving words like 'surrender' and 'forfeit'. These are words that a king never learns.

So Edward II did the logical thing. He invaded Scotland.

But Edward II was not his father. His end would come at night in Berkeley Castle, where he was alleged to have been assassinated by having a red hot poker rammed up his backside (through a cow's horn to leave no external marks . . . so cunning). It was said you could hear his screams a mile away. Like a particularly vigorous evening with Black Jack Randall.

But he wasn't to know about that when he mobilised 2000 cavalry and 25,000 infantry. The largest army ever to invade Scotland.

The Scots numbered about 6000 with a small number on horseback – small, nimble, pony-sized creatures, who could outmanoeuvre the English warhorse. Robert the Bruce divided his army into three 'divisions' or 'schiltrons' (massive spear formations), led by the Bruce himself, his brother Edward and his nephew Sir Thomas Randolph, Earl of Moray.

After years of raiding guerrilla-style, and nicking everything that wasn't nailed down in the North of England, Bruce's Tartan Army were tough as nails.

As Edward II crossed the border, he found his way blocked at Stirling by the Scots, on carefully chosen ground just south of Stirling Castle. To his east lay the natural obstacles of two 'burns' or rivers, Bannockburn and Pelstream, along with plenty of soft, boggy ground.

He filled the approaching roadway with pits to break the legs of advancing cavalry. This was going to be played as a defensive encounter. But before that could happen, one of the leading knights of Edward's army, Sir Henry de Bohun, spotted the Bruce.

Robert sat on a small horse armed only with a war axe.

Sir Henry was in full armour, sword and lance, and a horse that was the equine equivalent of an Abrams tank.

This was de Bohun's chance. Victory was within the grasp of his mailed fist. He was probably imagining victory parades, endless bouts of drinking and more maidens than he could shake a sword at.

Sir Henry de Bohun charged, lance tilted. He must have been elated at the thought that he was going to decide the battle singlehandedly. He was a renowned warrior. He was enormous, sat astride an enormous horse, carrying an enormous lance.

The Bruce just sat there as Henry barrelled towards him.

One can almost feel the collective holding of breath by both sides. The English sitting there sure in the knowledge that Sir Henry would teach this Jock upstart a lesson, preferably one that involved getting impaled on a lance travelling at 35 mph.

But in a moment reminiscent of Indiana Jones's encounter with the scimitar-wielding Arab in *Raiders of the Lost Ark*, the

Bruce simply stepped his horse to one side at the last moment and brought the full force of his war axe down on top of de Bohun's head.

Killing him instantly.

Robert wasn't even sweating.

You can almost hear the collective roar of victory from the Scots accompanied by phrases like, 'Get in their son!!!', and 'Take that, you English bastard!'

The Scots tore into the English. At one point it looked like the English might beat them back, but then Randolph's schiltron fell upon them from out of the nearby wood, catching the English cavalry completely by surprise.

An absolutely vicious melee ensued, but the sheer density of spearmen stopped the English breaking through. At one point they resorted to throwing swords and maces at them, rather like petulant schoolboys in the playground.

1–0 to the Bruce.

The English were depressed, but thought they could bring the Scots to a set-piece battle the next day and bring the power of their Welsh longbowmen to bear.

But fortunately for Robert, and unfortunately for Edward, one of Edward's top commanders decided to defect and spill the beans on everything Edward was planning. Adding for good measure that the English army was as depressed as me after finding a coffee shop that closed early.

So the Bruce decided to face Edward in open battle. They ate a hearty breakfast of oatmeal, cooked with the blood of dead Englishmen, no doubt. The Scots then joined the local religious leader in massed prayer, which Edward II mistook for them praying for mercy.

One of his commanders was said to have replied, 'They ask for mercy, but not from you. They ask God for mercy for their sins. I'll tell you something for a fact, that yon men will win all or die. None will flee for fear of death.'

I think Edward may have gulped in response to this cheery appraisal.

There followed what was a victory of tactical genius. Bruce employed his mobile schiltrons to great effect, driving the English one way and then another, leaving some trapped in boggy ground while others attempted in vain to flee.

As the English fled, the cry of 'On them! On them! They fall!' echoed across the battleground. Of the army that had invaded Scotland, only 3000 made it home.

Or as the song goes in 'Flower of Scotland':

Who fought against him,
Proud Edward's army
And sent him homeward
To think again.

Full time: 2–0 to Scotland

FAMILY OF BRUCE

SAM

The House of Bruce – which sounds like a private club in Soho – was a prominent lowland family and not a Highland clan. Contrary to popular belief, many Scots do not actually have a clan and therefore belong to families. Clans were all about power and protection and often included many members with no blood ties – The Old Fox, Lord Lovat famously offered a 'boll of meal' to anyone who changed their name to Fraser.

[*Graham: Now you'd have to pay* them *to have you!*]

The Bruces on the other hand were an aristocratic family with powerful connections. Like the Frasers, the Family de Brus (or de Bruis) were French nobility from Normandy, who popped over the English Channel in 1066 led by William the Conqueror and unleashed a can of whoop-ass on the unsuspecting Brits. What's amusing is that the Normans were descendants of Vikings or Norsemen who had settled in northern France, so it was essentially another Viking raid – only way more sophisticated.

After a successful Conquest of England, including taking out King Harold with an arrow in the eye at the Battle of

Hastings (which is apparently a myth – he was hacked to death), what followed was a land grab. William the Conqueror declared all land to be owned by the Crown and he rewarded his knights and barons by giving them vast tracts of it, much of which is still owned by the descendants of those Norman families today. In fact, William's 22nd great-granddaughter, Queen Elizabeth II, is still the legal owner of England and all the houses in it, so the English are but tenants to Betty Windsor!

Thankfully, this is not the case in Scotland. Phew!

Today, most members of the Scottish and English Bruce line can trace themselves back to Robert de Brus, 1st Lord of Annandale (William also handed out titles to his Norman buddies like I do protein bars to Graham), who arrived in England in 1106.

Fast forward six lords later and we come to Robert the Bruce, the 7th Lord of Annandale and Earl of Carrick inherited through his mother, the feisty Marjorie, Countess of Carrick. (I love the name Marjorie and obviously so did the Bruce, because he gave the name to his eldest daughter.) By now the Family de Bruce had done very well indeed, amassing vast estates in Aberdeenshire, County Antrim, Durham, Essex, Middlesex and Yorkshire. The Bruce family still resides at Broomhall House in Fife, which today is graced by the 37th Chief of the Name of Bruce and Head of the Family of Bruce, Andrew Bruce, the Earl of Elgin.

I actually met the Earl of Elgin at a secret gathering of the Masters of the Malt. An annual get together of the powerful players in the whisky business. Andrew Bruce, a small and charming man with a uniquely high singing voice, invited us to put our feet on the table as he sang an ode to Scotch. For the last rousing chorus, we were encouraged to stand on the chairs and tables and after much top-notch Scotch, we obliged willingly. Thankfully, Lord Elgin did not fall off the table afterwards and finished his song in spectacular fashion. Broomhall House is one of Scotland's grandest houses, and you can contact the Earl of Elgin directly to book a private tour via the website. One for *Men In Kilts 2*, Graham?

To Scots, Robert the Bruce is right up there with William Wallace, Sean Connery and Billy Connelly – total legends. He was a fearsome warrior, a freedom fighter and a king, and it was his paternal Norman lineage that gave him claim to the Scottish throne. In 1290, when heir apparent Margaret, Maid of Norway, died aged seven, the Bruce's grandpa Bob (they are ALL called Robert) exercised this claim. Unfortunately he wasn't the only claimant, as John Balliol, Lord of Galloway, also thought he had a shot at the title.

Edward I backed Balliol and John was crowned king. For a few years. Until 1296, when Edward I decided to invade Scotland. The Family of Bruce saw their chance and backed Edward's invasion plan, securing King John Balliol's removal from the throne and banishment to France. (There's a pattern, isn't there? The terrible threat of Frenchmen being sent back!)

Edward I was now in charge of Scotland and that's when the Family of Bruce decided to switch allegiances (again), this time with Robert the Bruce teaming up with William Wallace, a Scottish knight (played by Mel Gibson), with whom he jointly led an uprising against the English, kicking off the Wars of Scottish Independence that were to last until Bannockburn in 1314. The uprising failed and Bruce had all his lands confiscated.

However, in 1298, Teflon Bruce, along with John 'The Red' Comyn III of Badenoch (Balliol's nephew), was appointed a guardian of Scotland. Red Comyn was the Bruce's key rival for the throne, so in 1306, The Bruce stabbed him before the altar of Greyfriars Kirk at Dumfries. Job done.

The Pope was very cross about Red Comyn's murder, so excommunicated Robert – the equivalent of a Papal 'talk to the hand'. Edward I went one further and outlawed him – ghosting on a regal level. But Bruce didn't care. He moved quickly to seize the throne, and was crowned King of Scots at Scone on 25 March 1306.

Unfortunately, he was deposed a year later and went on the run, laying low on an island off Northern Ireland. His wife and daughters were captured and imprisoned and three of his brothers were executed. The path to absolute power is never an easy one! [*Comment from Graham – to come?.*]

When the time came for him to return to Scotland, The Bruce came back smarter and stronger like Rocky and whipped the English arses using guerrilla warfare tactics, which helped secure his victory at Bannockburn.

A little known fact is that Sir Alexander Fraser of Touchfraser and Cowie, a hero of Bannockburn, actually married Robert the Bruce's widowed sister, Lady Mary, in 1316, who'd been imprisoned in a cage by Edward I. What a git. So I'm practically related to Robert the Bruce.

[*Graham: You are not a FRASER!*]

7 June 1329 - Robert the Bruce died.

Robert the Bruce died at his manor house in Cardross, on the western bank of the River Leven in Dunbartonshire. He was buried at Dunfermline Abbey, but his heart rests at Melrose Abbey, after a failed attempt to take it to the Holy Land, via Spain.

There's a carved stone monument erected to Bruce near the dramatic and seriously fortified Stirling Castle. It faces south, towards Bannockburn. Designed in 1876–7 by George Cruikshank and sculpted by Andrew Currie, the statue depicts the King dressed in chainmail standing tall, his hand resting on his sword; an axe and shield at his feet. You should never pose for a portrait or a statue without an axe. It doesn't look impressive enough.

[*Graham: If they gave you a statue – and I strongly doubt they will – it would probably have an Audi in the background for product placement, both hands filled with bottles of your booze brand, your leg cocked in the Full Nash, your brow furrowed while staring into the distance, with an expression questioning whether you'll make it to the toilet in time.*]

[*Sam: Yours would have a latte in one hand, a scarf around your neck, surrounded by biscuit wrappers, perched on your treasure chest of money, legs astride in your kilt having still not mastered the art of concealing yer family jewels!*]

REGION OF THE MONTH
STIRLING AND DUNBARTONSHIRE

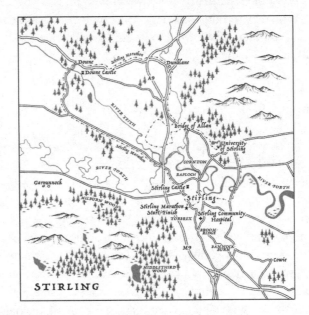

SAM

I love Stirling and, as you know I've run a marathon there [*Graham: Where HAVEN'T you run a marathon?*] and I also received my first honorary degree from the University of Stirling. I had a tour of Stirling Castle when I was working with *Outlander* and strangely I took a beefy American personal trainer, who dragged his knuckles all the way round, the experience and history completely lost on him. AND, he even complained about how many stairs there were – this isn't GRAHAM, but a fitness guru complaining about the stairs!

The castle is very close to where we film *Outlander* and Fraser's Ridge is only ten minutes away in a . . . secret location. When we were shooting Season Four, one of the Native American cast was shot in the leg by an arrow so he was taken to hospital in Stirling, still dressed in full costume. I'm not sure if any one believed the nurse when she told her friends and family later that she had triaged a Native American, who had been shot by an arrow but they probably locked the drinks cabinet!

The same excitable group, after sampling some Scottish hospitality one night, attempted to scale the walls of Stirling Castle itself, with one of them hitching a ride on the back of a police car home like a rodeo rider, without the cops ever realising! They once had a mass pillow fight in George Square, Glasgow, all twenty of them, until the police turned up. They are WILD, passionate, connected to their land and culture, generous, wise, now some of my good friends AND totally brilliant!

ADVENTURE OF THE MONTH
BEN LOMOND

SAM

Loch Lomond and the Trossachs National Park is just a wee way to the west of Stirling. And, if you haven't been, then go! You can even cycle there from Glasgow along the River Kelvin and canal system. There's the majestic scenery of the Arrochar Alps and Ben Lomond and the islands of Loch Lomond and the Falls of Dochart. The park is home to 21 Munros, 19 Corbetts, 22 large lochs and seven waterfalls – there is so much to see and do. The native woodland within the park includes some of the most important Atlantic Oak woodland in Europe – Scotland's rare temperate rainforests – a haven for rare plants, lichens and fungi, as well as a number of unusual animals.

One such site is Inchcailloch Island on Loch Lomond. Inchcailloch means the 'Island of the Old Women' and refers to a nunnery founded on the isle by St Kentigerna. You can take a boat across the loch and in April there is a sea of bluebells amongst the ancient oaks on the enchanting isle. I actually went to look at an island that was for sale on Loch Lomond. Once the home of the Countess of Arran, a power boat enthusiast, she held the record for the women's speed record on water (102 mph) and I imagined her zipping across from the island to get her daily bottle of milk and newspaper.

It was also the home to some wild wallabies, yes, mini kangaroos, though I'm sure they'd hate being called that. 'Here, gonnae no call me a kangaroo, pal, I'm a Scottish wallaby, ken?!' They were introduced to the island in the 1920s, but appear to have all vanished, possibly becoming the first (Scottish) wallabies to swim to Australia, or wherever they normally live. The island was beautiful, with the remains of an old lodge situated on the southern shore. I dreamed of owning the island, but then remembered the annual midge attacks each summer and couldn't blame the wallabies for escaping to a warmer climate. The price was also way out of my range, but it was fun to dream. Laird of the Wallaby Isle.

It was the first year of shooting *Outlander* and I was, let's say, rather green, having never been the lead of a TV show before. I assumed that it wouldn't last more than a year, or two . . . but almost a decade later, I'm still here! However, there was a point in that first year where it almost came to a rather sticky end. More on that later!

As I have said, I was rather inexperienced, but up for anything on and off set! So when my mate Marina suggested we go and 'bag a Munro' for the first time, I agreed enthusiastically. Marina was and is a really great friend and introduced me to the love of Munro bagging but it's just occurred to me that every time I've almost fallen off a mountain (twice) it's been with her! Lesson clearly not learned.

It was early April and a typical Scottish spring day – sunny, raining, snowing, foggy, sleeting and every other meteorological phenomena you can imagine. The sky would change every few minutes (four seasons in one day) and yet when filling up Marina's ancient battered car with fuel, and necking our second, extra-large Americano from a well-used travel cup, she muttered, 'Perfect weather for a wee hike,' and then gunned the car into first gear and headed for the hills.

As we drove north, the short 45-minutes to Loch Lomond (more like thirty with her driving) past Dumbarton Rock, and the Erskine Bridge, we neared the base of Ben Lomond and its lopsided shoulder, the Ptarmigan Ridge. The snow-capped peak disappeared into the clouds some 3000 feet above.

'Do you think we need snow shoes?' I asked, having no idea what they were, but knowing I'd seen some old black-and-white footage of mountaineers in the snow, wearing what looked like tennis rackets on their feet.

'Nah, we'll be fine, buddy,' Marina replied cheerfully.

Normally on a clear day, the peak of Ben Lomond is visible from the higher ground of Glasgow and across Strathclyde, with the West Highland Way running along the western base of the mountain by the loch, the largest in the UK (by surface area). On a sunny day, the grey waters of the loch appeal to locals and Glaswegians alike, looking for a day out. It's popular with water sports, sightseeing, dog walking or sitting by the shore eating a fish supper. Today, however, even the most brave souls had decided to remain indoors, with the ominously heavy snow clouds threatening us like a Highland bully.

'Go home!' they growled. 'Go back to that nice-looking bar just down the road . . . with the open fire. Cold beer. Hot food . . . And whisky'.

We made our way along the rough tree lined path. When we finally broke the cover of the trees we were treated to spectacular views of the loch and belond. We both took a sharp nip of smoky whisky from Marina's tweed flask and instantly felt braver. Which was important, as the path had now disappeared upwards into the low-lying snow.

'Ach, we just keep going up,' she said happily, as I pulled my thin windbreaker further up my neck and gave one last look back towards Glasgow, and home. We really aren't dressed properly for this, I thought. Hitherto, the sun had been shining and the views were magnificent. Now the dense clouds had drawn in and a howling wind made it hard to hear Marina's shouts ahead.

We soldiered on, blindly looking for any sign of the now well-covered path. Then we scrambled, using our feet and hands to pull ourselves up some steep scree. Loose stones fell away as we hung on to large tufts of heather. This didn't feel like a walk; this was mountain climbing. A few minutes later, as we stopped at a large overhang, trying to gingerly negotiate our way around it, the clouds briefly parted, showing we were actually on a rough cliff edge, the mountain falling away below.

'ITHINKIT'STHEWROOONGWAAAYY,' I screamed, the wind stuffing my words back into my mouth so hard I almost choked. Marina looked to be having the same thought, judging by her rudimentary hand signals and heavy frown. We circled back from the overhang and then 'lo and behold', there was the path! Or at least, a few stones rising out of the now deeper snow signalling a pathway of sorts.

We pressed on, thinking we must be nearly at the top. We could make out the narrowing cone of the mountain, maybe 100 metres above us. Eager to reach our goal and now wet through, we began to climb, cutting foot holes in the hard packed ice, frozen over by the bitter north wind. It was very steep. We made our way straight up (there is actually an easy way to walk up this mountain, I promise, but we were hopelessly lost). Ten or twenty feet up, I heard a faint 'Oop!' behind me.

I turned and watched Marina slide face down, gathering pace, desperately trying to dig her fingers into the ice and snow, but she couldn't get a hold. As she sped downwards my heart was in my mouth because the edge of the cliff was only a short distance to our right, and in the same moment, I too slipped onto my back and tobaganned after her! We finally came to a stop, having fallen some twenty feet or so. Both of us lay there on our backs, breathing hard.

'Perhaps we can come back in the summer? With the right equipment,' I said, staring up at the ever belligerent sky. 'With snowshoes?'

'And more whisky,' she replied, laughing.

DRAM OF THE MONTH
DEANSTON 12 YEAR OLD

SAM

The village of Doune in the Stirling district of central
Scotland is rather unassuming. A quiet village with a single
main street, grocery store, some gift shops, a cafe or two,
several bed-and-breakfasts and a nearby caravan park (ideal
for McTavish and his friends). The historic burgh was known
in the past for pistol-making as well as its well-fortified castle,
which some Scottish time-travel TV show took over and has
comandeered multiple times. In fact, we do tend to shoot a
lot of *Outlander* around Doune and the nearby area.

One place in particular I'm very fond of is the Deanston
Distillery. For Season Two of *Outlander*, we shot in the
bonded warehouse, the main stor room for their
delightfully aging barrels of whisky. It was to double as a
Parisien wine cellar and the base for Jamie's illegal
smuggling business. An 'accidental' death, ahem, caused by
Claire and Jamie forced them to hide the body in a cask of
Crème de Menthe in said wine cellar. I guess to keep the
remains minty fresh?!

That evening, as the film crew descended on the
warehouse, I noticed the strong smell of whisky. No, this
time it wasn't coming from me, but 'the angels' share', or
evaporating cask strength whisky inside the barn. For hours I
breathed deeply, trying to take in as much of the sweet barley
and oak fragrance that hung in the thick air. Some crew felt
lightheaded. I felt amazing. We went for another take, as I
rolled a large barrel for the tenth time to John Bell (playing
'Young Ian').

'ARRrrgh!' The 100-plus-gallon bourbon barrel landed on
his foot. Poor John.

'Breathe deep,' I said. 'The fumes will take away the pain.'

Hours later, the distillery generously gave us all a bottle of whisky and whenever I smell that dram, it reminds me of Doune and poor John's foot. (The whisky doesn't smell like his feet, I hasten to add.)

The Deanston 12 year old, aged in bourbon barrels (moved by myself – well, a fake one, but all the same) on the banks of the river Teith.

CRACKING CASTLE OF THE MONTH
DOUNE CASTLE

GRAHAM

Doune Castle, near the village of Doune, was home to the MacKenzies in *Outlander* (Castle Leoch), and scene of many a great day of location filming. We went back there for *Men in Kilts* to meet Iain MacGillivray and Charlie Allan. It was so lovely to return.

I remember going there a few weeks before we started on Outlander, with my eldest daughter Honor, to show her where Daddy would be filming. It was completely deserted. We were the only people there. I think that may well be the last time Doune Castle was that quiet!

It is also the setting for one of the funniest moments in *Monty Python and the Holy Grail*, where our heroes arrive before a French castle (Doune) and demand entry. For those who haven't seen *Holy Grail*, do so immediately. It is perhaps my favourite Python film.

I was lucky enough to become good friends with Terry Jones, one of the Python team and co-director of *Holy Grail*, when I was at university. Not only one of the funniest people I have ever known, but also the most fiercely intelligent and generous soul you could hope to meet.

I went on to work with him on *Erik the Viking* and *The Wind in the Willows*, written by that marvellous Scotsman, Kenneth Grahame. He was a lovely man, who explained to me that the reason they used coconuts to imitate the sound of horses' hooves was because they couldn't afford horses . . .

SAM

As Graham said, Doune Castle has been featured in many TV shows and films. Monty Python, *Game of Thrones*, *Outlander* (of course), and clearly the most iconic, *Men in Kilts*.

In front, on the grounds of Doune, Graham McTavish surprisingly feigned a hamstring injury during a particularly brutal game of shinty in Season One of *Outlander*, claiming he needed to sit out and rest for a few hours while his poor, tired stunt double was left to do all of the dirty work.

It was also here that Graham McTavish ate the entire contents of the actors' Tesco's snack bag (fruit and nut bars, Kit Kats, and the odd soggy biscuit) in Season One. AND where he made regular and unreasonable demands for protein shakes (only after seeing me drinking them!) Little did he know that the assistant director had run out of protein, so what McTavish was chugging down were in fact glasses of cloudy water!

Not far from Doune Castle is Old Newton of Doune. A small castle almost as old as Doune with the site dating back to the 1400s. It's where our original showrunner, Ron Moore, and his wife Terry stayed during production. It has thick fortress-like walls, arrow slits for windows, and has housed the likes of Bonnie Prince Charlie, Sir Walter Scott and the philosopher David Hume. Much of the furniture and decoration is from the same period and even features what can only be described as a 'period toilet'. The sound it made when flushed could wake an entire castle.

One late night, after raiding Ron's famous whisky collection, I decided to crash on a sofa in the tower, facing an antique painting of a jester. During the night I woke with a start, perhaps owing to the volume of expensive whisky, or the delicious meal Terry had cooked me. The only light shining was a faint bedside lamp, which cast an eerie golden shadow across the wall and fell upon the joker's face, his wry smile and squinted eyes laughing at me. I felt the picture watch me as I stumbled down the staircase to find the toilet, hoping not to wake everyone with the screaming cistern?

Luckily I managed not to fall down the dark staircase and returned to the tower to spend a tortuous and interminable night being watched by the jester, praying he wouldn't move or wink at me. I didn't sleep much, if at all and left for work super early (a first!). I'm sure McTavish was somewhere in one of the multiple rooms, snoring deeply, although I'm not sure how he managed to score a bed! But then again in true McTavish form he'd probably wangled the best room in the castle, complete with butler.

6 June 1944 - The Normandy Landings.

SAM

On *Men in Kilts*, as well as catching up with Charlie Allan and his collection of broadswords and Lochaber axes at Doune Castle, we met Iain MacGillivray, a farmer, piper and the youngest clan chief in Scotland. Iain told us about the history of the bagpipes, one of the most ancient forms of music in Europe – an instrument of beauty, but also a weapon of war. The pipes were meant to put fear in the enemies and were used at many great battles, including Culloden. Iain explained that when the British Empire spread, the Scots were at the forefront. Orchestral Scots in kilts with a set of bagpipes and drums!

In the Second World War, there is the wonderful story of Piper Bill Millin, personal piper to none other than Simon Fraser, the 15th Lord Lovat. Simon Fraser was a man who did things differently and his way – rather like his ancestor the Old Fox, the 11th Lord Lovat, whom we heard about in the month of April.

At the request of Simon Fraser, Private Bill Millin, aged twenty-one, stormed the beaches of Normandy in the D-Day landings still playing the bagpipes. When Millin pointed out that British Army regulations meant bagpipes were restricted to the rear, Lord Lovat replied, 'Ah, but that's the English War Office. You and I are both Scottish, and that doesn't apply.'

So wearing the same Cameron tartan kilt that his father had worn in Flanders during the First World War and armed only with his pipes and the *sgian-dubh*, upon Fraser's orders the young Bill marched up and down the Normandy beaches playing 'Highland Laddie', 'The Road to the Isles', and 'All the Blue Bonnets Are Over the Border'. For half an hour he played as his comrades fell around him. Bill learned later that the Germans had apparently stopped shooting at him, because they couldn't believe their eyes that someone could be that insane! What a complete legend.

However, the best part of our meeting with Iain was the surprise he had in store for the Grey Dog. He informed Graham than one of his relatives, a certain Simon McTavish of the North West Company (fur traders) in Canada, was the nephew of William MacGillivray, which made him and Iain distant relatives! Graham was overjoyed and to celebrate this TV gold moment, Iain played 'The Black Bear' on his bagpipes – one of the McTavish's favourite marches.

NATURE NOTES
OUTLANDER FLOWERS

SAM

Three flowers in bloom this month had great significance in *Outlander*, for very different reasons: St John's wort, forget-me-not and, wait for it . . . lavender (shudder!).

Perforate St John's wort (*Hypericum perforatum*), which flowers from June to September, was the first herb to feature in the *Outlander* series and was the first to be used on Jamie

Fraser as a pain reliever. The plant is still used to treat depression today and in the 1700s a pouch was kept under the armpits (or oxters) of people possessed by the devil.

Have you washed your 'oxters', Grey Dog?

The forget-me-not (*Myosotis*) is native wildflower of the British Isles. During the day the tiny blue flowers give off very little scent and are at their most fragrant during the evening. *Myosotis* can be found across areas in south-west Scotland and on the east coast. It is, however, not known to be found in the Highlands, Outer Hebrides, Shetland or Orkney, which is perhaps why Claire is so surprised to see a forget-me-not at the stone circle of Craigh na Dun.

Unable to take a closer look, because pagans are arriving to perform rituals for Samhain (in the book it's Beltane, which is a better fit for the flowering forget-me-nots), Claire returns to the stones to find the flower and, of course, falls through the stones and the rest is six seasons of *Outlander* history! My co-star Caitriona also collaborated with the good folks of the Garden Shed Gin company to create a gin by the same name. I'm waiting for my bottle, hopefully she doesn't forget . . .

Unlike the forget-me-not (*Lavandula angustifolia* – aka English lavender) is not a native of Britain but from the Mediterranean region, and is grown in gardens across Scotland blooming from June to August. There are 450 varieties and 45 species, of which Black Jack Randall would have had his subtle favourites. Because as we all know he's a big fan of the stuff. Usually associated with grannies' handbags or relaxation, in *Outlander* its association is far darker.

The air in Geillis Duncan's still room is thick with the scent of lavender (*Outlander*, Chapter 9) and, of course, villain Black Jack always carries a vial of oil of lavender with him for lubrication purposes, making it Jamie's least favourite flower. However, I do actually like the smell and have a regular bottle to keep my trailer smelling nice!

GREAT SCOT!

NOTABLE BIRTHDAYS, DEATHS AND SIGNIFICANT EVENTS

1 June 1946 – Brian Denis Cox CBE born in Dundee.

1 June 1991 – *Outlander*, written by Diana Gabaldon, was first published by Delacorte Press. The *Outlander* series has since sold over 25 million copies.

3 June 1945 – Actor William 'Bill' Paterson born in Glasgow; 'LBP' as we called him on set, played the brilliant 'Ned Gowan' – solicitor to the stars!

8 June 1772 – Robert Stevenson, engineer, who constructed 18 lighthouses around Scotland, born in Glasgow.

9 June 1942 – First US troops (over 10,000 men) disembarked from the *Queen Mary* on the River Clyde.

10 June 1688 – James Francis Stuart born. In honour of the 'Old Pretender', this is known as 'White Rose Day' in Jacobite circles.

10 June 1719 – The Battle of Glenshiel.

GRAHAM

On 10 June 1719, the only pitched battle of the first Jacobite rebellion was fought in the stunningly beautiful narrow pass of Glenshiel. The two sides turned up with comparable numbers, roughly one thousand each.

Present among them was a character that we have already spoken about, Lord George Murray (who would be at Bonnie Prince Charlie's side at Culloden). At the time of Glenshiel, Murray was a sprightly youngster, only twenty-five. Also there was the legendary Rob Roy MacGregor, who was a comparatively ancient forty-eight years old at the time of the battle.

The rest of the Jacobite forces were made up of Clan Mackenzie (Tulach Ard), the Camerons and MacDougalls. Joining them (before they decided the best bet was siding with the Government) were the Campbells and about 200 Spanish troops from Galicia.

It is a strange thing to note that the week before the battle, one of the Spaniards died of heatstroke, such was the unusual heat of the Scottish summer that year. Anyone who has strolled around Glen Shiel would find it hard to imagine dying of anything other than hypothermia.

There is a hill there that, to this day, is called *Sgùrr nan Spàinteach* (The Peak of the Spaniards). Perhaps there is another smaller hill nearby, called 'The hill of that one Spaniard who should've stood in the shade and worn a hat'?

On the Government side were, among others, the Munros, Sutherlands, MacKays and, yes, you guessed it, the Frasers.

The Government troops were using a new type of small mortar, which they used to great effect by bombing the crap out of the Jacobites. Through superior tactics, and dropping high explosives from a distance on the struggling followers of King James, the Government forces prevailed.

The Jacobites, along with a badly wounded Rob Roy MacGregor, retreated up the glen, the mocking jeers of James Alexander Malcolm MacKenzie Fraser's ancestors no doubt echoing down the glen.

18 June 1746 – Flora MacDonald met Prince Charles Edward Stuart and persuaded him to wear women's clothes as part of the escape plan from the Outer Hebrides to Skye.

19 June 1937 – J.M. Barrie, the author of *Peter Pan*, died.

GRAHAM

Peter Pan was the first film I ever was when I was five years old at my local Odeon cinema. It made such an indelible impression on me and one that I've remembered when my own children have watched animated films.

You see, I totally believed it was real. I didn't see a 'cartoon', I saw a real life adventure. A child's mind doesn't distinguish between real life and make-believe. The pathways between the two worlds are wonderfully open to children. It's more than imagination, it's an ability to inhabit parallel worlds. What a gift! And how sad it is when that open pathway becomes blocked.

As adults we still enjoy fiction and emotionally invest in it as if it is real using our 'suspension of disbelief'. It always amazes me as both a performer and audience member that, especially in theatre, an unspoken contract exists between those two sides of the stage that allows us all to believe completely in what is happening. That despite the fact that our rational mind knows watching a 'play' in a theatre, with props and fake scenery, with actors performing scripted dialogue (mostly) – and that as audience members we bear witness to this – we still allow our imaginative self to fall headlong into the story. To be swept along by its drama, laughing at its comedy, shedding tears over its tragedy.

So it was that my five-year-old self saw *Peter Pan*. Not as fiction at all. Peter was real. In fact he was so real that when the cinema stopped showing it and they took down the posters, I remember distinctly asking my parents, 'Where has Peter gone?' Because, to me, Peter Pan 'lived' in that cinema. It is one of my first memories as a child, such was the power of Pan.

Cut to about thirty years later and I was given the chance to play Captain Hook in the TAG theatre company's version of *Peter Pan*. It was wildly imaginative. As Hook I wore a red velvet frock coat, white trousers and Doc Marten boots up to my knees, with a long curly black wig, and, of course, a large silver hook! My first entrance was in a shopping trolley. My foot on the front, like the prow of a ship, being pushed by Smee played by Thane Bettany (father of Paul). It was one of the best entrances I've ever had.

[*Sam: 'stifles self'.*]

It is the most extraordinary play, and like the open pathway that I spoke of earlier, it examines what it is to be a 'child', never to grow up, and the curse of adulthood that Hook somewhat represents.

One night I was doing the play. Children used to come dressed as their favourite characters, Peter, Wendy, Smee, and some dressed as Hook. During my speech in which I refer glowingly to 'a holocaust of children', out of the inky darkness came the clear voice of a child saying simply, 'I love that man.'

I honestly think *Peter Pan* is one of the abiding reasons I have spent my life, to some degree or other, trying NOT to grow up.

29 June 1946 – My parents, Alexander Graham McTavish and Ellen Patricia Alexander married six months after meeting for the first time.

[*Sam: Graham was just a twinkle in Alex's eye.*]

JULY

Clan Douglas
Motto: *Jamais Arriere* (Never behind)
[*Graham: Clearly not the motto of Black Jack Randall.*]
Lands: Lanarkshire, Galloway,
Dumfriesshire, and Angus

172

REGION OF THE MONTH
OUTER HEBRIDES (AKA THE WESTERN ISLES)

SAM

Whilst on tour with the Traverse Theatre, I was lucky to visit many remote locations in the Highlands and Islands. It was a magical trip, but not quite as glamorous as the previous stint in the Edinburgh Festival and London's Royal Court, where I was nominated for a Laurence Olivier Award, for most promising performer. I remember being at the ceremony, drinking free champagne and thinking, 'Oh God, please don't let me win, this champagne has gone straight to my head,' as I hadn't prepared an acceptance speech. Fortunately I didn't win and I was very thankful for the free bevvy.

At midnight, I changed out of my hired kilt in a public toilet without being propositioned once and boarded a night bus back to Scotland. Eight hours later, I stumbled off the bus and shuffled blearily into the building next door, for my 9 a.m. class at drama school. The previous night's festivities and champagne were a mere stain on my rented kilt and a thumping pain in my head. I thought expensive champagne was supposed to be hangover free?

[*Graham: Is that the sound of Laurence Olivier turning in his grave?*]

During the tour of the play *Outlying Islands*, with the entire cast bundled into a people carrier and the director driving the whole way, we visited amongst others, Easdale Island. Eilean Eisdeal is the smallest island in the Inner Hebrides and seems to be made entirely of slate. It has also been home to the world stone-skimming championships, due to its abundance of perfect skimming stones. I gave a few a good try, but I don't think I would make the podium.

Easdale is less than 60 hectares and you can walk around the whole island in around forty minutes. It's also only 200 metres from the mainland, so you have to take a small boat to reach the island. In fact EVERYTHING goes by this tiny boat, as no cars are allowed on the island. I've no idea how we managed to transport our whole stage and set there, but we did.

In the local community hall, the inhabitants (sixty people or so), plus a few 'mainlanders' crushed themselves in front of our small stage. The play, set on the remote island of North Rhona, is about two young ornithologists who go to the island to study the wildlife and mistakenly end up killing the local farmer (oops!), who happens to have a lovely daughter that both the lads fall for, over a delightful meal of stewed puffin.

It's a dark and beautiful play, about the loss of innocence, and foretells the darkness of the coming Second World War – with a little Laurel and Hardy thrown in for laughs. Our set, a dark bothy (remote mountain shelter) was like a small cave. In the community hall, with all of the island inhabitants gathered together, their communal breath held as my character fought for the love of the local farmer's daughter. The loss of life, the seagulls nesting in the roof of the actual building and the waves outside crashing against the slate island, provided very real sound effects and a spellbinding evening.

As the play climaxed my co-star's character commits suicide by jumping off a cliff into the coming storm, just as a very real storm was also starting to blow up outside. Despite the short distance to the mainland, it became too dangerous to transport the audience back home, plus they were by now well-lubricated by single malt whisky. So after the show finished, the entire island, actors, crew and 'foreigners from the mainland' met in the boat-keeper's house and sang, drank and laughed until morning, whilst the locals played traditional cèilidh music on a chanter and fiddle. I don't remember where I slept, but thankfully I made the short crossing the next day back to the mainland, without having to swim.

On the same tour, we visited the Outer Hebrides and on the Isle of Lewis, we ate dinner with my Gaelic poet and playwright friend Iain MacLeod. He later wrote a play that I performed in called *The Pearlfisher* – about the last of the Scottish traveller folk and freshwater pearl fishers. Subsequently I invited Iain to appear in an episode of *Men in Kilts*, discussing the age-old rivalry and bitter grudge between the MacLeods and the MacDonalds.

In the Port of Ness, on the north-west tip of Lewis, as massive waves crashed against the black cliffs looking out to the North Sea, his father still weaves traditional Harris Tweed. He showed us his simple loom, operated by hand, in the same way that it had been for hundreds of years before. We wanted to visit the island mentioned in *Outlying Islands*, North Rona, that lay some forty-four miles north-east of

Lewis, the most remote island ever to be inhabited in the UK, with its neighbours being the Faroe Islands.

It's so remote, it is normally omitted from maps of the UK. Small and windswept, it has only the North Sea, strong winds and screaming birds for company. In Old Norse it means 'rough island', which feels very apt. Back in the Dark Ages, St Ronan set up a small Christian community there, and it must have felt like being on the edge of the world.

We jumped into a fast rib, (a large speedboat), with bright orange life jackets keeping us warm, and settled in for a bumpy journey across the raging sea. For several hours our orange vessel bounced happily across the water, spotting only the odd seal or gannet (traditionally eaten by the locals on Lewis and called 'Guga' – apparently it tastes as bad as it sounds).

Finally, our eyes clouded by too much sun, wind and sea, we could just about make out a tiny rocky pinhead in the vast ocean. Safely on land and walking the windswept island, we saw the remains of the holy settlement, inhabited centuries ago. It really is an island on the edge of the world, which only a few people have or ever will visit. It's magical, but I wouldn't plan your next vacation there. It is definitely best left to the gulls and grey seals.

Another epic boat trip I have undertaken is the journey crossing the Minch, the channel which separates the mainland and the Western Isles. We filmed it for *Men in Kilts*, as I tried to impart some mythical knowledge bombs to my prosecco-doused companion. The clans that dominated the coast and islands were very powerful, because they controlled access to the sea and in those days it was the fastest way to travel. However, it was also the most dangerous, and the Scottish seafaring culture is packed with folklore and mythical creatures, such as the storm kelpies (Scottish Gaelic: *na fir ghorma*).

Known as the 'Blue Men of the Minch', they looked for ships to sink and sailors to drown. The same size as humans but blue in colour, they could create storms at will. No wonder the Minch is also known as *Sruth nam Fear Gorm*, 'Stream of the Blue Men'. (I imagine they all have large white beards, bald heads and a love of frothy coffee.)

In *Superstitions of the Highlands & Islands of Scotland* (1900), John Gregorson Campbell suggests the origins of the strange blue men: 'The fallen angels were driven out of Paradise in three divisions, one became the Faeries on the land, one the Blue Men in the sea and one . . . the Northern Streamers or Merry Dancers in the sky.'

The 'Merry Dancers' were a name for the Northern Lights, which we'll come to in the month of October.

Other mythical creatures included the nuckelavee, a horse-like demon of which Islanders were so terrified, they wouldn't utter the creature's name without saying a prayer afterward. It was found near the beach, but amusingly enough wouldn't come ashore if it was raining, so not that often then! The beast's breath could wilt crops and spread disease to livestock, but like many other scary sea monsters it couldn't survive in freshwater, so throwing yourself in a river or a loch was a sure-fire method to get away should one be chasing you!

However, you might come face to face with a shellycoat instead . . . Argh! These relatively harmless creatures lived in rivers and streams and were more mischievous than malicious, particularly enjoying getting wanderers lost.

BEST OF FISHERMEN'S FOLKLORE
- Don't EVER talk about salmon aboard a boat. I don't know why, just don't do it.
- Ditto a pig and a rabbit.
- Never take a banana aboard. Ever, ever, ever. Even today. (Unless you're on a banana boat.)
- Don't whistle into the wind – you'll create a storm. (Impossible to do btw.)
- If you see a vicar or a woman on your way to your boat, go home!
- Wear a single gold earring. (Graham?!)
- Carry a sprig of hawthorn.
- Always turn right out of the harbour.
- Put a coin in your sock.
- And, whatever you do, don't save someone from drowning . . .

. . . because many hundreds of years ago in the Shetlands, Orkney and parts of the north-east, it was forbidden to save someone at sea, as people believed a life was a necessary sacrifice to the spirit of the sea. Hence the reason a lot of islanders and fishermen never learned to swim!

'The sea takes the saver of life instead of the saved. The sea maun hae it's nummer,' so goes a nineteenth-century saying from Peterhead, Aberdeenshire.

COMPETITION CORNER
SURF'S UP!

GRAHAM
One of the other 'sporting' events that Sam had put into our schedule was surfing. I've always had great admiration for surfers. Their athleticism, balance, and bleached blond hair.

[*Sam: Hair . . . I mean, he literally sets them up for me!*]

I remember *Baywatch*. Who doesn't? (Well, I suppose anyone under thirty-five to be fair.) But the sight of scantily clad women racing across sun-kissed sand in California was an abiding memory of the 1980s for me.

I always thought, one day I'll try surfing. Those friends I know who do it regularly attest to how addictive it becomes, leading them to check the surf forecast and sometimes travel hours to a beach, simply to catch a wave at dawn.

My dream of surfing was always tempered by my deep suspicion of the ocean. I've seen *Jaws*. I saw it when it first came out. I think EVERYONE who saw that film in the 1970s ALWAYS thinks of it when they are in the ocean. I know I do.

You really don't know what's beneath you in the ocean, coupled with the fact that surfers look like tempting seals to a shark, which adds up to a deep-seated reluctance to swim too far out in the sea.

But when I had these thoughts, these dreams of surfing, I never imagined them in connection with the icy tip of the Isle of Lewis and the North Atlantic. I can assure you that the Beach Boys weren't thinking of Uig Sands in Lewis when they sang 'Catch a Wave'. As for sharks, I doubt Lewis has a big problem with Great Whites, as the shark would die of hypothermia first.

When Heughan suggested surfing, I was game, but I never imagined he would turn it into a competition. Looking back I can see how naive I was. For Sam everything is a competition: boiling an egg, getting dressed, making a pot of tea. If ever sleeping became a competitive sport, Sam would train for it.

[*Sam: Game on! zzzzzzzz.*]

So it was on our one day off that week, Sam went to practise surfing, just so he could beat me the next day. I have no shame admitting that he did. I could barely get the board in the water, let alone stand up on it.

We were lucky with the weather when we shot Season One of *Men in Kilts*, but the weather gods chose our surfing day to make up for the sunny days by battering us with horizontal rain, wind and ball-freezing temperatures.

We were given wetsuits. I think I probably put a wetsuit on top of my wetsuit. I definitely wore gloves and a cap. The overall effect was that I looked like a giant baby in a romper suit, as I wrestled my surfboard down to the water.

[*Sam: Did you pee yourself? Honest question?*]

Any attempt at dignity was abandoned after a few yards. My surfboard literally took on a life of its own. It was like struggling with Duncan Lacroix after he's had one too many whiskies and has heard there might be a bar open late down the road.

When I eventually got in the water, it was actually a relief. I paddled out atop my board and managed to delude myself into believing I was part of the surfing community. In between gulps of salty sea water and the feeling of being slapped about the face by the waves, I glanced over to see Heughan attempting to stand up on his board.

I waited for what I thought might be a wave that would help me glide effortlessly inshore. When it finally happened (when I wasn't tipping off the board and floundering and gasping like an infant wildebeest), it was a great feeling.

After I stayed on the board for more than ten seconds, I realised, at that moment, why people enjoy surfing. This was fun! This was effortless!!! And then I would try again, only to have Poseidon give me a right doing as I battled my way back into the waves.

Of my roughly 15–20 attempts, I think I might have stayed on twice, and that was probably by complete chance. I lost track of time and, amazingly, I wasn't cold!! Well I *was* wrapped up like a man in a sleeping bag, covered in a duvet while wearing a space blanket.

Meanwhile I took another furtive look at my competitive compatriot. Of course, there he was standing on his board (admittedly like a giant toddler taking his first steps in the romper room), but he WAS standing.

Good for him, I thought. (Well, no, that's not what I thought. More like, God, I hope he falls!)

Eventually I realised that I would probably have to stay in the water for the rest of the day, possibly the rest of my natural life, before I could stand up on a surfboard, so I called it a day and began the insane walk back onshore, resembling a man carrying an unruly wild animal under his arm.

Surf might've been 'up' that day, but McTavish definitely wasn't. One of the leading surfboard builders in the world is called McTavish. Obviously we are not related.

SAM

The sea wasn't cold, McTavish, it was warm! Surprisingly warm. The dip in the Sligachan pools on the Isle of Skye, though . . . ooohhh – now THAT was testicle-retracting stuff. I was speaking with a squeaky voice for a good hour afterwards.

But for surfing the sea was a balmy 13°, because the Gulf Stream brings warm currents from the Gulf of Mexico, which keeps the west coast waters warmer than on the east coast of Britain. The sea here never gets below 9° even in winter, so yet again, Graham is being characteristically high maintenance. And as for sharks, basking sharks are harmless, but whoa the dogfish, Grey Dog, they are deadly. I don't know how you survived!

The first time I ever went surfing was with my marine biologist friend, Taylor Chapple. The day before we went, he took me out in a twelve-foot boat along the coast of Monterey Bay, to tag Great White sharks. On the way we saw dolphins and a couple of Orca whales and, OH, did I mention GREAT WHITE SHARKS!

Less than two minutes after we (he) put the lure into the water (a piece of his mum's carpet), seven Great Whites were circling our boat. I held firmly to the handrail and watched as Taylor tagged shark after shark. One had obviously watched *Jaws* and did its best to recreate a memorable scene from the film. It swam off, turned around and came straight for the boat, out of the water and started biting the outboard motor. Just when I really thought my heart couldn't take anymore, they suddenly all disappeared.

'Where did they go?' my voice trembled.

'There must be a big one,' Taylor replied cheerfully, hanging out over the water.

I scanned the horizon, my heart in my mouth. Phew, nothing – only the large wave coming towards us. No. Wait. That WAVE is being caused by something . . . a sixteen-foot Great White, as wide as it was long (almost), glided under our miniature boat and I realised that we were not studying them, they were studying us. Clever fish.

But back to the Outer Hebrides and a balmy day on the beach, teaching an old dog, new tricks. I'll set the scene . . .

Graham was dressed in a double wetsuit, extra thick for extra protection, and what was more ridiculous was that he wore the wetsuit hat. I mean no one wears the wetsuit hat, right? So I made sure to have our brilliant stylist Laura suggest that he wear it, fully expecting him to refuse. But nothing – no tantrum, grumpiness or refusal. Graham willingly donned the oversized head condom and he looked so hilarious, it was wonderful.

Maybe it felt nice to have something on his head for a change.

It was windy. Actually, it was very windy, so when we both carried our surfboards down to the shore, Graham was being blown around violently as he tried to keep hold of his board and his dignity. We arrived at the water's edge and ah, what sweet bliss as I pushed my board out into the waves and started to paddle, leaving a stiff and disgruntled Graham on the shore behind me, still struggling to hold onto his board in the wind.

I paddled out some more, enjoying the immense freedom that surfing gives you. The water was so clear, you could see through the emerald green waves to the golden sand below. This is Scotland, not the tropics!

I looked back at Graham and could see he was waist-high in the water trying to keep a hold of his surfboard. By now he was shouting something that sounded Gaelic, but more likely random expletives. I smiled to myself and paddled onwards, trying to remember what my instructor had taught me in Hawaii.

Graham: Oh, yes, I'd forgotten you had lessons there. So you're practically a professional.

Sam: Okay, so I admit it, I'd surfed in Hawaii, America, and had secret practice lessons the day before.

Graham: But of course you did.

Sam: We actually invited you to come with us, but the idea of working on your day off was met with a look of disbelief and a contemptuous guffaw.

As I enjoyed the waves despite the fierce wind, Graham swallowed as much salty water as he could manage, staying in for about ten minutes. He had been knocked off his feet countless times by the baby waves that broke gently in those exceedingly shallow waters.

Let's face it, the outcome was always going to be the same, for here was a man more suited to lying on a lilo in an infinity pool, a cold glass of Whispering Angel in one hand, his agent on his cell phone to his ear, whilst someone busily made a gourmet three-course lunch for him inside his luxury (borrowed) villa!

This is what happened to poor George, his driver-cum-butler, who had to wait patiently that day on Uig Sands for his master, like Greyfriars Bobby, holding his blue fluffy dressing gown, monogrammed slippers, hot water bottle, tartan-patterned flask of latte and emergency protein bar, all as requested.

I mean, talk about above and beyond, McTavish makes even Mariah Carey's legendary demands look reasonable!

CLAN MACNEIL

GRAHAM
I love this clan. Small but mighty, and well known for being rather marvellous pirates. (And who doesn't love a pirate!)

The main stronghold of the MacNeils is Barra, with MacNeils also looming large on the islands of Colonsay and Gigha. The Colonsay MacNeils actually had a long-standing dispute as to which island had been the MacNeils' the longest.

Barra won first prize.

Sometimes you really do think the Scots will argue over anything!

Until recently, it was believed that the MacNeil clan was descended from Ireland. Specifically from one man – Niall of the Nine Hostages.

(I have to pause here and take a moment to reflect upon this name. Niall of the Nine Hostages. A bit like Duncan of the Seven Castles. Did he start out as Niall of the Couple of Hostages, building up to Niall of the Half Dozen Hostages, until finally settling on nine?)

'I need more hostages!!!!'

'But my lord, you've got five hostages. That's way more than Billy of the two hostages down the road.'

'Noooooo!!!!! I want bloody nine hostages. NINE!!!!! Find me four more of the bastards!!! You!!!!! You can be a hostage!!!'

'But I'm your sister.'

'Doesna' matter. You're a bloody hostage now!!! And YOU!!!!!!'

'Yes, Dad?'

'Hostage!!!!'

Did he have marks carved on the castle wall for each hostage?

'You'll be running out of room soon, my lord.'

'Shut up!!! You can be another hostage.'

I wonder if Niall ever let the hostages go, or was it like my journeys with Heughan and the hostages developed some kind of medieval Stockholm syndrome.

The MacNeil motto is *Baidh No Bas*, which translates as 'Conquer or Die'. Pretty binary choices there, then. No room for misunderstanding. No danger of confusion when it comes to options for the enemy.

However, after some recent DNA testing, it has been discovered that the MacNeils are really descended from Vikings. One look at the pirate ship of choice, the burliss, would confirm this. It is basically a replica of a Viking longboat. It was in these that the MacNeils tore around the seas being very Long John Silver.

One of the MacNeil pirates stole a number of Elizabethan ships during the reign of James VI. When dragged before the King to explain himself in Edinburgh, MacNeil simply said that he thought James would be pleased that he'd been raiding the ships of the woman who had killed Mary Queen of Scots. The King was so stunned by this response that he let MacNeil go.

The first Viking on Barra, according to Norse saga, was the wonderfully named Omund the Wooden Leg. Not surprisingly this was because, like any good pirate, he had one leg. Possibly a parrot, but we can't be sure.

Maybe Omund and Niall met? A wooden leg and nine hostages, what a fun night.

The MacNeils were staunch Jacobites, and at Killiecrankie in 1689, Viscount 'Bonnie' Dundee was supported by no less than Black Roderick MacNeil. I imagine this refers to his reputation rather than his Caribbean origins.

Finally, it is worth noting the daily call given by the faithful retainer of the MacNeil Clan Chief at Kisimul castle.

Each day he would stand on the battlements and blow his horn, followed by this news: 'Hear o ye people, and listen, o ye nations. The great MacNeil of Barra having finished his meal, the princes of the Earth may dine.'

I think I'm going to use this myself whenever I'm next out to dinner with Heughan.

BATTLE OF THE MONTH
THE BATTLE OF THE WESTERN ISLES, 1585–6

GRAHAM

It's slightly misleading to call this a battle. A battle implies two armies meeting to fight it out on a given day and to the victor the spoils.

This was more like a series of betrayals, deceits, atrocities and slaughter. The islands upon which this sequence of events centred are so beautiful, it's hard to believe they harboured so much enmity.

But, oh boy, they did!

The 'battle' centred on the islands of Jura, Islay, Mull, Tiree and parts of Kintyre. Although it is called the Battle of the Western Isles, which usually means the Outer Hebrides, these are all in the Inner Hebrides.

It all happened between 1585 and 1586 between two branches of Clan MacDonald (Sleat and Dunnyveg) against the MacLeans.

It started when one group of MacDonalds did what Highlanders did best and stole some cattle. But what made this different was that they made it look like another MacDonald had done it, a chap by the name of Donald Gorm Mor. Cheeky wee buggers!

The owner of the cattle was Lachlan Mor Maclean. Not a man known for his peace-loving nature and, knowing this, the thieves also knew that the first person Lachlan would blame was poor Donald Gorm Mor.

Sure enough, Lachlan jumped in a ship with some vengeful MacLeans and went straight to pay Donald a visit. Before Donald could even offer them a cup of tea (or whatever he was brewing at the time, perhaps a latte?), Lachlan killed sixty MacDonalds. Donald Gorm Mor and a few others managed to make their escape.

Needless to say, Donald was not a happy chappy.

He called upon all the other members of Clan Donald to join him in beating seven shades of shite out of anyone unlucky enough to have MacLean as their name. He even prepared to invade Mull.

Now at this point they discovered that actually it was a couple of MacDonalds who'd done the stealing in the first place . . .

'Eh, Donald, can I have a wee word.'

Donald Gorm Mor is bent over sharpening his axe.

'Aye, what is it!!!'

'Well, it's quite funny really, but you know those cattle that were stolen?'

'Aye, the ones we got the blame for??? Complete hashed-up fabrication by those bastard MacLeans.'

'Yes, well about that . . . turns out it WAS a couple of MacDonalds who did the stealing.'

'Really?'

'Yes, they tried to pin the blame on youse. Quite hilarious really. So does that mean we'll call off the attack by hundreds of our men against the MacLeans, who were justifiably pissed off about their cattle being nicked by MacDonalds?'

'No, it bloody well doesn't!!! I'm going to give them a right doing once this axe is sharp enough.'

So there you have it. Never let the truth get in the way of a good revenge attack.

Enter the King.

James VI of Scotland urged the MacDonalds to stop all this killing nonsense and come to peaceful terms with the MacLeans.

As a result, Angus MacDonald of Islay rowed across to Skye

to talk to Donald Gorm Mor of the very sharp axe and persuade him to come to peaceful terms with Lachlan Maclean.

On his way back he stopped at Duart Castle (perhaps for one of Lachlan Maclean's famous lattes), to try and persuade Lachlan likewise to choose the path of peace.

Lachlan (obviously caffeinated up to the eyeballs) chose instead to seize Angus and his attendants, insisting that Angus hand over lands on Islay to him.

To make sure he did, Lachlan took Angus's sons James and Ranald as hostages.

By the time Angus got home, you could say he was very, very upset indeed.

Lachlan Maclean duly went to Islay to take possession of his new lands and stayed at the local fort, rather like a sixteenth-century Holiday Inn. For three days, he kept inviting Angus MacDonald and his men to visit him at the castle.

'Come on, come up and have a few bevvies!!!!'

Finally Angus gave in and, along with eighty-six of his men, went up to the castle to spend the night.

Lachlan entertained him in grand style, but when he offered to put Angus up for the night, Angus said, 'No, thanks,' he preferred to stay with his eighty-six mates in an outbuilding and, 'Oh yes, I'll be taking your son James with me for safe keeping.'

Later that night, Lachlan felt the inexplicable urge to go down to the outbuilding and invite Angus up for one more drink.

Unusually, though, he took 400 men to back up the drink invite.

It turns out that Angus was a man who never accepted a drink invite without holding a sword to the throat of a hostage. This was the sight that greeted Lachlan Maclean as Angus opened the door.

'Ah, Lachlan, I see you've brought some drinking companions. Four hundred of them.'

'Ah, Angus, I see you have a very sharp pointy sword held against the throat of my wee son, James.'

At this point Lachlan did the sensible thing and said if Angus gave up his son, he and all his men would be spared.

Incredibly, Angus believed him.

Two of Angus's guys said, 'No thanks' (they were the ones who'd killed a mountain of MacLeans), so quite understandably they were burnt alive inside the outbuilding.

Lachlan then kept his word and released Angus, but not before killing every last one of the prisoners.

Yup, Lachlan was not quite telling Angus the truth, was he?

Enter the King, again.

He asked Archibald Campbell, Earl of Argyll, to mediate.

Angus agreed, provided he was pardoned for his crimes, and provided Maclean gave him eight hostages and also agreed to stop killing anyone who even looked like a MacDonald.

So far so good.

Angus then decided to take a wee holiday in Ireland and, while he was away, Lachlan thought it would be a good idea to ignore the fact that Angus had eight hostages. Instead, he went over to Islay and laid waste to it.

When Angus got back from his Irish vacation, amazingly he spared the hostages, deciding he would rather invade Mull and Tiree and kill everyone there who even looked up when the name MacLean was called out.

I bet the census was a lot of fun that year in the Inner Hebrides!!! And very short.

Enter the King.

AGAIN!!

Having had enough of these shenanigans, James VI dragged both men to Edinburgh Castle and imprisoned them until they'd come to their senses.

This they eventually did, presumably because there was literally no one left on Islay, Tiree and Mull left to kill.

And so ended another busy year in the Highlands between the MacDonalds and the MacLeans.

NATURE NOTES
SHEEP

SAM
Across the islands and mainland of Scotland there are more sheep than people. In fact, part of the reason for the Highland Clearances (1750–1860) was to empty the landscape of people in order to fill it with sheep, which back in the day were worth more than crofters and tenants to unscrupulous landlords. The first clearance of an entire township to make way for woolly farm animals was as early as 1770.

In an extreme case, the Duchess of Sutherland and her husband the Marquis of Stafford removed 15,000 people to make way for 200,000 heads of sheep on their 1.5 million-acre estate between 1811–21. And, it wasn't just the British who were responsible for the clearances, the ruling Scottish nobility and clan chiefs were all blameworthy, as they tried to adapt from warlords to landlords in the aftermath of Culloden.

As well as many Jacobites, who were forcibly shipped to far-flung parts of the new world, the first wave of the clearances in 1763 saw around 10,000 Highlanders emigrate to North America, often tacksmen, who were both educated and enterprising. Tackmen were middlemen who leased land from a laird (often a relation) and sub-let portions to tenants from whom they collected rent. After the collapse of the clan system, these 'middlemen' were the first to become redundant.

The next people to find themselves surplus to requirement were the crofters and tenants, as the newly styled landlords sought to make their estates more efficient and streamlined, and that's when the sheep started to arrive in growing numbers. Often Scots left voluntarily, as the alternative was starvation or watching their crofts burn down.

Over 150,000 Highlanders and Islanders were cleared from their homes, which given the total population of Scotland was 1,608,420 in 1801 according to the census, puts it into stark context. The lost citizens of the Highlands are remembered by monuments across Scotland, in particular the Emigrants Statue in Helmsdale.

Graham and I have met our fair share of fearsome Scottish sheep in our time, and lest we forget, Dolly the sheep – not an ex of Graham's, but the world's first cloned sheep – was made in Scotland by scientists from Edinburgh University.

Our most recent time in the company of these woolly ruminants was on *Men In Kilts*, with hosts Alasdair MacLeod, Donald MacLeod and Calum MacInnes, not bloodthirsty clan chiefs, but benevolent crofters on the Isle of Skye. Three generations lived on the farm, father Alastair and son Donald, who had a little boy, perhaps one or two years of age.

Graham took a total shine to this child and became 'Daddy Graham', making a fuss and wanting to hold him. It brought a fair tear to my eye and I'm sure the poor boy was equally traumatised.

They were such a kind and happy family, living in a beautiful but often brutal and barren landscape, and their contentment reminded me of the Gaelic word *dulchas*, which conjures a sense of belonging and a deep connection to a place that so many of us have 'misplaced' nowadays. They were rebuilding their croft, so were living in a static caravan, but they let us take it over, mainly as Graham's dressing room. [*Graham: YOUR dressing room, you mean, for your daily three-hours in make-up with your personal make-up artist, Wendy.*]

They grazed their sheep on the Quiraing (the landslip on the eastern face of Meall na Suiramach), where Graham complained about his bike being 'not fit for purpose' both up and down hill. Donald explained that keeping sheep at an elevation of over 400 metres meant it was pretty challenging to find them! He would have to hike up and cover a vast area, sometimes taking all day.

At the farm they showed us how to round up the sheep

into pens using sheep dogs. Graham was overly exuberant and I was slightly suspicious as to why. He gave a constant running commentary, as if it were a sport.

'Oh my god! It's amazing – look at the dogs. Look! They're going *behind* the sheep! And now the sheep are going *towards* the pen!'

I feared he might still be drunk from the night before, or fancied himself as a bucolic sheep hustler.

There were seven sheep dogs, including Spot, who was full of energy, enthusiastic and pumped ready for action. He was constantly circling the sheep, saying, '*Come on! Let's go, go, go!*' There was also an elderly dog that been brought along for the ride, who was just about still going but very, very slow, and had to be lifted into the back of the truck, panting and exhausted.

I leave you, dear readers, to come to your own conclusions as to whom these canines might just remind you of.

It was soon Graham and my turn to be the sheep dogs and round up the woolly beasts into the pen ourselves. AND we almost bloody managed it . . .! Until they escaped, running towards the soundman, Merlin, who dumped his recording equipment on the ground and legged it across the field, as if a herd of stampeding wildebeest were thundering after him and not a few wee lammies. We watched helplessly as the sheep leapt over Merlin's equipment, landing on it and covering it in sheep shit! Graham was tickled pink.

Sound equipment wiped down and reunited with its operator, our hosts showed us how to shear a sheep. Now, Graham considers himself a man of the land, but not in a rustic sort of way – no, in the pastoral idyll of his muddled mind, he is laird of all he surveys. I looked at him watching silently, crook in hand, as Donald turned over a ewe and expertly began to remove its fleece.

[*Graham: I was childishly delighted to observe that Sam had to abandon trying to turn the sheep over. Unlike a rock, sheep fight back.*]

Graham looked back at me and whispered that we must go down on our knees to watch the extraordinary agricultural haircut, which I thought was VERY strange indeed. I was happy standing.

'Come on, get down on your knees. We've got to get really close to the sheep.'

'We don't need to do that,' I said.

'I mean we were only at the Baa-bers!'

[Graham: This pun is pish.]

[Sam: Ewe feeling sheepish?]

GRAHAM

As I'm sure all of you readers are aware, sheep were amongst the first livestock to be domesticated. This happened, somewhat amazingly, as part of multiple domestication episodes all over Europe and Asia. Different sheep became domesticated at different times, but with the same result – we kept them for milk, wool and meat.

Meat came first (being humans, if it has flesh our first thought is, can we cook it – well, that's my first thought anyway). But milk and wool joined the trifecta of sheeply delights as far back as 4–5000 years ago.

There were no sheep in Britain 6000 years ago (hard to imagine now), but those remains that have been found from archaeological digs were short-tailed, multi-horned types and a lot smaller. They would need to have been tough to survive the wet conditions of Northern Europe, and none wetter than the Hebrides.

[Sam: Graham has read a 'fascinating' book on sheep. Prepare to drift off. Or imagine counting sheep, jumping over a fence, their little fluffy faces, so happy and joyful. zzzzzz.]

There's a marked genetic difference between the fluffy white-woolled sheep we are most familiar with and the 'outer' sheep. They were found in the Hebrides, Isle of Man, Iceland and Scandinavia, and are quite literally a breed apart.

Even the females often have horns.

One wonders what a regular sheep would make of one of these horned beasts. I also wonder if these Hebridean sheep are the ones who began the somewhat belligerent attitude towards cars and people that you frequently encounter in Scotland.

Whereas a sheep in southern England will run a mile if approached, Scottish sheep stand their ground, glaring aggressively at you, daring you to pass.

I remember one particular summer's day after climbing a mountain in Perthshire, finding myself surrounded by sheep led by one particularly aggressive ram. As I left to descend the mountain, they literally followed me and made sure I was leaving.

'That's right, son! This mountain is OURS!!!!'

The smaller, dark-haired, horned sheep of the far north were, at one time, even kept as ornamental sheep by the aristocracy.

Fortunately these wonderful creatures are found more and more often all over Britain, standing proud, looking like the ovine equivalent of a motorcycle gang. It is interesting to note that as well as being referred to as a flock, the other collective noun for sheep, is a mob . . .

Coincidence? I think not.

SAM

If you ever make it to Harris – and I hope you do – one thing you need to do is see the weavers at work using the humble flock and spinning it into this iconic, handwoven wool fabric: Harris Tweed®. It is only produced there and has a history going back hundreds of years. The success of the industry was largely down to one woman named Lady Catherine Murray, Countess of Dunmore (née Lady Catherine Herbert), who inherited the isle of Harris on the death of her husband (and was also left with four children). She improved social conditions on the island, built churches and crucially encouraged home industry, sponsoring women to learn spinning, knitting and embroidery so they could earn a wage from home.

Catherine devoted herself to the burgeoning Harris Tweed® industry and promoted the woollen wear to her aristocratic friends, as well as mainland markets such as Edinburgh and London. Her efforts paid off and Harris Tweed became incredibly successful and is still one of the main industries of the Outer Hebrides today, with three Harris Tweed mills currently in production.

Identified by the historic Orb trade mark, it is the only fabric in the world protected by an Act of Parliament and the Harris Tweed Authority, and it is still woven by weavers at home in the Hebrides.

GRAHAM

I must mention my epic cycle ride across the Outer Hebrides back in 1995.

Here was my itinerary:

Ferry to Barra from Oban (probably drunk)
Castlebay – Lochboisdale, South Uist
Lochboisdale – Benbecula
Benbecula – Lochmaddy, North Uist
Lochmaddy – Tarbert, Harris
Tarbert – Callanish (must have stopped for snacks and a five-
    star meal?)
Callanish – Stornoway
Stornoway – Ullapool
Ullapool – Lochinver
Lochinver – Scourie
Scourie – Cape Wrath
Cape Wrath – Lairg
Lairg – Train home

[*Sam: I can't imagine him doing this without constant feeding, frothy lattes and a whole entourage following him in support. Less Tour de France, more Tour de Gramps.*]

One of the high points of that trip was visiting the Callanish Stones and it was great to see them again on *Men in Kilts*. The inspiration for Craigh na Dun in *Outlander*, this place is the definition of awe-inspiring. You stand amongst them in stunned silence as you take in their enormity, and their solemn presence.

It is amazing how they have survived. Standing remote and unchanging over millennia on this obscure corner of a Scottish island.

It is a long journey to reach them. A ferry from Skye to

Lewis and then a substantial road trip to a remote part of an already remote island. But it is well worth the trip. In fact, the journey helps make it that much more special.

When Sam and I went, we were blessed with a particularly beautiful day. The sun shone on those ancient stones and you could not deny the powerful feeling as you stood next to them.

The stones are old. I mean, really, really, really old.

They are made from Lewisian Gneiss, the oldest rock in Britain, dating back some 3000 million years. When you touch that rock, it is easy to believe you are travelling back in time. In fact, standing inside the circle, you are can transport yourself back to the time they were built. The area has no buildings visible nearby, and the view will not have changed much over the centuries.

The stones themselves are shaped into a sort of distorted Celtic cross.

Known as 'The Stonehenge of Scotland', it actually predates Stonehenge, going back to 2900–2600 BC. Compared to Callanish, Stonehenge was an upstart, modern piece of construction. The people who erected these staggering monoliths would not have had access to the resources of those who put up Stonehenge.

The largest, central stone – the one that Claire touches and is the cause of all that trouble in *Outlander*, notably my brutal murder at the hands of my treasonous nephew and his monstrous accomplice!! (Bitter?? Not me!!!!) – is about nineteen feet high and weighs around 5.5 tons. Can you imagine what went into getting that upright 5000 years ago?

It has thirteen other smaller stones around it, with an avenue of nineteen stones leading towards it. In the centre is a burial pit, which has been found to contain human remains. We don't really know why it was built or what it was used for. It is believed to be a kind of enormous astronomical observatory, for tracking the movements of the moon.

More circles have recently been discovered through archaeological surveys, hidden beneath the peat, including one with evidence of a gigantic lightning strike. It's hard to imagine what people would've made of lightning 5000 years ago!

It's construction, beggars belief. Callanish wasn't put up over a weekend.

One wonders which popular member of the tribe came up with the idea.

'I think we should build a stone circle.'

'Good idea, I'll go and pick up a few rocks and make a circle, shall I?'

'No, I think the main stone should be nineteen feet high and weigh in at five and a half tons.'

'YOU WHAT?????'

'Yes, and there should be about thirty more stones a wee bit smaller. If you start now, you should be finished in about a couple of years.'

Local myth has it that the stones are the frozen remains of giants, cursed for not becoming Christian.

But whatever the reason they were built, how, and by whom, it is believed that they were abandoned in around 800 BC . . .

. . . and we have no idea why.

But, for the same reason that we can't explain why Sam Heughan childishly likes to torment his friends and is obsessed with peddling his own whisky, some things are best left unexplained.

SAM

Back to yer epic cycle trip for a moment, Bradley McTavish. I have to say, for a man who says he's cycled all over Scotland, I've never actually seen you DO much cycling. In fact, I'm very suspicious whether you've really cycled or just eaten your way around the country, driven in a car by some poor unfortunate companion, your bicycle attached to the bike rack at the back. Sound familiar, people?

I mean he's *supposed* to have cycled the islands and Ireland and all over, but whenever I have presented Graham with a bicycle, he's complained bitterly about it. He grumbled about the bikes on *Clanlands*. He whinged about the bikes on *MIK* – not only about the tandem, but also the single bicycles. He's never happy – they were never fast enough, or comfortable enough, he moaned about his arse being sore – none of them were ever good enough for him. On Skye we got on two great bicycles and cycled down the Quiraing, then he complained the brakes didn't work. Then we raced up the Quiraing and I left him in my wake (as usual) and he said his gears were rubbish!

Graham's idea of cycling is very slow and therefore I would have thought these old-fashioned bikes would have been right up his street, because that's what they're built for. But maybe I should get him the best type of racing bike next time – like a Chris Hoy-style carbon fibre bike, with a full-body Lycra skin suit, and a crazy sperm helmet. Graeme Obree, aka the Flying Scotsman, built his own bike out of a washing machine, won all the races, broke the world hour record twice, and never protested that his washing-machine bike wasn't fast enough or comfortable enough!

GRAHAM

I feel it is becoming my familiar duty to correct some of Heughan's wilder assertions. I believe the entirety of his cycling experience is going from London to Brighton one day.

'How far is that?' I asked.

'About eighty-odd miles,' came his confident reply.

It's actually fifty-four miles.

[Sam: It was after my unintentional diversion . . . ahem. Lost somewhere near Gatwick.]

I wonder if he completed it on a lump of iron rescued from the Spanish Inquisition, such as we were treated to on Men in Kilts. I suspect not.

I also suspect that Sam is one of those cyclists who goes full spandex, with a top emblazoned with sponsors and brands whom he is tapping for cash.

I further suspect that Sam thinks the North Coast 500 is only a particularly lengthy tour of whisky distilleries.

When I was seventeen, I did my first long-distance cycle from Welshpool via the Welsh mountains down to southern England. The following year my friend and I cycled from

Edinburgh to the south coast. The bikes had five gears, with not a piece of carbon fibre in sight.

Since then I've cycled the west and east coasts of Ireland, the Outer Hebrides across to Ullapool and Cape Wrath, as well as Arran across to Kintyre, Gigha, and then north to Mallaig.

Perhaps Sam can provide a photo of his faux Tour de France outfit next to his carbon fibre eighteen-speeder.

[Sam: I really do have a spandex cycling top with a whisky logo! And I also competed in a triathlon at Blenheim Palace, so I've done my fair bit of pedal pushing!]

As for beating me to the top of the Quiraing, I hate to remind him, and apologies to fans of the show who thought we did cycle up that hill, but our ride to the top went for about fifty yards before they shouted, 'Cut!'

It is true, however, that I probably did need a latte by then.

My cycling experiences were not confined to holidays. My first job out of university (in-between banging on theatre doors trying to convince people I was an actor), was as a cycle courier.

[Sam: Did I mention I've delivered sandwiches by bicycle all over London? In the winter.] [Graham: Giving yourself lunch doesn't count as a job, Sam!]

I joined the first company of its kind to use cyclists as couriers, called 'On Yer Bike'. We were based in a side street off Smithfield meat market in London (somehow it seemed fitting that it was where William Wallace had been hung, drawn, and quartered).

I was given a walkie-talkie, a sack with a strap (which later became fashionably known as 'a courier bag'), and I was sent on my way.

I would cycle all over London delivering packages, letters, anything at all. What was surprising was that a pushbike could do the distance between the West End and the City of London faster than a van, or even a motorbike.

I think it was partly for this reason that van and taxi drivers did their best to kill me. I still can't see a white panelled van without thinking of them as 'the enemy' – drivers who looked upon cyclists with barely concealed contempt, and homicidal rage.

I used to finish the day looking like a coal miner. No masks or helmets for us in the early 1980s. In fact, one of the reasons I stopped after eighteen months was because I HADN'T had an accident.

Before this I'd been a postman between leaving school and starting university, and yes, I was on a bicycle.

Everything you've heard about postmen and dogs is true. The postman who trained me suggested I carry a piece of 2 x 4 wood strapped to my cross bar.

'Attack them before they attack you,' he told me. These were words he lived by.

Some addresses didn't have mail delivered to them because of their dogs.

There was one Cujo-like beast that used to stare malevolently at me from the window. I would have to pretend not to be delivering to the house and then at the last moment leap from my bike and run up the front path, ramming the mail through the letter box – as I heard the Hound of the Baskervilles' claws sliding along the wooden floor, before slamming into the door and tearing the mail to pieces in its slathering jaws.

I also managed to have one young woman time the collection of her milk bottles to coincide with when I was walking towards her house. Dressed in nothing but a negligee and a broad smile, she would bend down to pick up the milk bottles as yours truly, a painfully shy eighteen-year-old, handed over the letters with a shaking hand.

I even had the door opened by a naked woman once. Thankfully, no dog was present.

All in all, I cycled everywhere until my mid-forties. I didn't own a car until I was forty-six [*Sam: Because people have been driving you everywhere! Your mother was probably still doing your washing then too!*], but I actually loved it. Cycling is, and always will be, my favourite way of getting around. (Except on a tandem with Sam Heughan.)

All this talk of cycling is making me hungry.

Famished in fact.

SAM

Well, one recipe you should get your butler or doting friends to rustle for you is Masala Lobster. You know, the one we recreated in *Men in Kilts*?

[*Graham: Oh yes. Mouth-wateringly good.*]

Lobster is in season in Scotland from April–December and many are caught off the coast of the Outer Hebrides. Here's Tony's amazing recipe.

Er, you're welcome!

TONY SINGH'S MASALA LOBSTER

Ingredients

250g pureed fresh local tomatoes
2 lobsters killed and sectioned into tail and claws
150g butter unsalted
25 garlic cloves (finely chopped)
4 finely chopped green finger chillies (also known as serrano chilli)
50g finely chopped ginger
50ml Sassenach whisky
150ml fish stock
100ml rapeseed oil
½ tsp turmeric
1 tsp garam masala
1 tsp salt
150ml water

Method

Heat oil in pan. Add garlic and cook until it has a touch of colour (approx. 1 min).

Add ginger and cook for a further minute.

Then add all spices and cook for 1 more minute.

Flame with the whisky, add tomatoes and cook till the oil splits out of the sauce.

Add lobster and fish stock and water and cook till done then season with the salt and serve.

ADVENTURE OF THE MONTH
BEN MORE

SAM

The islands north of Skye and the Cullins have no Munros, however Mull has one, Ben More – the large mountain. I started out at the colourful and picturesque Tobermory, with each house in this fishing village painted a separate bright colour, from red to blue, yellow and green. I drove right around the island, which isn't that far but takes slightly longer as it's mostly single track, and you never know if one of the friendly local sheep is going to stare you down on the next bend. The sun was blazing and the ocean was emerald blue.

Parking next to the beach, and setting off in shorts and T-shirt, I knew the route would be relatively straightforward. The path follows a stream that reveals a number of small waterfalls and one large natural bathing pool, which I just had to jump into on the way down. A steep climb and you reach the top, to be greeted by a stiff breeze and epic views across to the mainland and Iona to the west.

It's maybe not the most dramatic ascent, but the views are so rewarding!

DRAM OF THE MONTH
LEDAIG 10 YEAR OLD

SAM

After climbing the only Munro on Mull, I found myself on the shores of Loch Scridain. It was summer and the peak of Ben More looked way higher than it had felt whilst climbing it some hours before. I pitched my tent and built a fire on the sandy beach and popped open a bottle of the local single malt, Ledaig. As the sun went down, a family of seals swam to the nearby island, some 200 metres away. They looked at me quizzically, their big eyes like some Disney character, almost human, as the sun set and dusk drew in.

I can understand why they are referred to as Selkies, and some Celtic traditions claim they can appear in human form by shedding their skin. Or perhaps it was the whisky speaking! Each sip of Ledaig was warming with a hint of smoke, a reward for the steep climb earlier that day. A little sand grit had gathered on the lip of the bottle (who needs a glass!?) and the driftwood fire added yet more smoke and heat. I stayed up late, listening to the waves lap against the shore and sang to my seal family.

Waking groggily the next morning to bright daylight, my seal friends were long gone fishing as I stumbled out of my tent. What a cracking whisky. What a beautiful island. What a tremendous hangover. I slept it off that afternoon, watching the sunlight play on the water and the distant mountain range of the mainland, lying in the summer warmth and shade of the trees. Magic. I believe in Faeries and the Selkie people that populate the deep green waters surrounding the island.

Ledaig is 10 years old, sweet, medicinal and spicy. Drink with close friends before they turn into seals.

GREAT SCOT!

NOTABLE BIRTHDAYS, DEATHS AND SIGNIFICANT EVENTS

1 July 1782 – Proscription Act repealed, allowing the wearing of tartan and the carrying of weapons.

2 July 1266 – Treaty of Perth, Norway renounced claim on the Hebrides.

11 July 1274 – Robert the Bruce born at Turnberry Castle.

21 July 1796 – Robert Burns died in Dumfries, aged thirty-seven.

23 July 1745 – Charles Edward Stuart landed on Eriskay at the start of the 1745 campaign.

24 July 1411 – The Battle of Harlaw.

31 July 1965 – J.K. Rowling, British author and philanthropist, born in Yate, England, resident of Edinburgh.

AUGUST

Clan Farquharson
Motto: *Fide Et Fortitudine* (By fidelity and fortitude)
Lands: Invercauld, Aberdeenshire

KEY DIARY DATES

1   Lammas/Lughnasadh
6-30   Edinburgh International Festival
        Edinburgh Festival Fringe
        Royal Edinburgh Military Tattoo
Last weekend: Cowal Gathering, the world's biggest
        Highland Games
Late August-Early September: Largs Viking Festival,
        North Ayrshire

1 August 1746 - The Proscription Act became law.

SAM

After the Battle of Culloden, the Law of Proscription was formed to cut off the head of Jacobitism and neutralise the clans by the forced removal of weapons and banning of Highland dress (or plaid), a symbol of Highland identity and clanship. Kilts were replaced by trousers and, because people could no longer wear plaid, many traditional skills used in dyeing and weaving were lost in a generation, including various ancient patterns.

This is an extract from the Dress Act, 1746:

That from and after the first day of August, One thousand, seven hundred and forty-six, no man or boy within that part of Britain called Scotland, other than such as shall be employed as Officers and Soldiers in His Majesty's Forces, shall, on any pretext whatever, wear or put on the clothes commonly called Highland clothes (that is to say) the Plaid, Philabeg, or little Kilt, Trowse, Shoulder-belts, or any part whatever of what peculiarly belongs to the Highland Garb; and that no tartan or party-coloured plaid of stuff shall be used for Great Coats or upper coats, and if any such person shall presume after the said first day of August, to wear or put on the aforesaid garment or any part of them, every such person so offending . . . For the first offence, shall be liable to be imprisoned for 6 months, and on the second offence, to be transported to any of His Majesty's plantations beyond the seas, there to remain for the space of seven years.

The law was eventually repealed on 1 July 1782, but it was the beginning of the end for Highland culture, though not for *Men in Kilts . . .*

COMPETITION CORNER
RUGBY AT MURRAYFIELD

SAM

In August 2020, Graham and I were destined to compete with each other in another great Scottish sport, nay the greatest Scottish sport of them all, the king of sports and my favourite game in the entire world: RUGBY. I have tried to watch every match Scotland plays, live or on TV. I've watched from my bed at 5 a.m. in America, in a raucous sports bar in South Africa and in the capital city of Scotland itself, as the ice-cold north wind blew at Fortress Murrayfield. I even attended the first ever Six Nations match against Italy in Rome – which we lost, but we still celebrated like we had won.

On the plane over to Italy, a friend and I were wearing our rugby tops and quaffing multiple cans of Peroni, the strong Italian lager we purchased in the airport lounge, pretending we were cultured and trying to 'acclimatise' ourselves to the Italian cuisine. The air hostess was confused, as we happened to be on the same flight as the rugby team, and she went to ask the head coach if it was okay to serve us booze.

'They're not with us,' the coach shook his head, horrified, as we happily toasted him and the team from the back of the plane: 'Salute! Here's to you, lads!'

The journey back, however, was a different story. After a long weekend that culminated in teaching the local Romans how to cèilidh dance, 'stripping the willow' in the Piazza del Popolo and losing our St Andrews flag in the Trevi fountain, we narrowly made it on to our return flight. The Azzurri, renowned for being voracious fans, were, let's say, surprised and impressed by our 'energy and enthusiasm' to celebrate the inaugural Six Nations loss, with as much Chianti as we could imbibe. '*Non tranquilo!*' they cheered as they slapped us on the back and ushered onto the bus to the airport.

My friend lay his thumping forehead on the seat in front of him, groaning quietly, his face painted with the Scottish saltire and a damp Italian flag draped around his shoulders. His rugby top stained with last night's frutti di mare and pieces of dried-out tiramisu. Our friendly rugby coach, accompanied by the legendary lock that is Doddie Weir, stopped on the way to the restroom.

'Alright, pal?' Doddie's six-foot-six towering figure lent over and whispered. 'Fancy a game of chess?'

My companion groaned, as his suffering had reduced his ability to speak, he lifted a weary arm and waved off the giant of sport with a limp wrist. He was too hungover to realise that one of his greatest idols had invited him to hang out with the team. Though more likely, Doddie was taking the piss. (Recently, Doddie has set up a foundation to raise awareness, funds and support for those affected by MND (Motor Neurone Disease). Go to www.myname5doddie. co.uk for more information.)

I really do love rugby and would happily travel the length of the world to watch a game. (I would love to visit NZ and see the legendary All Blacks play, plus visit McT in his natural habitat.)

[*Graham: Which is rather odd really, considering you've never even played it. Not even touch rugby. Ever. Rugby in the practical sense just passed you by. You are not a participant but a voyeur, etc.*]

Anyway, to go to Murrayfield on *MIK* was beyond a fantasy . . .

GRAHAM

Yes, Murrayfield: home of Scottish rugby, the temple of tears, where (as Sam so aptly put it) Scotland has too often snatched defeat from the jaws of victory.

To help Sam and I with our rugby were two legends of the Scottish team, Al Kellock and Chris Paterson.

Chris was the classic smaller rugby player. Nimble, quick, and with a fantastically accurate kick. Not for Chris the steamrollering of the opposition, the clash of heads, the straining of every muscle in your body. Chris was the stealth bomber, the guided missile of the team. Deadly in his deployment and cool under pressure.

[*Sam: Not to mention an idol of mine. Chris Paterson is arguably one of the best kickers in Rugby Union history. A legend. He has single-handedly won many a victory for Scotland, being the highest Scottish point scorer and most-capped player by the accurate strike of his right boot. I was in awe to meet him and mortified that I may have to kick a rugby ball, having never touched one in my life.*]

One look at Al, however, told me that here was a man who was no stranger to violence on the field.

His ears.

They looked like someone had repeatedly stomped on them and then invited a particularly vicious dog to use them as a chew toy. Then, when, the dog was done gnawing at them, taken a small hammer and tongs and beaten his ears into the shape of a calzone pizza on an anvil.

Lovely fellas, though, and very patient with the pair of us.

[*Sam: Al is a total gent. Also a legend of the sport, having captained Scotland. He even invited me to play touch rugby with him and a group of ex-players. Perhaps merely an excuse to trample on a soft actor or torment me, at least the guys playing were all seniors – though none as old as McTavish.*]

When I played rugby at school, I played winger. The winger is basically the fastest runner on the pitch, and, in my case, the one who least likes playing rugby, and most dislikes being tackled and piled on top of by fourteen other sweaty men who are much bigger than you.

[Sam: Exactly. Already a distinct advantage. No excuse really . . .]

While we were chatting with our two 'coaches', I noticed Sam's outfit. Resplendent in Scottish colours, Sam looked every inch the rugby player. I think he may have had his name on the back in large white letters.

All that was missing was any actual experience playing rugby.

Yes, that's right. The man who loves rugby, bellows out all the lyrics of 'Flower of Scotland' at international games and proudly wears a rugby shirt at any opportunity, has NEVER played the game.

When he casually let this slip on the pitch at Murrayfield, I nearly choked on my own amazement!

Never?

Even at school?

Apparently Sam had managed to go through his entire childhood, teenage years and young adulthood without participating in a single game of rugby.

Instead, I was standing on this hallowed ground with a rugby voyeur, a pretend player, a poseur of the pitch.

[Sam: My brother played, for Lismore, Boroughmuir and briefly for Newcastle. I prefer to be the cheerleader than the quarterback. Wrong sport, but you get my drift.]

It was decided that our 'competition' would be a series of rugby drills.

We were given a line of cones to sprint towards, perform a single burpee and then sprint back to 'pass' the rugby ball into a wheelie bin.

[Sam: I had spoken to the guys before and added the burpee aspect, knowing McTavish would dislike it and possibly be slower than me. Just 'levelling the playing field' – ahem.]

'Go!!!'

We ran backwards and forwards, Sam edging ahead in the sprints much to my boiling rage and self-disgust. We went for the passing and after three balls, we were neck and neck.

[Sam: Despite me finishing first, I think a bonus point should have been awarded.]

It would all come down to the kicking.

Our task was to drop kick the ball some distance and have it land within a marked-out square. Then Chris Paterson demonstrated and made it look ridiculously easy.

Next up was Sam.

He kicked the ball.

Well, to call it a kick may be stretching the definition of the word. A part of his leg made contact with the ball. It may have been his shin, or ankle, perhaps even his knee. Either Sam was genuinely unaware which part of his anatomy was his foot, or he had never kicked a ball in his life. Any ball.

If the rugby ball had weighed 200 pounds, Sam would definitely have excelled at this sport. Perhaps the lightness took him by surprise. I wouldn't be shocked to discover that Sam was unaware that a rugby ball was filled with air, rather than rocks.

It sailed into the air and landed . . .

. . . outside the square.

[*Sam: I kicked it the way I had been instructed, with the ball angled backwards and apparently in the manner that would apply more accuracy, or so Al told me – the second row scrummer who basically never kicked the ball. (Why didn't I listen to Chris!?) Graham however, just 'hoffed' it. Like a battering ram. No accuracy, sheer blunt force.*]

I took the ball and knew that if there was ever a moment that I needed to channel any schoolboy muscle memory into a single action, now was that time.

Using the joint that connects your big toe to your foot I hit it, being sure to follow through.

The ball arced through the air and landed with a satisfying thunk . . .

. . . smack bang . . .

. . . in the middle of the square!

My childish delight was captured on film, but I make no apologies.

This was my Olympic moment, my crossing the line first at the world championships, my winning leap over the high jump bar.

It was sweet

And it was mine.

I think, after that, Sam may have stayed until nightfall practising his kicking until it was too dark to see.

But it was all to no avail.

The kick had been taken

When the pressure was on.

And when that ball needed to land in the middle of that square

Only one ball made it

And that ball had my boot mark all over it.

[*Sam: I did spend the next hour or so, running around the pitch like a madman. I worked out how to kick the ball with accuracy and loved charging around the national stadium, pretending the crowds were cheering me on. Alas, only a weary, overly proud McTavish watched on, wallowing in his narrow victory. Just wait until he sees what I've got lined up next.*]

Ahem . . . I can't help noticing that Sam's version of events focuses heavily on excuses and 'what might have been', and 'I was much better when no one was watching', while mine simply states what happened.

Otherwise known as . . . 'the facts'.

SAM

The sad, sad truth of that fateful day at Murrayfield was that my on-screen grumpy uncle had kicked my arse in the sport that I hold so dear – and to add insult in injury, he'd rubbed my face in it in front of my sporting heroes, wearing his triumph like an ignoble kilt, in which he did a hip-swinging, thrusting dad dance mocking my defeat. It is not an image I want to think about for very long. At all.

So, the scores on the doors for our *Clanlands* competition are:

Drinking – Sam

Axe wielding – Graham

Complaining – Graham

Golf – Graham

Abseiling – Sam

Surfing – Sam
Dirk Dancing – Graham
Rugby – Graham

The testicle-retracting reality of being *au buff* in the North Atlantic inched ever closer . . .!

REGION OF THE MONTH
THE CAPITAL OF SCOTLAND: EDINBURGH

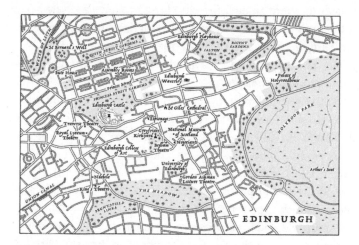

SAM

Welcome to the capital of Scotland! But more importantly, my home town! The Old and New Towns of Edinburgh gained UNESCO World Heritage status in 1995, recognising the extraordinary architecture and street design – medieval in the Old Town, Georgian in New Town.

King David I established the town as a royal burgh in the twelfth century. It has seen many a siege since then, but what is most striking about Edinburgh today is how culturally electrifying it is. Theatres, museums, restaurants, architecture, gardens, festivals – it just keeps on giving. From my time as a teenager at school here, to legendary nights out and incredible festival experiences, this is a city that casts a deep impression which never ever leaves you.

EDINBURGH FESTIVAL MEMORIES

SAM

So, Edinburgh was where it all started and one of my first experiences of the Edinburgh Festival was when I was sixteen working as a poster boy. I was not gracing the posters at this time, but was the poorly paid youngster responsible for plastering them all over the city! I used to have to cycle across Edinburgh on my rickety bicycle (a bit like the one I gave Graham on our *Clanlands* road trip, only smaller) with a big bag of posters, and then go into bars, restaurants and theatre venues to put them up.

At that time of year, everywhere becomes a crucible of entertainment, even a dingy basement or a one-bedroom flat. EVERYWHERE is a potential stage. It was exciting to get glimpses into these other worlds, but to be honest I didn't exactly excel at flyering, opting to flyer the interior of a trash can on the odd occasion when I couldn't face cycling up the Mound for the 100th time that day.

I quickly opted for a career move and I landed some work experience, first at the Traverse Theatre and then the Lyceum Theatre. Not on the stage, rather behind or underneath it. At that point I had an inkling I wanted to be an actor, but didn't know that I *could* be an actor – or even that it was a real job. At both stagehand jobs I had to be really practical. The trouble is that I'm about as practical as Graham is low maintenance.

A current example of how impractical I am is that I recently bought a new camera. I got the wrong case delivered, the wrong handle delivered, and finally realised I'd been taking hundreds of photos without a memory card in! After almost maiming the stage manager when I dropped a piece of decking on his hand, my days of stage (un)handiness were put firmly behind me and stage managers the length and breadth of the country let out a collective sigh of relief.

At the Lyceum, unsure what to do with me, they gave me the seemingly straightforward task of making cucumber sandwiches for a scene in the play *Rough Crossing* by Tom Stoppard. I got even that wrong, because I didn't make them as one would expect. I was told the crusts had to be cut off, to use less butter, and only very fine slices of cucumber, so as to prevent the actor from choking (he also didn't really like cucumber). I remember thinking at the time, God, this is so weird, I mean, it's only a cucumber sandwich, but they were so particular about it.

I also had to make papier-mâché vases, which were broken during the play . . . they were disappointing specimens to say the least and I was, well, crap at it. I didn't get the sack, but let's just say you can only get moved sideways so many times!

However, although in the wrong job spec, these backstage experiences had sparked the fire within, which was to become my burning passion for acting. The actor largely responsible for igniting the flame was Tom McGovern. I was in awe of Tom and had followed his career. He was athletic and his command of the language muscular, his delivery distinct. As those of you who have read *Clanlands* may recall, one day I found myself standing outside his dressing room at the Traverse, and I told him I wanted to be an actor. Tom told me to get as much experience as possible, which I did, including joining a dramatic society in Edinburgh. Graham: I just spoke to Tom. Apparently he has a restraining order out against you. Join the club, Tom!

During my time with them we did a couple of plays at the Festival, including a walking *Macbeth* performed through the city. I played Macduff and it was truly amazing going through from Greyfriars Kirkyard (where we shot *Men in Kilts*) down the Royal Mile and ending up near Holyrood, with the whole audience following us on this journey. It wasn't the best performance, and the costumes were thrown together, but it was an atmospheric experience.

The next time I returned to the Traverse Theatre was to realise my dream and this time I was on stage, as opposed to behind it. *Outlying Islands* started as a Fringe play first, which transferred to the Royal Court Theatre in London.

The atmosphere during the Festival is electric. There are fireworks every night from the Military Tattoo at the castle, and people from all over the world visit to see this prestigious military event, not to mention the main Festival plays and music, the Fringe events, comedy and general vibe. The pubs and bars are open really late. The format is essentially: you meet a mate for a drink and go and see a show, whilst someone else is going to watch something else, and then you all meet up at a different bar afterwards and have a drink and then go on to another stand-up event, and you keep doing that all through the night!

The Traverse was my number one, because you'd get to see people coming in and out, there was a real buzz, then you'd go on to the Gilded Balloon to watch some comedy, and then a sticky, seedy nightclub like Espionage (I was always on the bottom floor – dance music and drunken teenagers), where it all went long and wrong!

We'd end up in the Negociants, which was a bar/nightclub open until late and I remember doing a bit of a *Trainspotting* number one night, when we forgot to pay the bill (perhaps too many libations?!). The security guards were running after us and for some reason someone shouted RUN, so we all started legging it and we were singing 'Lust for Life' (the *Trainspotting* theme tune). We all felt like legends in the moment but, of course, we did go back and pay. Eventually!

I saw the brilliant one-man Charles Dickens show by Simon Callow, who joined us as the scheming Duke of Sandringham in Season Two of *Outlander*. I also loved watching comedy and one act in particular was the Flight of the Conchords – 'the biggest band in New Zealand' – a double act who played funny songs and bantered in-between. They now have their own HBO show, but it was great to see them so early on in a tiny venue. That is the unique magic of the Festival, watching great acts and up-and-coming stars in dingy boozers you would never be able to find sober.

During many Festivals, I was working hard in various restaurants, bars and other establishments. [*Graham: I can only imagine the 'establishments' that you peddled your wares in between acting jobs.*]

As a teenager, I worked in an African cafe called Ndebele. It was a terrific place, full of otherworldly sounds, people and smells. I learnt to cook Boerewors (beef pork and coriander sausage) with a sweet tomato and mango relish, served Mrs Ball's Chutney with ostrich, and chewed on Droëwors, chilli beef and Kudu Biltong.

The cafe was run by an incredibly energetic and vibrant lady called Jenny, and at times she'd treat us to an ice-cold Castle lager, or a warm cup of malted-chocolate Milo. The cafe attracted a lot of creative people and the staff were comedians, actors, writers and musicians. It was such fun to cook Durban curry, or on my break, go downstairs to play on the Djembe (African drums), much to the amusement or horror of the paying customers.

I even worked with a Zulu chief, who was visiting the UK and had been assigned to wash dishes. I felt embarrassed to be ordering him around and made sure he got as many snacks and breaks as he wished. At the end of his shift, his friend interpreted for me: 'The Chief would like to give you a Zulu name, "Sipho" – meaning "gift" or "young man".' I was delighted and perhaps it became my first acting role, the young Zulu warrior 'Sipho' from Scotland, serving sandwiches and carrot cake to the locals. Though I don't remember ever serving a grey-bearded thespian with a penchant for caffe lattes and white wine . . .

In the evening we would squeeze into the local pub next to the Kings Theatre, where other creative types, actors and crew from the theatre opposite would meet us to talk and share music – it had the best jukebox in Scotland.

It was here that I first met Martyn Bennett - the amazing Celtic DJ and bagpipe player. A softly spoken islander, with long dreadlocks and an impish smile. Quiet and shy in person, on stage he would transform. Famous for mixing traditional scottish folk songs and ballads with modern dance music and high tempo samples, his music was electric and to top that, he played the bagpipes on stage, in his kilt, whilst the audience raved below. His music used songs of the traveling people (Roma) and the Gaelteachd traditions of the Hebrides, he used a lot of the "real" folk culture of Scotland. Less tartan and shortbread, he used the songs and music that had been orally passed down for generations by a people that were all but lost now. Most of the music was passed to him this way or the samples he used were recordings of earlier work, from as far back as the 1950s.. One of his songs, Blackbird, was sung by Lizzie Higgins, a well known traveller. Martyn had heard the traditional song when he was 12yrs old. Sad and plaintive, the singer mourns the loss of her lover. It's a sound you've never heard before and is utterly stunning. I believe Lizzie had passed away and so Martyn had sampled her voice and set it to some beautiful music.

What a voice, what a voice, what a voice I hear
It's like the voice of my Willy dear
But if I had wings like that swallow high
I would clasp in the arms o' my Billy boy

What a voice, what a voice, what a voice I hear
It's like the voice of my Willy dear
But if I had wings like that swallow high
I would clasp in the arms o' my Billy boy

When my apron it hung low
My true love followed through frost and snow
And noo my apron it is tae my chin
He passes me by and he ne'er spiers in

There is a blackbird sits on yon tree
Some says it is blind and it cannae see
Some says it is blind and it cannae see
And so is my true love tae me

We lost Martyn way too early but his music, his genius and creativity still lives on. I was fortunate to witness a full orchestra, DJ and piper, play the whole album, live on stage at Celtic Connections (see JANUARY's Key Diary Dates). To hear the traditional strings and brass, paying alongside the beat of a turntable and the distinct call of the pipes, was beautiful and powerful. I couldn't wait for the last song, Mackays Memoirs, and the final moment a lone piper plays a Pibroch, piobaireachd or ceol mor, a traditional piece that has no regular tempo or structure and is as technical and ancient as Scotland itself. The Scottish National Orchestra does regular performances with his earlier album "Bothy culture" performed in 2019.

One year, in 1998, I was working as a waiter in a sushi bar. [*Graham: How very Human League of you.*] It was the first of its kind in Edinburgh, probably in Scotland, and I knew nothing about Japanese food, but like everything else in life, it didn't hold me back! One night a handful of New York actors were dining there, they were all really hot and starring in this intense play with dark and disturbed performances, and I remember talking to them, in awe, only a kid pretending to know what sushi was! It was another moment where I can recall really wanting to be part of that world. And not serve cold fish.

However, I was to continue being a waiter/cocktail barman/cycle courier/etc. on and off until the ripe old age of thirty-four, when I landed the role of Jamie in *Outlander*. It was very much part of my life.

Just before *Outlander*, I was working as a waiter for a cocktail company (that much is true). It was owned by an actor friend in London and we used to do grand events such as the Natural History Museum soirees. I remember popping Champagne and the cork flying right through the skeleton of the Blue Whale. There were many wonderful times, as we would get to meet incredible guests and later enjoy the free booze, and sometimes we were given after-show tickets to exclusive parties. It was hard work and long hours, but great fun.

At one event, I was head barman at London Fashion Week, and one person's job was to stand near the door with a tray and hold people's drinks, whilst they went for a smoke. I was standing there chatting to a friend who was doing that, when up walked Richard Madden, whom I know from Scotland. He was just starting *Game of Thrones* at that point. He didn't see me or recognise me, and simply handed me his drink to go out for a cigarette, which he duly smoked, then returned inside, collected his cocktail and walked up the stairs before I even had a chance to say, 'Hi, Richard, it's me!'

I remember that moment so clearly and the sinking feeling that I must work even harder to get to that place. I was nowhere near where I wanted to be in my chosen career. I thought to myself, one day I will be in that situation. One day. It certainly made me aware and appreciate all waiting staff, knowing how hard they work, but also that they could be the next big thing!

Cheers, Richard!

GRAHAM

I first went to perform at the Edinburgh festival in 1983, around the time that Sam was getting potty-trained no doubt. I have a vision of me traipsing the streets of Edinburgh leafleting unsuspecting passers-by while 'he of the golden locks' was bumping into furniture and making charming belching noises (come to think of it, little has changed there).

[*Sam: Uuuurp!*]

I was graduating from the University of London and I was part of the London University Drama Society. I was cast in a play called *No Exit* (looking back this was indeed a prescient title that could well be applied to my time with Heughan), written by Jean Paul Sartre.

I played the character of Garcin in a four-hander that all takes place in a single room. It contains the famous line, 'Hell is other people' (never were truer words spoken), and the room was, literally, Hell.

It's a great play and we performed it at Edinburgh College of Art at 10.15 a.m. The Edinburgh Festival of 1983 was very different to that of today. Then there were a total of 875 shows performed over the four weeks of the Fringe, today it is nearly 3500 shows. It has always had an amazing atmosphere, and for anyone who hasn't been, it is a 'bucket list' must to visit it during August, and is a baptism of fire for many young performers.

For me it was my first time at any festival. Nothing prepared me for the numbers of people, but also the camaraderie and the support of fellow companies. At night we would invariably all gravitate to the Fringe Club, which was housed in Edinburgh University.

Smoke-filled rooms, raucous music and conversation, the floors sticky with spilt beer and crammed to the gunnels with actors, comedians, dancers, singers, circus performers, all letting off steam and regaling each other with tales of their day, and getting horribly drunk in the process. But being twenty-two, I wouldn't even have the suggestion of a hangover the next morning. Ah, those were the days . . .

We were fortunate enough to get good reviews, so that even at 10.15 a.m., the venue was packed. I remember us all sitting in the bar looking at the newspapers, hot off the press and nervously scanning the reviews to see what the verdict was.

Once we'd had a good review in *The Scotsman*, I knew we were okay. I don't remember if we even got paid expenses, let alone a wage, but that experience marked the moment when I absolutely knew this was what I wanted to be.

I loved it so much that I returned the following year with an actor I'd worked with in *No Exit*, Nick Pace. We had become firm friends and we decided to go back with another play, this time a two-hander, *The Zoo Story* by Edward Albee.

Another great play, and an even greater showcase for the two actors. Nick and I ended up touring it around London along with the one-man play *Krapp's Last Tape* by Samuel Beckett, which I had used to get my union card for acting.

It was *The Zoo Story* that prompted Nick and I to write our own two-hander that became *Letters from the Yellow Chair*, about Vincent and Theo Van Gogh, which we ended up touring all over the world. (But more about that another time.)

In 1984, we performed in the then Roxburgh Hotel on Charlotte Square in a converted space that, with exquisite irony, later became the production office for *Men in Kilts*. Life is indeed strange.

Apart from the show, which went down well (so well we came back with it again the following year), my abiding memory was walking up and down the streets of Edinburgh with a pot of wallpaper paste and a brush putting up posters for the show. Nowadays you probably need a license, but in 1984 it was a cut-throat business of putting your poster over someone else's. In the competitive world of Fringe theatre, there was no room for sentimentality.

My fourth, and most recent Festival performance was at the Royal Lyceum in 1994, in *Armstrong's Last Goodnight* by John Arden. This time as part of the 'Official' Festival. No wallpaper paste then, but lots of rather tedious festival events that we had to attend where I practised my hoovering of canapes and guzzling of Champagne.

I love the Festival. It is truly unique, even with 3500 shows, and I feel privileged to have been a part of it on so many occasions in so many guises.

Maybe one day Sam and I will do a *Men in Kilts* live show there, during which, no doubt, I will be fired from a cannon by him as part of the horrifying finale.

GREYFRIARS CHURCHYARD

GRAHAM

Whilst on our *Men in Kilts* adventure, Greyfriars was one of the many locations that Sam lured me to in order to subject me to some kind of ordeal. In this case, trial by Heughan. I will, of course, reference many aspects of my second journey across Scotland with the be-kilted one, but I knew from the outset that on this day he was going to do his best to terrify me.

Since finishing the second road trip (yes, I fear there will be a third, perhaps a fourth . . . just as long as the Rohypnol lasts), I have often imagined what Sam thinks of when he wakes up in the morning.

No, not that.

Does he wake up, brush his teeth, perform a ridiculous feat of strength in his bathroom, and then pause to wonder, 'How shall I ruin Graham's day today?' If he kept a diary (which I highly doubt, given that I've never had proof he knows how to write by hand – even his signature resembles that of a Bonobo monkey), every entry would end with: 'Another great day of torturing grey beard.'

[*Sam: tick.*]

At Greyfriars, I knew he was up to something. Every other moment I could see a diabolical smile playing upon his lips. Our guide, a self-described 'death historian' (always a great conversational ice-breaker at parties, I bet), took us into the Covenanters prison. This was an open piece of ground where 1000 Covenanters were held prisoner in 1679. They were kept for four months, exposed to the elements, with four ounces of bread a day. Most of them, unsurprisingly, died miserable deaths from exposure and starvation.

The 247 who survived were taken to be transported to the West Indies (not a popular holiday destination in 1679, more like a hell hole of disease, misery and squadrons of mosquitoes). Their ship, however, sank off the Orkney Islands, drowning all but forty-seven. Given their abominable luck, the surviving forty-seven probably all got struck by lightning a few days later.

The prison is a very creepy place. I knew this was where Heughan was going to put his monstrous plan of terrifying the bejesus out of me into action.

If you watch the episode, I was glancing constantly to my right and left. So far, so good.

[*Sam: Muahahahah . . .*]

Then we reached the black mausoleum. This was a dank, dark, cavernous structure, where a rather unpleasant individual by the name of George Mackenzie (yes, probably Dougal's ancestor) was interred.

Picture the scene, the opening is covered by a locked iron gate. Our 'death historian' delighted in telling us it was haunted by a poltergeist. She even provided charming photographic evidence of Mackenzie's poltergeistering (yes, I know that's not a word!). As she opened the gate (which creaked loudly, of course), Sam suggested I enter first.

This was where it was going to happen! I was convinced.

He was practically quivering with malevolent delight, like some imp on steroids. I entered . . . slowly.

Nothing!

We walked in, trying to look brave (actually I didn't bother trying – my naked fear was all too obvious). Our guide then locked us in while she told us unspeakable tales and I stared in horror at the very large dark stain on the roof.

Eventually we exited. I double-checked again for anything designed by Samwise to scare the crap out of me.

All clear.

I'd made it. The segment was over. We were leaving. All that remained was for Sam and I to do our ident to camera (we'd done them at every location), an attempt at witty repartee between us. Our death guide stood to one side, smiling.

It was then he struck!

While I grinned like a simpleton, safe in the knowledge I had survived, Heughan had engineered for some bloke in a costume invented by H.P. Lovecraft to come and grab me from behind.

For those who have seen it, this is where I literally jumped in the air, swearing like a trooper, threatening death to the ginger one. My assailant was dressed in an ankle-length leather coat, and a plague doctor's mask. You know the kind, with the enormous hooked beak. I believe he was also wearing goggles. Apparently these items were from his own private collection. As the partner of the 'guide of death', one can only imagine how unusual their private life is.

To say I nearly shat myself is not an exaggeration.

Just to top it off, Heughan continued to make me jump at regular intervals throughout the rest of the day, indeed month. As I say, a monster.

[*Sam: Ah, revenge. What joy. Elation. Indeed, it really delights me to see the bearded one jump. All his macho persona forgotten and rather like a timid animal or camp pantomime dame, he jumps several feet in the air and grasps on to whomever or whatever is close by, for comfort. Unfortunately that is usually me. Then the tirade of abuse. Some words I don't think even existed before now. Even in Gaelic. Graham is very creative.*]

CRACKING CASTLE OF THE MONTH
EDINBURGH CASTLE

SAM

Not only the setting for the amazing Military Tattoo, the eleventh-century castle dominates the skyline of our capital city from its prominent position on Castle Rock, which has been occupied since Iron Age times.

Fortress, military garrison, royal residence and prison, the castle has seen its fair share of sieges. The final attempt to capture the castle was by the Jacobite army in 1745. Led by the Bonnie Prince, they captured the city but not the castle, and after being forced to retreat from Edinburgh later that year, they marched homewards to Culloden Moor. And we know how that ended.

Over the centuries, the stronghold has been fortified with an increasing number of cannons, including Mons Meg, a six-ton siege gun that was once capable of firing a 330lb gunstone two miles! I wonder if anyone has tried to lift it? Boasting a barrel diameter of 510mm, Mons Meg (named after the Belgian town where she was made) is one of the largest cannons in the world by calibre and was given to James II in 1457.

The castle's other famous gun is the One o'Clock Gun, fired at 1 p.m. every day except Sundays. Dating back to 1861, when a businessman brought the idea back from Paris, the original 64-pounder gun helped ships in the Firth of Forth set their clocks. Since 2001, a modest 105mm field gun has been fired from the Mills Mount Battery, just outside the Redcoat Cafe.

In 2006, Bombardier Alison Jones became the first woman to fire the One o'Clock Gun in its history. I would like to put my name in the hat to have a go at firing it, too.

Or even better, Mons Meg . . .

BOOOOOOOOOOOOOOOOOOOOOOOOOOOOOOOOOOM!

ADVENTURE OF THE MONTH
ARTHUR'S SEAT

SAM

Not a Munro, in fact it's probably about a third of the size of one, but Arthur's Seat stands proud and protective over the granite city of Edinburgh.Great for a wee sledge or ski if it snows enough in winter. I grew up as a teenager near the gates to Holyrood Park and access to Arthur's Seat and the Salisbury Crags. The 640-acre royal park is a short walk from Edinburgh's Royal Mile and adjacent to Holyrood Palace. The highest point is Arthur's Seat, an ancient volcano, which sits 251 metres above sea level giving some stunning views of the city, and on a clear day you can see across to the Kingdom of Fife.

As a lazy teenager, the hike up to the top felt difficult and way too far, but it is pretty simple. Either a direct scramble straight up, or a more leisurely walk along the road that circumnavigates the park, then it's a short stroll to the peak. On the top is also the site of a large and well-preserved fort. This is one of four hill forts dating from around 2000 years ago.

It was on this walk that we invited our 2019 Peakers (members of My Peak Challenge) to join us, as part of our annual gala weekend. I took the lead in front of several thousand banner-waving Peakers and gave the command to start our hike around the hilltop. We had the Glencorse Pipe Band marching in front of us, pipes and drums skirling in the wind and setting the pace to the bass drum (no McTavish this time).

A few hundred metres in, I realised I had never 'driven' a pipe band, observing that they needed plenty of space to turn and wheel around. A small gang of gnarly trees ahead were getting closer and threatening to disrupt our musical march. I signalled for the band and several thousand passionate Peakers to change direction, and we narrowly avoided complete pandemonium.

We continued on, passing the Salisbury Crags – a series of 150-foot cliff faces that are cut into the side of the rock and are sandstone red or orange in the setting sun. It's a remarkable place to grow up and I now love to visit it and climb to the top, to remind myself where I come from (and how much easier it is to climb, now that I don't mind a bit of exercise). I advise you to not take a large group of musicians with you, however – you'll be bound to lose the bass drummer first!

DRAM OF THE MONTH
WHATEVER YOU LIKE . . . WE'RE ON A BAR CRAWL IN EDINBURGH!

SAM

Surprisingly, until recently, Scotland's capital city didn't have a whisky distillery. I'm sure there were many in years gone by, legal or not but it's only in the last decade that a number of distilleries have been established, including the Holyrood Distillery and Port O'Leith. However, both distilleries have only completed their first batches and the new spirit is still resting in oak barrels, awaiting the minimum four years before it can be classed as 'whisky'.

There has always been a lot of trade in Edinburgh, especially around Leith and the docks. Gin and rum were traded and travelled through here to the south of England, Europe and beyond to the New World. As I have mentioned, my youth was mispent in the dark alleys and wynds of Auld Reekie and therefore I would like to suggest a few good places for a refreshing drink or dram:

- **The Bow Bar** – a no frills bar serving a great selection of whisky and beer, on the picturesque cobbled Bow Street, just up from the Grassmarket. A short stumble to **The Last Drop** (site of the hangman's noose).
- **The Meadows Bar** – a regular watering hole during my teenage years, next to the Meadows park.
- **The Black Cat** – open until 3 a.m. and one of the many bars on Rose Street, the challenge is to drink a half pint in each bar on the street . . . impossible!
- **Bennets Bar** – established in the 1830s, it is like going back in time. I'd nip in for a dram after work at a café nearby.
- **SMWS** – on Queen Street, mostly a members' bar, but they have a small visitor section and access to an infinite number of special bottlings. Could spend days here.
- **Voodoo Rooms** – stunning decor and service.
- **The Devil's Advocate** – a spooky spot close to the Royal Mile with a huge selection of whisky.
- **The Sheep Heid Inn** – after a bracing walk over Arthur's Seat, a pint in this sixteenth-century boozer is the ideal refreshener. Graham probably remembers when it opened.
- **Hector's** – in classy Stockbridge, it used to be where I'd go for a Bloody Mary on a lazy, hungover Sunday, or to impress a friend for a chilled late-night cocktail. More McTavish's style.
- **Cask and Barrel** – I worked here for a time on Broughton Street and loved match days, the punters coming in before the football for cold pints and plates of homemade stovies.
- **The Cumberland Bar** – a swanky area and an even prettier pub. Worth a visit. Graham: I can't believe you've left out The Blue Blazer?! Synonymous with after-show boozing of actors and crew from the Royal Lyceum. It is a wonderful no-nonsense establishment with a wonderful selection of cask ales and a small but impressive choice of whiskies.

GRAHAM

Just when you think you've exhausted the most violent of the Scottish clans, you come across a gang like Clan Douglas and have to search for new and ever more extreme adjectives to describe their history.

The Douglas Clan's most famous family member was Sir James Douglas. Known by the Scots as 'Good Sir James', he was dubbed by his enemies (basically all of England) by another name.

'The Black Douglas'.

This was on account of two things, apparently – his black hair (rather like calling Sam 'The Ginger Heughan'), along with a truly fearsome reputation. The English believed he was, in fact, a demon sent from Hell. (The comparisons with Sam just keep getting stronger.)

He began getting that reputation when he was about eighteen years old and he decided to re-take his family seat, Castle Douglas, from the occupying English garrison. He chose to do this on Palm Sunday, knowing that most of the garrison would be at Mass in the church. Clever bugger.

Not one to stand on religious ceremony, Black Douglas entered the church with his horde screaming their war cry, the easily memorised 'Douglas! Douglas!' (Imagine the embarrassment if one of the clan forgot the war cry? 'Er, it begins with D . . . don't tell me, it's on the tip of my tongue!')

The ensuing massacre was charmingly known as 'The Douglas Larder', on account of the fact that any survivors were taken to the cellar and beheaded.

Not content with wholesale decapitation, Black Douglas then ordered all of the severed heads to be mounted on a stack of broken wine casks.

Just for good measure, he set fire to the heads.

Then he burnt down the castle.

Clearly he had a lot of pent-up rage.

'What shall we do with the prisoners, chief?'

'Cut their heads off.'

'Fair enough!'

'Hang on! See those wine casks? Smash them to pieces and then stick the severed heads on top.'

'Right, chief.'

'Then set fire to all of them.'

'Set fire to them? Okey dokey.'

'Oh, and then burn the castle to the ground.'

There was a popular lullaby at the time among the English of the north. It went:

Hush ye, hush ye, little pet ye
Hush ye, hush ye, do not fret ye
The Black Douglas shall not get ye.

A folk tale says that on one occasion as the lullaby ended, a calloused hand gripped the mother's shoulder and a voice like gravel said, 'Don't be too sure about that!'

Black Douglas once took Roxburgh Castle by covering himself and his men with cowhides, and crawling on their hands and knees to the castle before bursting in and slaughtering the inhabitants.

Some maintain he could've beaten Wallace in a fight, which is saying something.

He certainly had an impressive list of victories: 57 victories to 13 losses (and those losses were basically tactical withdrawals, not defeats as such). He was a bit like the Lionel Messi of killing, the Tom Brady of butchery.

When he was busy besieging the castle of Berwick upon Tweed the Pope intervened, telling him to stop AT ONCE, or risk excommunication and eternal damnation. The Black Douglas's reply gives you some idea of who you were dealing with: 'I'd rather enter Berwick than Paradise.' (Come to think of it, I think we should start a campaign to make this Berwick's new official town motto.)

He eventually died on his way to the Middle East, while carrying the heart of Robert the Bruce in a casket around his neck (naturally). Surrounded and alone, he basically decided to fight it out single-handedly, armed only with sword, axe and balls of steel, with around 200 of the enemy.

The power of the Douglas clan then grew and grew, first through his son, Archibald 'The Grim'. (I know, I know, where were the Scots with names like 'Sean Who Loves a Good Sing-song' or 'Alastair the Painfully Shy'?)

The Grim's son was called the equally charming, James 'The Gross'. (I'm truly not making any of this up, by the way.)

They grew to become known as 'Douglas of the Six Castles', sadly one short of our dear friend, 'Duncan of the Seven Castles'.

Their power became such a threat that King James II decided to invite them to dinner at Edinburgh Castle.

The dinner arrangements were organised by Sir William Crichton and they persuaded the Gross's nephew, William the 6th Earl of Douglas, and his brother to come and have a slap-up meal.

'Come to dinner!!! No need to bring wine.'

In the middle of the dinner, a black bull's head was brought in.

Now Willy and his brother were probably hoping for chicken, maybe a nice turkey, and would've known exactly the significance of a black bull's head.

It symbolised death.

Sure enough, they were quickly dragged outside to Castle Hill, given a mock trial and beheaded.

(Oh, by the way, James II was ten years old at the time.)

The moral of that tale is always check to see if bull's head is on the a la carte menu, and never accept a dinner invitation from a small child.

This incident became the inspiration for George R.R. Martin's 'Red Wedding' scene in *Game of Thrones*, prompting Martin himself to say: 'No matter how much I make up, there's stuff in history that's just as bad, or worse.'

And, let's face it, most of it is Scottish.

NATURE NOTES
THE MIDGE

GRAHAM

From the *Ceratopogonidae* family (try saying that after a few drams of cask strength whisky!). For those who don't know what a midge is, or what one looks like, here is a picture:

This is not life size . . . fortunately

Midges are tiny, I mean really tiny and they love nothing more than sucking human blood. They make mosquitoes look like albatrosses. To spot an individual midge is quite a challenge, but fortunately (or unfortunately) they tend to travel in battalion-sized swarms. They appear as a moving cloud of flying specks and they have ruined many a Scottish summer holiday.

Now, we are not all created equal in the eyes of midges (tiny weeny eyes at that). They definitely have their favourites, and like so many *Outlander* fans, one of their absolute favourites is Sam Heughan.

Maybe they all sit in front of their midge-sized TVs and simply can't resist the ginger locks and slabs of beef that make up the 'King of Men', and perhaps they have equally seen my performance as Dougal MacKenzie and thought, we'll steer well clear of baldie! But midges just DON'T like me.

They leave me alone.

They give me a wide berth.

They merely wave with their tiny midge wings at me as they descend like squadrons of besotted *Ceratopogonidae* onto Jamie Alexander Malcolm MacKenzie . . . (well, you know the rest!).

For those who have watched *Men in Kilts*, there is a scene where we sit for our Gaelic lesson. The scene comprises the delightful Gaelic teacher, Sam, myself and approximately eight thousand midges that maintain a permanent orbit around Sam's head.

The poor soul. He sat like a man experiencing a prolonged fit, spasming and jerking, windmilling his arms around in a vain attempt to ward off his miniature fans.

Sam suggested that I must've created some kind of diabolical midge farm for the sole purpose of tormenting him. I cannot confirm or deny this. All that I can confirm is, if you watch the scene, the midges leave me entirely alone.

In contrast to Sam's St Vitus dance of despair, I am relaxed, legs crossed, a small smile playing upon my lips as I wrestle with the Gaelic, while out of the corner of my eye I witness a strong man reduced to a gibbering wreck.

A man that can lift a 200 pound rock, run a marathon, and climb many a Munro, emasculated by insects smaller than of a grain of salt.

I admit it, I hoped the Gaelic lesson would never end. After all that he had pulled at my expense on the MIK series, the sight of him LITERALLY putting a bag over his head while furiously slapping himself suddenly made the world seem a more comforting place.

When he finally fled the interview, his face was a boiling mass of helplessness (somewhat reminiscent of Edward Munch's painting 'The Scream') and the seething cloud of devoted midges followed him en masse.

If I closed my eyes, I imagined I could almost hear their tiny little midge voices calling in unison: 'Don't go, Sam, don't go! We love you . . .!'

GREAT SCOT!

NOTABLE BIRTHDAYS, DEATHS AND SIGNIFICANT EVENTS

6 August 1881 – Birth of Sir Alexander Fleming, who discovered penicillin.

9 August 1757 – Civil engineer Thomas Telford was born in Dumfries.

9 August 2014 – *Outlander* premiered on Starz. The show, now in its sixth season, has received over 71 nominations and 31 awards from Golden Globes and Emmys to Scottish BAFTAs and Critics' Choice TV Awards. Also where Mr Heughan found his victim McTavish.

13 August 1888 – The birth of John Logie Baird, who developed the television.

15 August 1771 – Novelist and poet Sir Walter Scott born.

16 August 1766 – Birth of Carolina Oliphant, Lady Nairne, a popular poet and author of many Jacobite songs, including 'Charlie is my Darling'.

17 August 1947 – First Edinburgh International Festival opened.

19 August 1745 – Charles Edward Stuart raised his standard at Glenfinnan signalling the start of the 1745 uprising.

20 August 1897 – Ronald Ross dissected a mosquito and established the link with malaria, and was the first Scot to win a Nobel prize in 1902.

[*Sam: I'd like to dissect a few of the bastard midges! Or reprogramme them to get Graham.*]

23 August 1305 – William Wallace executed.

25 August 1930 – Actor Sir Sean Connery born in Edinburgh. He died on 31 October 2020.

SEPTEMBER

Clan Mackenzie
Motto: *Leceo Non Uro* (I shine, not burn)
Lands: Ross and Cromarty, Isle of Lewis

KEY DIARY DATES

Meteorological start of AUTUMN: 1 September–30 November

1	Start of Autumn
Early Sep	The Braemar Gathering (Highland Games)
22	Autumnal Equinox (Astrological start of Autumn)
	Mabon – Pagan Harvest
Mid-Sep	Stranraer Oyster Festival

REGION OF THE MONTH
ABERDEENSHIRE, BANFFSHIRE AND MORAYSHIRE

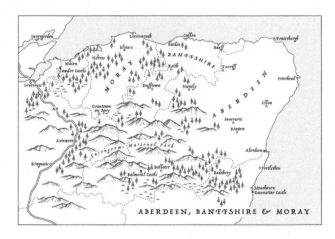

ABERDEEN, BANFFSHIRE & MORAY

GRAHAM

It might make more sense to talk about the Cairngorms in this chapter, which focuses heavily on Braemar, but Samwise declared the National Park of the Cairngorms synonymous with love and picnics in February, and we all know how sentimental he is, so we can look at Aberdeenshire and Morayshire here, with a particular focus on the stunning Moray coast. It might make more sense to talk about the Cairngorms in this chapter, which focuses heavily on Braemar, but Samwise has made that region forever synonymous with his romantic history and the kind of picnic that Renoir might have painted. Whilst I applaud his sentimentality and sensitivity (words not normally associated with the galloping Galwegian), we must look further afield in this chapter for natural inspiration.

So we journey to Aberdeenshire and the Morayshire with particular focus on the Moray coast.

It's an often neglected part of Scotland, being well off the beaten track for explorers of the Highlands but it's well worth a visit.

Just north of the Cairngorms is the town of Nairn. It was here that the government forces led by Cumberland camped out before Culloden. This location was so much better for a pitched battle than the boggy quagmire known as Drumossie Moor, aka Culloden.

It happens to be a temperate microclimate as well as being one of the driest places in Scotland.

It is worth speculating on what the outcome of that battle would've been if the Jacobites had successfully sneaked up on the enemy the night before, while Cumberland and his troops were celebrating the Duke's birthday, instead of marching for 12 miles and getting hopelessly lost. As a result they ended up exhausted, soaked to the skin and demoralised fighting on a piece of land that, if it had a microclimate, it seemed like it was the focus of all the rain in Scotland during the month of April.

If they'd been lucky enough to be in this corner of Scotland during the summer months, and feeling particularly energetic, the Jacobites could have enjoyed the 45 mile Moray Coast trail going from Forres to Cullen. But, given they'd just marched to England and back perhaps they would've preferred watching the seals and dolphins frolicking off the coast from one of the many hidden white sandy beaches that dot this beautiful coastline.

It's a lovely thought isn't it: Bonnie Prince Charlie's tartan army picnicking on the beach applauding a pod of dolphins.

Early September - The Braemar Gathering (Highland Games).

SAM

The Highland Games are an amazing celebration of Celtic culture through sporting competitions, music and dance. There are over 100 Games held the length and breadth of Scotland and even more worldwide.

Largely a Victorian invention following the Clearances, many of the sports themselves predate recorded history. The first reference was during the reign of King Malcolm III (1031–93), when he summoned men to race up Creag Choinnich near Braemar to select the fastest runner to be his royal messenger.

There is also a letter from the Chief of Clan Grant ordering his men to a gathering with all their weaponry, as early competitions were about selecting the best soldiers.

The Cowal Gathering at Dunoon is the largest Highland Games in Scotland and the Braemar Gathering arguably the most prestigious, as it's attended by royalty, being not far from Balmoral Castle, the Queen's Scottish residence. However, Grandfather Mountain in North Carolina is perhaps the largest Highland Games in the world with 30,000 spectators!

The main events:
- Caber Toss – lifting, running and flipping a telegraph pole
- Stone Put – shot put with a rock
- Hammer Throw – think sledgehammer x 2
- Weight Throw – lobbing a ball and chain
- Weight Over the Bar – Lobbing a lump of iron over a massive high jump

- Sheaf Toss – tossing a 20 pound bag of straw with a pitchfork vertically
- Tug of War – eight men trying to get a rope back from eight other men
- Whisky Drinking – well, it should be a recognised sport

All with the ambiance of bagpipes, Celtic bands and traditional dancing.

COMPETITION CORNER
MY CABER'S 'BEGGAR' THAN YOUR CABER!

SAM

Of course, it was only right that Graham and I had a go at some of these Highland games so I set it up on *Men in Kilts*. Yet again, Graham had totally forgotten what he'd let himself in for . . .

We arrived in Braemar after a long drive from Inverness via the Highland ski resort of Lecht for a freezing cold group photo opportunity, despite it being the height of summer, as the north-east wind blew. In the winter months, the hills would be covered in snow, and even in the height of summer it felt cold enough for it. We obviously stopped for lunch (to placate Mr Hungry), which I remember that day was a packed lunch with a sandwich, pork pie, apple and carton of juice, Graham was extremely upset. He'd tried to make three-course lunches with wine as part of his contract, but I had firmly refused, being the senior producer on the show.

We drove a long way that day and I remember feeling really stiff from the campervan. [*Graham: Getting your excuses in early, I see.*] After a quick freshen-up at the Fife Arms – an amazing hotel in Braemar – we drove to the Duke of Fife Memorial Park, where the Highland Games are held.

We were properly attired wearing white vests, kilts and socks with garters. I remember Graham's nipples were distractingly erect. The first thing Kyle Randall, our 28-year-old Highland Games champion coach, said was, 'Never go commando – in case you get up-ended.'

Having had no fear about today's lesson, my nether regions suddenly felt very anxious. Kyle, who told us he spent his time running about the Highlands of Scotland 'throwing shit', went on to tell us that he tore the left side of his stomach from hammer throwing and now lived 'in constant pain and sadness through the seasons'. The nervousness rose upwards like a flood.

Our first activity was hammer throwing and, yes, I knew I'd be good at this. I mean, REALLY GOOD. Well, at least I thought I would be. There are two types of hammer: the Scots hammer, the 16lb one with a flexible shaft (ooh, matron) – and the one I got, the Braemar hammer, a 22lb monster with a different handle, which Kyle used.

[*Graham: I think it's only fair to mention in the spirit of full disclosure that Kyle and I have stayed friends since the day at Braemar. Me: 'Hey, Kyle, what were the weights that Sam and I used in the hammer throw?' Kyle: 'You both used the 16 pound hammer.' Hmmmmm. The prosecution rests . . .*]

Now I don't know what happened to the handle, whether it was Kyle or some kind of sabotage by Graham, but it was covered in a thick, sticky resin. Or even super glue.

It came to my turn to throw the hammer and as I started spinning around and around as Kyle had shown us, I tried to let go, but I couldn't because the handle had bonded to my hands. Round and round and round I went in spinning, stomach-churning (and tearing) circles, but I couldn't get rid of it. I was stuck to the fucking thing and *gah!* – five times, six times, seven – I kept spinning.

It finally flew off into the sky, falling almost immediately to Earth like lead and taking my ego with it. It was a disappointingly short throw. I internally berated myself. This was meant to be a good day. It was sporting sabotage, but I could never prove it. The prickly heat of impending defeat danced on my chest as I watched Graham pick up the lightweight, no, bantamweight hammer, without adhesive on the handle, spun a few times on his pointy toes using his training from the bullshitshoi, let go and the thing went MILES.

Things improved immeasurably with the caber toss. The word 'caber' derives from the Gaelic *cabar*, meaning wooden beam, and competitors pick up a large telephone pole made of larch weighted at one end, run with it and attempt to flip it over. I mean, it really looks like a tree trunk. Yet again, there were two sizes: the intermediate caber and the Braemar, which was about 19 feet 6 inches (5.94 m) tall and weighed 175 pounds (79 kg).

I only tossed the intermediate, but I succeeded in flipping it over. Graham had a go, but he couldn't even get it up (snigger), let alone run with it and toss it! I tried with the Braemar a couple of times and I managed to get it up, but running and tossing such a chunky pole proved too much for me as well. I wonder if there's such a thing as caber Viagra?

Then we had the tug of war and we got all the crew involved and Graham was upset with the distribution of strength. So while I was off tossing the caber, he was working on Kyle, telling him he could get him a part in the next Hobbit movie: 'Kyle, you're a natural in front of the camera. That doesn't come easily – Heughan had to work at it, but you were born with it. We could have our own show, Kyle, *if* you help my team with the tug of war. What do you say?'

He, of course, said yes and Graham's team won, which the grey-bearded-one was delighted about.

Especially, as he knew that it meant he'd won our sporting competition and I would now have to swim, stark bollock naked, in the Atlantic Ocean – and with the longest run up to a wild swim ever before witnessed, because Graham had timed my dip perfectly with the tide being out. I literally had to run a mile to find the sea, out there,

239

watched by some Scandinavian couples from their campervans, who didn't bat an eyelid at my bouncing crown jewels because, let's face it, they are a nationality who are always in the nuddy – around the house, on TV and in their saunas. In fact, I was worried they would think it was an invitation or a Scottish tradition, and they would start running in behind me.

His Majesty surveyed my swim from the shore, wrapped up in blankets like the Queen Mother, a flask of warm tea served by George, raising his expensive Swiss binoculars to his eyes and letting out a contented chortle.

NEXT TIME, GREY DOG. NEXT TIME . . .

GRAHAM

I've long been an admirer of traditional Highland Games. I've gone to several around the world and marvelled at the abilities of men and women to lift and throw enormously heavy objects.

The hammer, the caber (a gigantic log), the farmer's walk (carrying enormously heavy weights in each hand and walking as far as you can before your joints separate), tug-of-war, the shot put (basically getting hold of a giant rock weighing between 20–26 pounds and sending it as far as possible with one hand), and weight for height (taking hold of a 56-pound weight with a short handle and throwing it up and over a raised horizontal bar. With each throw the bar gets higher and higher. The record stands at 20 feet 3 inches, which is nearly the size of a three-storey building!!!!).

The older traditional events of haggis tossing and dwarf throwing have (thankfully in the case of the latter) slipped into obscurity.

Needless to say all of these had Sam's name written all over them. (Not the dwarf throwing obviously.) His feverish delight in lifting anything heavy for any reason is a primary force in his life. When he goes to his hotel room at night, he probably bench presses the bed, or relaxes by throwing full whisky barrels around in his house.

It was with all this in mind that I approached the games in trepidation.

It was not a warm day and Sam is correct when he says my nipples were standing out like chapel hat pegs.

Kyle Randall was the man chosen to instruct us. As he walked towards us, I kept thinking he had arrived, like some optical illusion, until finally he stood before us, but he kept getting bigger and bigger. He claims to be 6 feet 5 inches, but he seemed much taller. A behemoth with hands like meat plates and a handshake like a meat grinder.

He was also sporting quite an alarming moustache.

We had been told not to mention the moustache beforehand, so here I am doing it from behind the comparative safety of a computer keyboard. It was a bold choice as a moustache, black and foreboding, as if from a bygone age.

He smiled a lot, but somehow the moustache merely added to the overall impression of quiet menace.

When I asked Kyle what he did for his job, he was quite coy, preferring to say simply that he was used to helping collect things for others . . .

I think I may have gulped, again, at this moment, as he released me from his bear-like grip.

We started with the hammer throw. Kyle introduced us to the two hammers (the 16 and the 22). He proceeded to apply some resin to his hands for better grip. (God knows what it was made of, perhaps the distilled salty tears of his competitors.) He then took hold of the shaft of the hammer and began to work his hands around it. I couldn't help being put in mind of a giant practising his throttling technique.

More gulping from me.

Then it was time to throw.

We did a few practice swings of the hammer (I was convinced I was going to herniate a disc at any moment), and then Sam stepped into the circle.

He began the swing.

Kyle and I looked on encouragingly.

The swing continued.

Kyle and I began to look slightly concerned.

Still swinging . . .

Kyle's moustache had grown noticeably by now.

And . . . more swinging.

The light was fading . . .

And . . . he let go.

[*Sam: The skin on my hands accompanying the hammer on its flight.*]

It sailed in an arc and landed, creating a satisfying divot.

Kyle and I woke up and cheered Sam on.

My turn.

I took the hammer from Sam and wandered into the circle.

I was preparing myself for the humiliation of falling well short of Sam's effort but, like a prisoner ascending the gallows, I dutifully gripped the hammer and started to swing.

Bloody hell, it's heavy.

I decided on not swinging as much as Sam (not difficult as there was a noticeable hole in the ground now from the number of times Sam had turned on the spot like a ginger corkscrew).

I let go (or perhaps it was the hammer letting go of me).

It arced.

It landed.

I heard Sam bark in surprise uttering the words, 'They're . . . so close.'

We measured out the distance to Sam's divot.

Then to mine.

Suffice to say it took us longer to reach mine.

Yes!!! I had thrown it further.

I was amazed.

It was at this point that I fell to my knees and looked to the heavens and bellowed out my joy.

[*Sam: It was primal. Like a wild animal. Or an angry hobbit, receiving his food after a year spent in isolation and starvation.*]

Sam stood nearby (well . . . by his divot, so actually about two metres away). His expression was a semi-pout coupled with a baffled squint.

When I'd finally stopped bellowing and capering like a lunatic, it was time for the caber toss.

This was going to be hard. We both tried it after Kyle had demonstrated (he made it look like he was flicking away a toothpick).

Our attempts ended in failure, but much to Sam's credit, he wasn't going to give up.

He tried again and YES!!!! He flipped it over. I was mightily impressed (believe me it is NOT easy), and I could see how much it meant to him. He also had the good grace not to rub it in my face (well, not immediately anyway).

Our final event was the Tug of War. We divided the crew between us. Our host, the master of ceremonies at the games, was the umpire.

I took up the end of the rope. Sam took up his.

I love tug of wars. They're just great fun. This was no exception. We took the strain (as they say) . . .

And PULL!!!

It was very even and then Sam persuaded Kyle (the behemoth) Randall to join his side.

Suddenly we were struggling.

NOOOOOO!!!! I thought.

Then, to the rescue, came the master of ceremonies. He jumped on our side and together we pulled Sam and his crew over the line.

Another day of raging competition over, we thanked our muscular hosts and I retired to warm up my nipples.

SAM

Afterwards we stayed overnight at the Fife Arms and ended up having a massive party. One of our runners could play the bagpipes and we were 'Stripping the Willow' and cèilidh dancing in the street until late, and got told off for it.

The Fife Arms is one of the best hotels we've stayed at – it's incredible and I thoroughly recommend it. It's got famous works of art including a Picasso. Very contemporary Scottish and high-end, strong cocktails and good food. Actually, Graham was nowhere to be seen – he'd probably written to the Queen to stay at Balmoral instead.

The 'Fighting' Farquharson Clan! When you know that a clan's nickname has the word 'fighting' in front of the name, you know these guys mean business. It wasn't as if other clans are known as the 'Peaceable' Mackintoshes, or the 'I'd rather be at home reading a good book' MacDonalds, but to have 'fighting' attached to you before you've even been properly introduced, says a lot about them.

It all began when Donald Farquharson (pronounced Farker-son by the way, in case you were wondering), married Isobel Stewart. They had a son, Finlay Mor (Finlay was a big lad!), who went on to be the King's deputy standard bearer at the Battle of Pinkie Cleugh (more later).

Finlay fell at the battle, but not before he had managed to father nine sons (nothing 'deputy' about that side of his life!). The Farquharsons from then on became known as Clann Fhionnlaigh, the descendants of Finlay. It's tempting to imagine Finlay coming home after a day's savage fighting and immediately fathering yet another son. If he hadn't died at Pinkie Cleugh, who knows how many sons he could've managed. Twelve? Why not twenty-five?

As it turned out, nine lads were enough to set up the Farquharson headquarters in the lands of Upper Deeside, enjoying the protection of the natural fortress of high mountains surrounding them on three sides. Only one way in, and one way out, and that was guarded by the nine testosterone-filled sons of Big Finlay. (Probably similar to a sort of Scottish Cerberus guarding the Underworld).

Just to be sure of protection, however, they joined the Highland super clan, Clan Chattan, the tartan version of La Cosa Nostra.

They continued to set a fearsome reputation as people who enjoyed a good punch up, with Donald 'Og' Farquharson of Monaltrie becoming Montrose's most successful commander in those Covenanter battles.

John Farquharson of Inverey fought alongside 'Bonnie Dundee' at Killiecrankie. He was known as the 'Black

Colonel', a name that probably wasn't meant as a reference to the preferred colour of his clothing. This was a man who was actually outlawed in 1666 – coincidentally the year of the devil!

They supported the Jacobite cause in 1715 and 1745 and their clan chief was captured, only to be pardoned on the very morning of his execution. One can imagine how he felt when he got THAT bit of news. (Once he'd changed his underpants, of course.)

But perhaps the most inspiring Farquharson was Anne, or 'Colonel Anne' as she became known. Married to a Mackintosh, she raised the 'Mackintosh regiment' in his absence and led them to the Battle of Culloden. She was briefly held prisoner at Inverness and then released.

Don't 'Fark' with a 'Farquharson'.

Perhaps my favourite Farquharson, though, was the truly astonishing individual who encompassed the whole breadth of the Jacobite cause. He had fought as a young lad of fifteen alongside Montrose at the succession of Jacobite victories, and lived long enough to see his last son fall at Culloden and the hopes of Jacobites die with him.

At the extreme age of 115 he wandered the land, desolate and forlorn, visiting the graves of those he had known whom had died. He was known by the Gaelic, *Fearchar gaisgach liath*, which translates, most suitably, to . . .

. . . 'The Grey Warrior'.

Oh yes, it is worth noting that the current Clan Chief, Alwyne Arthur Compton Farquharson, turns 102 years of age this year.

CRACKING CASTLE OF THE MONTH
BALMORAL CASTLE

SAM

Bought from the Farquharsons, who still own Braemar Castle today, Balmoral was purchased in 1852 by Queen Victoria and Prince Albert and remains a private property of Queen Elizabeth II. Known as Liz's holiday home, the castle grounds and gardens are open to the public and you can visit the Garden Cottage where Victoria would write letters or, as I like to imagine, tuck into a full Scottish breakfast with Albert. Or even a breakfast roll from the local Braemar cafe.

Oh my God, I literally dream about this breakfast roll. It was so good. From The Bothy in Braemar I would drive there right now to get one. I was slightly hungover and Davy, my driver, had an extra one and gave it to me. It was two square sausages, an egg on top with brown sauce in a bread roll, freshly baked, soft on the inside but crusty on the outside, it was that incredible. Argh, I sound like Graham . . .

In fact, there's another reason why I want to go back to Braemar, which is to see the pyramid in the forest at Balmoral. Yep, there's an actual pyramid in the Cairngorms!

One of eleven cairns on the estate, the Prince Albert Cairn, was constructed as a memorial to Victoria's husband:

> *To the beloved memory of Albert the great*
> *and good Prince Consort.*
> *Erected by his broken hearted widow Victoria R.*
> *21st August 1862.*

Cairngorm means 'blue cairn' in Gaelic and a cairn is a pile of stones over a burial chamber, so it seems really fitting to use these traditional piles of stones in the area. And, there's a walking route to many of the cairns, including Prince Albert's, which is something I definitely want to do. As well as eat another breakfast roll. I'm dribbling on my keyboard. Why don't they do Highland Deliveroo?

There was also another cairn erected by Queen Victoria in memory of Mr John Brown, her personal attendant and ghillie when he died in 1883, however her son, Edward VII, removed it. Brown was most memorably played by Billy Connolly in the eponymous film and no one quite knows the nature of their relationship, but Victoria obviously regarded him highly. There is a bronze statue to him in the woods to the south-east of the castle, a kilted figure, cap in hand, inscribed: *Friend more than Servant, Loyal, Truthful, Brave, Selfless than Duty even to the Grave.*

Like Victoria, our current Queen loves Scotland and enjoys hill walking, riding native ponies and picnicking here every summer. I've never met her personally, but I have met Prince Charles a few times. Graham probably knows them really well and gets them to cook for him or drive him when he's in London.

I was actually invited to Buckingham Palace in 2018, when I was asked to compere at a concert. It was an evening of music from the Royal Conservatoire of Scotland, where I trained as an actor. HRH Prince Charles is the patron of the Conservatoire. It was an interesting evening to say the least. Firstly, you're not able to take photographs in the palace at all and we were backstage, but desperate to take photos. Prince Charles's aide walked in and we knew instantly from his terrible, bright red corduroy trousers that this guy was an officious type. Teamed with his red trousers were yellow socks and brown brogues. Let's just say that in the UK, red trousers and custard cords are a sure sign (but not always) of a total bawbag.

Enough said.

He sidled up to me and said, 'What would your mother say, wearing boots with a kilt?' I ignored him, but things got worse when the conductor, after leading an amazing piece of Armenian music, stood up to talk about the music. But he wasn't supposed to and the officious bawbag went bright red with rage, perspiring, pacing and muttering loudly behind the stage. 'What is he doing?! He shouldn't be doing it! No. No. NO!!!'

I went to speak to one of the waiting staff, who laughed and said, 'Ah, so you've met Red Nose, have you?!' I asked them what they meant. 'When he gets angry, his nose gets redder and redder.'

That night it made the palace look like the red light district.

Sadly, I found out later I was actually meant to have dinner with the performers, Prince Charles and everyone afterwards, but Old Red Nose never let me know – maybe penance for me wearing 'my boots with a kilt'.

I snuck out of the front door of Buckingham Palace, walked out of the gates towards the Victoria Memorial roundabout in my kilt (and boots), and hailed a cab, while scores of tourists gawped at me wondering who the hell I was!

The moral of this story: never trust a man in red trousers.

ADVENTURE OF THE MONTH
LOCHNAGAR

SAM

Lochnagar is a 1155-metre Munro in the Grampians which sits on the royal estate of Balmoral, five miles south from the great river Dee. In 1848, Queen Victoria pulled on her hiking boots and tweeds for a quick tramp up to the top. The summit is referred to as *Cac Càrn Beag*, meaning 'small cairn of faeces' in Scottish Gaelic, or less euphemistically, 'little pile of shit', and I wonder if old Queen Vic would have been amused?

No doubt she carried a hip flask with her, to toast reaching the top and admire the views across the Cairngorms and down to Braemar. However, the weather that day was crap (excuse the pun) and she saw nothing, famously writing: 'But alas! Nothing whatever to be seen; and it was cold, and wet, and cheerless.'

But it is a dramatic and well-celebrated Munro, in the right weather conditions. Lord Byron (1788–1824) spent some time there as a troublesome teenager, and wrote this poem:

Lachin y Gair – Dark Lochnagar
England! thy beauties are tame and domestic,
To one who has roved on the mountains afar:
Oh for the crags that are wild and majestic,
The steep, frowning glories o' dark Lochnagar.
Lord Byron, 1807

DRAM OF THE MONTH
12-YEAR-OLD ROYAL LOCHNAGAR

I can imagine Queen Victoria taking a large swig from her gold-trimmed hip flask to warm herself up, her flask perhaps filled with whisky from nearby Royal Lochnagar Distillery. Both Victoria and Prince Albert visited the distillery and likely sampled as much as they could of this delicious spirit. It's a small distillery that is mostly used for production of the top-end Johnnie Walker blend, but they do bottle their own spirit. Whilst shooting *Men in Kilts* in Braemar, it became the whisky of choice for the crew and we managed to empty quite a few bottles before leaving the Highlands. Interestingly, the distillery has burned down twice in the past, but thankfully we didn't leave it in flames and it still stands near the River Dee in the north-east Highlands.

BATTLE OF THE MONTH
BATTLE OF PRESTONPANS, 21 SEPTEMBER 1745

GRAHAM

For those familiar with the TV show *Outlander*, you will remember there is a whole episode called 'Prestonpans'. This places myself and Sam at the heart of a battle that marked the first great victory of the Jacobites. Dougal MacKenzie and his soon-to-be treacherous, murderous nephew, Jamie Fraser (yes, my bitterness continues), ran alongside each other and attacked the Governing forces.

The main difference between then and 21 September 1745 is that the actual battle was like something from a butcher's yard, whereas our battle took place in a giant white tent with fake smoke, and stuntmen who kindly allowed us to pretend to kill them in-between having coffees brought to us and sipping on protein shakes. (However, I suspect there is a part of Sam that believes he was actually AT the real battle.)

Prestonpans was everything that Culloden later was not. Apart from being a stunning victory by the Jacobites, it showed the devastating effectiveness of the Highland charge.

To set the scene: how the armies met was almost a comedy of errors. The British Government had only two regiments in Scotland to deal with this uprising. Led by Sir John Cope, they marched north to meet Bonnie Prince Charlie (BPC), while the latter marched south.

Almost like being driven around the Highlands by Sam, the two armies managed to pass by, oblivious to one another. BPC went on to take the completely undefended Edinburgh on 17 September 1745.

Realising the only enemy he was going to meet marching north would be belligerent sheep and the odd wild haggis,

Cope turned right, went to Aberdeen, took the fastest ship he could and headed south to the coast just east of Edinburgh.

Meanwhile BPC headed out to meet him.

The two men and their respective armies then met on 20 September.

Charlie-boy decided to occupy the high ground above Prestonpans (actually two separate places: the village of Preston, and the salt 'pans' nearby). His plan was to charge down the hill and deliver a brutal blow.

Clever old Charlie.

Cope meanwhile deployed his men to deal with the attack facing north to south. He had positioned his men with the walls of two country estate houses on his flank to help channel any charge into a ready-made bottleneck.

Clever old Cope, I hear you say.

Unfortunately for BPC, he discovered that the ground between them was littered with bogs and coal pits and to charge through that would be like watching Sam and I trying to do a highland sword dance (that is, embarrassing and horrific).

The Jacobite army settled into lots of arguing (this was to become a feature of their entire campaign). Cope, however, knew none of this.

The Jacobites moved left.

Cope moved right.

The Jacobites moved right.

Cope moved left.

It was like some really terrible dance, where neither partner knows who is supposed to lead.

All this toing and froing was doing nothing for the nerves of the red-coated soldiers who, quite rightly, surmised that no one knew what they were bloody well doing.

Night fell, and apart from the odd frustrated musket shot from either side, bugger all happened.

Enter Robert Anderson. He was a local man in the Jacobite army, who took it upon himself to let Lord George Murray know that there was a shepherd's path leading east that they could follow, which would outflank government forces.

Murray told BPC and the word went out: 'Follow Bob Anderson!!'

At 3 a.m., they set off. There was hardly any moon that night and one can imagine the scene as a couple of thousand men walked single file along the track. Those with broadswords probably muffled the sound inside their plaids. Others carried little more than farming implements, or blades tied on to poles. The Jacobites had no cavalry, and therefore no horses to alert the enemy.

Good old Bob Anderson must have been a student of history, as this was exactly how the Persians outflanked the 300 Spartans at Thermopylae (or maybe he was just a lot smarter than the men in charge!).

Too late Cope's troops saw them and fired off a signal gun. Cope hastily deployed his men in line, but his artillery of six guns had no opportunity to get into position, so all those cannons were bunched on the right-hand side.

BPC wasn't going to wait any longer, and nor were the Highlanders. At last, there was the enemy, right bang in front of them. As dawn broke, to the scream of 'Claymore!', the Highlanders charged.

The enemy regular soldiers who faced them had literally never seen anything like this.

They were used to armies standing facing each other and politely firing cannons and muskets at each other from a distance. Here was a horde of barefoot savages sprinting towards them, their plaids flying, their broadswords raised, screaming together in a language entirely foreign to them.

It must've felt like they'd been dropped onto another planet. One minute you're sleeping and the next minute you're hearing the drone of the war pipes, and thousands of men bellowing at you in Gaelic.

Cope's men managed to fire their cannons only once. The noise of the cannons spooked the horses of their own Dragoons who had, incredibly, never been trained to fight under fire. They bolted. They didn't stop until they reached Edinburgh, where the gates to the castle were locked to them and they were threatened with being shot for their cowardice.

Meanwhile back on the open plain, the ululating war cries of the clans echoed around the remaining infantry. The MacDonalds of Appin, the Camerons, the MacLachlans, the Robertsons, the MacDonalds of Glencoe (yup, them), the MacGregors, and the MacDonalds of Glengarry, Keppoch and Clanranald. These were the men who ran across that plain that day. Perhaps there was a Dougal MacKenzie and Jamie Fraser in there too.

The opposition managed a couple of volleys before the solid wall of homicidal plaid smashed into them. The first to batter into their line were Clan Ranald and the Camerons, followed by the rest.

It is useful to imagine the scene that September morning. Men standing with sleep still in their eyes trying to make sense of what was happening. They were the Government army, for God's sake, and now they were meeting something utterly different. As they hastily attempted to reload their muskets, they would've looked up and basically seen a wall of Charlie Allans. Not marching towards them but SPRINTING, screaming, mouths open, faces twisted in hate, carrying a host of broadswords glittering in the fading moonlight.

The sound of thousands of bare feet thumping across the soft ground, the faint swish of their plaids, perhaps a jingle of metal. They might as well have been facing a pack of rabid dogs. In the time it took them to fully register the horror of what was happening, they were already watching their friend being dismembered next to them by a local farmer baying for blood.

Men with broadswords, dirks, pitchforks, axes and cleavers were literally lopping limbs off them, or slicing off the top of their heads like an egg.

So they did what any sensible person faced with thousands of bearded, screaming, spitting maniacs would do . . .

They ran.

Unfortunately they ran straight into the very walls they had hoped would create a bottleneck for the Highlanders.

Instead, it became the place where the majority of the Cope's men met their end.

Showing little mercy, the Jacobites killed 450 of them and captured a further 1500. Only 170 enemy soldiers escaped.

The Highlanders had lost thirty men.

What had happened in the space of fifteen blood-soaked minutes of total horror was the complete destruction of the only Government field army in Scotland. They had been beaten by an army of shepherds, crofters and volunteers led by a 25-year-old with no experience of battle.

It's highly likely that good old Robert Anderson survived. One wonders how he was thanked. I suspect, knowing the army, it was a firm handshake and an extra ration of whisky rather than a knighthood.

But there is no doubt, but for Bob the shepherd, the result would've been VERY different. I wonder if he made it to Culloden . . .

NATURE NOTES
HEATHER

SAM

The late flowering bell heather (*Erica cinerea*) accompanies ling on the moorland in September and is an even bigger magnet for bees. There are two main species of heather in Scotland: ling heather (*Calluna vulgaris*) and bell heather. Heather usually blooms twice, in the early summer and the late summer/early autumn.

One of Scotland's national symbols (along with the thistle and the Scots pine), it covers over five million acres of hills, glens and moorland and ranges in hue from pink to purple with white being very rare indeed.

The Many Marvellous Applications of Heather (The flower not the lady!)

- As good fortune.
- To ward off evil.
- In thatching and construction of houses.
- To dye cloth and wool – such as tartan.
- Medicinally, treating stomach complaints, coughs, rheumatism and anxiety.
- In soaps and salves.
- In mattresses.
- In Heather Ale. Four thousand years ago on the Isle of Rum, Neolithic settlers were fermenting alcohol from heather using pottery flagons that still bear traces of the residue. It was a potion popular with the Picts, too.

Heather Ale: A Galloway Legend

From the bonny bells of heather
They brewed a drink long-syne,
Was sweeter far than honey,
Was stronger far than wine.
They brewed it and they drank it,
And lay in a blessed swound
For days and days together
In their dwellings underground.
Robert Louis Stevenson, 1890

GREAT SCOT!

NOTABLE BIRTHDAYS, DEATHS AND SIGNIFICANT EVENTS

3 September 1745 – Prince Charles Edward Stuart proclaimed his father as King James VIII of Scotland at Perth.

3 September 1752 – With the adoption of the Gregorian calendar, 3 September 1752 became 14 September. Crowds flocked the streets demanding, 'Give us back our eleven days!'

6 September 1715 – The Earl of Mar unfurled the standard of the 'Old Pretender' in Braemar at the start of the first Jacobite Uprising.

11 September 1297 – Battle of Stirling Bridge.

SAM

Whilst running the Stirling marathon in 2018, and in the eighteenth mile as my legs were really starting to burn, I caught sight of the Wallace monument. It marks the site of the Battle of Stirling Bridge, where Wallace defeated the English and became a national hero, given the sobriquet, 'The Guardian of Scotland'. Purported to hold his Claymore double-handed sword measuring about six feet long and taller than Dwalin the angry Dwarf, he was a fearsome warrior. His memorial can be visited today and, via a narrow spiral staircase of 246 steps, you can reach the top to receive a dramatic and windy view.

It's a rewarding climb, just don't do it after running a marathon.

GRAHAM

Much has been heard of William Wallace, mainly thanks to Mel Gibson. (Gibson is a fine Scottish name, and I feel sure Mel was righteously inspired to make a film eulogising the man who started the War of Independence in Scotland.)

Now, I love *Braveheart*. I've probably seen it three or four times, but Mel made one crucial mistake in his portrayal of William Wallace . . . he simply didn't make him violent enough.

In a culture that seemed to give birth to bloodthirsty maniacs on a daily basis, 'The Wallace' stands head and shoulders above most.

This is partly because it is rumoured he literally stood head and shoulders above the rest. At a time when most folk settled at five feet four inches, Wallace's claymore alone is said to have been six feet long. You can look at Wallace's sword in the Wallace monument, hanging in a very large glass case. The hilt is said to have been bound with the skin flayed from the spine of one of his enemies.

See what I mean . . .

William Wallace was probably an average peace-loving Highlander until a few English soldiers tried to take away his fishing catch of the day by force.

But first a wee bit of background.

The crown of Scotland had fallen vacant after the death of the previous Scottish king, and the subsequent demise of his two-year-old infant successor. In their desperation, the Scots went to the very last person they should have asked for help, Edward I of England, known affectionately as 'Longshanks'.

It would be like begging a wolf to be your shepherd, while you went into town for a night out. Edward was the kind of guy who probably flossed his teeth with the bones of his many enemies and drank his own health out of cups made of human skulls. Oh, and he hated Scotland.

His response was entirely predictable. He grabbed the Scottish crown, rammed it on his own head, and said, 'Thanks very much. I'm King. Me. Only me. So the rest of you can fuck right off.'

This is the land WW found himself in when he went beer drinking and fishing in Lanark. All was well, until he encountered five absolutely blootered English soldiers, who insisted he give his entire catch of the day to them.

When Wallace quite reasonably offered to share it rather than lose everything, they threatened him with treason.

William's next response was less reasonable. He smashed in the face of one of the soldiers, stole his sword and proceeded to cut the others to pieces, probably while humming a sea shanty.

The sheriff came round to William's girlfriend to find him, and when she told the sheriff she had no idea where Wallace was, he had her summarily executed.

Oooops.

William was not happy.

In fact, he only regained a modicum of his happiness after he'd butchered the sheriff, probably wearing his face as a sporran, and slaughtered the entire garrison at Lanark.

And he was only getting started.

He and his growing band of followers then proceeded to kick the arses of every English soldier in Scotland, probably beating half of them to death with the severed stumps of other victims, while posing with the severed heads of anyone who didn't sound Scottish enough.

Meanwhile Edward, 'Lord Vader' Longshanks, was getting mightily pissed off.

Having executed most of the generals who had so far let him down as an encouragement to others, he sent the pride of England to meet Mr Stroppy Wallace at Stirling Bridge on 11 September 1297.

It should've been a foregone conclusion.

A well-trained and equipped English army, many on horseback, against a mob of peasants often armed with little more than a really bad temper.

The English outnumbered them five to one.

Wallace didn't even consider surrender. He probably stood there on the other side of Stirling Bridge looking well, glaring malevolently towards the English, his great kilt barely able to contain his gigantic brass balls, no doubt while fashioning a warm jacket out of the stitched-together hides of his fallen enemies.

The English were so enraged that they decided to cross the bridge in force. As soon as the first part of the army was over the bridge, Wallace ordered his men to charge out of the surrounding woods and batter them like a pack of hyenas in one of those David Attenborough documentaries. You know the kind of one, where the slow, dim-witted wildebeest is separated from the herd and literally torn to pieces, while Attenborough gently narrates the unfolding scene of diabolical horror.

If only Sir David had been at Stirling Bridge: 'And here we have the traditional group of Highlanders falling upon the bewildered English army. Note how the Highland swords work particularly well at disembowelment and decapitation. Goodness me! That's a lot of blood!'

The English, instead of concluding wisely that they should forget about fighting something resembling a berserker convention, instead sent their heavy cavalry across the ridiculously narrow bridge.

Big mistake.

Old Billy boy had previously weakened the aforesaid bridge (probably with his teeth), and the bridge collapsed with the English knights plunging into the river.

While the stranded rearguard of the English army looked on helplessly, Wallace's rabid horde of extras from *28 Days Later* slaughtered everyone with an English accent.

William concluded the day's fun by flaying the corpse of the English commander and using his skin to wrap around the hilt of that truly enormous viscera-coated sword.

There was a lot more bloodshed in the months to come, culminating in the Battle of Bannockburn, which we heard about earlier in JUNE.

27 September 1958 – Novelist Irvine Welsh born in Leith, Edinburgh (*Trainspotting*, etc.).

30 September 1928 – Announcement of the discovery of penicillin by Ayrshire-born Sir Alexander Fleming.

OCTOBER

There's no place on earth with more of the
old superstitions and magic mixed into its
daily life than the Scottish Highlands.
Diana Gabaldon, *Outlander*

Clan Cameron
Motto: *Aonaibh Ri Chéile* (Let us unite)
Lands: Lochiel

Black History Month

4   Catriona Balfe's Birthday (born in 1979)

Early-mid October: Royal National Mòd

20   Claire Randall's Birthday (born in 1918)

Mid-end October: Scottish International Storytelling Festival

31   Samhain (Halloween)

1 October - International Coffee Day.

GRAHAM

I love a latte. I'm trying to remember my first latte, but I like to think it was in the month of October and I was probably in London.

Prior to the arrival of widespread espresso in London, pretty much all you could get was tea. The drinking of coffee was rare, mainly because of the scarcity of coffee shops. Nowadays you can barely walk fifty metres down a high street without seeing a coffee shop, but in the early 1980s there was nothing.

I think my first latte was in 1986. It was at a Costa coffee shop (these are now ubiquitous, but then they were as uncommon as an episode of *Outlander* where Jamie Fraser isn't topless).

I wish I could remember that first sip. It was probably an accident that I tried one. You have to remember that prior to this, coffee in Britain was freeze-dried granules. Instant coffee. We would have big cans of instant coffee in rehearsal rooms. If you had Nescafe Gold Blend, you knew you were in a posh theatre.

[*Sam: So true! I honestly remember when the first coffee shops in Edinburgh started selling caffe lattes, it was a revolution! Some ten years behind London and the rest of the world, but we finally got there!*]

So the idea of espresso coffee was as unlikely as a quiet evening with Duncan Lacroix.

But my love affair had started (with latte, not Lacroix). I don't know how many lattes I've had since then, but it has to be in the region of 25,000.

I graduated from Costa Coffee to the Monmouth Coffee shop in Covent Garden. There I came to encounter the almost zen-like, religious qualities of great coffee-making. It became a place of pilgrimage for me and my friends. Tiny, wooden booths, the swoosh of the steam wand, the pressing of the coffee, the aroma of the beans.

Since then I have sampled lattes all over the world. Sometimes cappuccinos or flat whites, but I always return to the siren call of the double-shot latte with whole milk. None of this soy/oat/fucking almond milk pish! Whenever I see a cow, I give silent thanks.

The only thing I cannot abide, which is associated in some quarters with the latte, is the absurd tall glass that narrows at the base with a tiny little handle near the bottom. A handle so tiny that only a five-year-old with a precocious espresso habit could hold it in their hand.

They frequently come with a very long spoon.

I hate those glasses. It would be like creating a plate that was an inch wide with a knife and fork made for Bilbo Baggins.

Much has been made of my latte love affair by Heughan. It must be pointed out now, however, that all lattes are not created equal.

I loved working on *Outlander*, I really did, and I loved the crew.

[*Sam: Wait for it . . .*]

However, from a latte point of view, they won't be winning any barista competitions anytime soon. I admit I had been horribly spoiled shooting *The Hobbit* in New Zealand. In that country, coffee-making is akin to a religion, beaten only by their obsession with the All Blacks rugby team. Everyone who worked on *The Hobbit* that was a New Zealander could make a great latte/flat white/Americano/macchiato, etc., It's as if it is part of their school curriculum. Or maybe it's hard wired into their DNA, similar to their ability to make all vowels sound interchangeable.

Even the coffee at the airports in New Zealand is fantastic. It's incredibly hard to get a bad cup of coffee there. If it happens, it is a moment of shame for the barista and awkward embarrassment for the customer. It's a little bit like you've let the whole country down. It might even be grounds for revoking your citizenship . . .

Whenever I have worked in other countries, I have to find a good coffee shop. I have developed a bloodhound-like ability to hunt down a good one. Once found, this temple of delight becomes the place I go to EVERY day. My fanatical devotion to the cup is similar to that of a religious zealot.

On *Outlander*, I would keep up a steady order of the latte. Unfortunately, it was reciprocated with a steady stream of frothy dishwater masquerading as coffee. It was not unusual to ask for a coffee during filming (when you can't go anywhere because you're dressed as a kilted Highland war chief on horseback), and for the coffee finally to arrive as night fell.

I can only imagine that the long-suffering crew member in charge of the coffee order had decided to walk miles and miles to the nearest town to get the cup and then was, perhaps, abducted on the way back, held hostage, and finally ransomed off just in time for him to deliver the aforementioned cup as a cold, congealed mass of tasteless bog water.

[*Sam: I have to agree, it would be carried in a large kettle and most likely stewed over a few hours. Not that we are coffee snobs, but caffeine is so important on a film set. When your call times are maybe in the middle of the night and you are expected to function in a freezing cold field or bog, a cup of coffee somehow offers some relief and comfort. Unless it's not up to McLatte's exacting standards.*]

At the other extreme, there is the latte that almost defies you to drink it because it is so perfect. Those moments when it appears Michelangelo or Leonardo da Vinci has turned his hand to barista work. You know the kind of latte I mean. Swirls of delicious colour creating an artful top, slightly bouncy with a definite curve to the meniscus. It has weight, texture and perfect temperature. It's practically singing to you. It feels like a desecration to take a sip. Like taking a hammer to the Sistine Chapel. At moments like these, there is not a word invented to describe it. Even Shakespeare would've struggled to do it justice.

In fact, time for a break. I'm off for a dose of the divine.

Sam: My thoughts on coffee are simpler. I like a STRONG black Americano. Double shot, a little water. Just enough to make the caffeine liquid enough to pour down my throat, reach behind my eyeballs and jolt my brain awake! That's all I need. No fuss. None of the frothy nonsense. Milk is for babies. The way we take our coffee says so much about us, doesn't it?

Graham: I agree. Your coffee of choice is simple, unimaginative and lacking in sophistication. I rest my case.

Sam: To a connoisseur, what you do to coffee is tantamount to savagery!

COMPETITION CORNER
CASKET WEAVING

SAM

Now Graham's restored by his Ovaltine – let's face it a latte's not far off one of those elderly milky night-time drinks, is it? [*Graham: Harsh!*] – we come to competitive basket weaving.

Yet again it's another tenuous victory that Graham would like to claim.

His long and nimble fingers, like those of Silas Marner fondling his golden coins, were infinitely suited to the craft of basket weaving and who knew it could be so competitive?

I fell a new reality TV format coming – forget *Bake Off*, *The Great Pottery Throw Down*, *Selling Sunset* and *MasterChef* – 'The Great Scottish Weave Off' happened first on *Men in Kilts* at Wormiston House!

I really enjoyed weaving baskets, though make no mistake it's tough on the fingers. The practice is as old as humans and there have been discoveries of fragments of ceramic with imprints that suggest the clay was pushed into a basket before being fired to make a pot. Which means the basket came first. The willow is grown all over Scotland and used when it still smells fresh and green.

Graham was convinced he would automatically be a master weaver, owing to the fact his second great-grandfather was a basket weaver (his great-great-grandson is a basket case!) and he did not stop going on about it. It was in the blood, apparently. Well, as those of you who have read *Clanlands* will know, my uncle from Eigg is also a basket weaver and makes cool massive structures for Scots to set fire to – like the fiery crosses that we used on Season Five of *Outlander* and stags (as seen in Season Two). It's a closer link and what's more my uncle had TAUGHT our tutor, Lise Bech, who knew Uncle Trev very well.

The basket weaving wasn't even meant to be a vicious competition, but the Grey Dog started one by ingratiating himself with Lise and trying to be a teacher's pet, meanwhile eating all the freshly boiled potatoes that were to be used as a prop. I was quite happy to sit there and have a go, but he was desperate to show off by weaving faster than me and seeking her approval like the school swat.

Unfortunately, Lise played up to his old tricks, telling him how wonderful and ambidextrous he was when he weaved, and the fact he used his left hand . . . and he LOVED it!

[*Graham: I think you'll find the word she used was Excellent. She said my work was excellent.*] [*Sam: Excrement?*]

Wicker baskets are very versatile, so Lise showed us you could use one as a colander and had cooked the said potatoes freshly harvested from the walled gardens in the grounds of

Wormiston to show us. Of course, Graham's eyes lit up and he proceeded to munch on them throughout the afternoon as he continued to work on his basket, despite just having had lunch. But so fast were his long, nimble counting fingers, and pumped with carbs, that whilst I was still weaving the bottom inch of a colander, he had managed to construct a vast basket, oblong and over a metre in length.

[*Graham: Actually I think your uncle made it . . .*]

Less of a basket, more of a casket, he had attempted to weave a wicker coffin for me! We found a larger sized one that Lise had 'woven earlier' and filmed a whole scene where we were driving around in the campervan with a big wicker coffin in the back, me looking slightly concerned, and Graham vigorously denying that it was a coffin.

[*Graham: I merely wanted him to lie down in it to check its dimensions.*]

It 'just happened' to be the perfect size for me. Unfortunately, Starz found it too dark and 'not in keeping with the show'. I found it highly disturbing and I still wonder how he made such a perfect fit. I shall sleep with one eye open from now on.

[*Graham: Obviously, the very idea of bringing a wicker coffin and forcing Sam to climb into it (which would probably have required me to break his arms and legs to cram him inside) was, clearly, THE very last thing I was thinking of . . .*]

GRAHAM

I wasn't aware that there was such a thing as competitive basket weaving. Only Sam could create a competition out of this. He probably practises competitive bed-making as well, or perhaps competitive toe-nail cutting?

All I was aware of was the simple, and incontrovertible fact that I was better at it than him. There are, of course, so many things Sam is better at than me (definitely lifting lumps of rock, and the use of emojis, I'm sure there must be other things), but basket weaving isn't on that list.

[*Sam: I beg to differ. Happy for a rematch any time, basket case.*]

I had never woven anything in my life before (Sam's only

previous experience in the weaving realm, of course, involves webs of deceit), but I did have a great-great-great-grandfather who had come from Argyll with that skill and used it to make money when he arrived in Edinburgh.

Perhaps Sam's right, though, as he says in *Men in Kilts*, maybe my distant relative was terrible at the weaving. Possibly his baskets were unusable lumps of tangled twigs that people only purchased out of pity.

'Ah, look, there's McTavish, trying to weave a basket again.'

'It looks like something a horse might have made using its hooves.'

The irony is that Sam has an uncle who is a master of weaving. Tremendous woven structures that often seem to be set on fire. A sort of weaving pyromaniac.

When I sat and started weaving, I could see how it could become a delightful meditative pastime. Our hosts were indeed complimentary about my dexterous fingers. Beginner's luck? Or maybe it was because I was sat next to a man for whom learning to weave was like attempting to teach a dog a card trick.

I could tell from Sam's expression that he was wishing there was an extremely heavy wicker basket he could pick up. (Sam gets restless if he's not dead-lifting large objects at any opportunity.)

2 October 1263 - The Battle of Largs.

SAM

The Battle of Largs was a small but decisive battle between the kingdoms of Scotland and Norway, fought on the Firth of Clyde near Largs (now a popular beach resort for the local Glaswegians), which was finally to put an end to 500 years of Norse Viking invasions and depredation. I mean, we Scots love a dust-up and a feud, but even by Highland clan standards this one had dragged on a bit.

After a failed attempt to buy the Hebrides from the

Norwegian King Haakon, the Scots launched a military assault to take the islands back by force. King Haakon responded by sending a vast fleet, comprising over a thousand ships, to deal with the matter. King Alexander III of Scotland realised he was outnumbered, so came up with a cunning and very Scottish plan – he would protract diplomatic negotiations as long as he could to gather new troops AND enter a period of more inclement, unsettled autumn weather, utterly unsuited for invasions.

As planned, negotiations eventually broke down in late September, just as the balmy days of Scottish summer came to an end! Everyone sunbathing on the beach had dispersed, and discarded ice-cream cones were all that remained. Haakon was primed to invade and brought his fleet to anchor at the Cumbraes. However, on 1 October 1263, a massive storm hit and many Norse vessels were run aground at Largs.

The next day, whilst the Norwegians were recovering their ships, the Scottish infantry and cavalry arrived, not looking for a sun tan and piña colada, but ready to give the enemy a right good doing. They pushed the invaders back onto the beaches at Largs and, after fierce skirmishing, the Norwegians retreated, stopping only to collect their dead. They then pushed off to Orkney to see out the winter.

Haakon fully intended a rematch, but died in Orkney that same year. His son, King Magnus Haakonarson, signed the Treaty of Perth in 1266, leasing the Inner and Outer Hebrides to King Alexander III, who was thenceforth known as 'The Tamer of the Ravens'. Meanwhile, the people of Scotland were delighted to be able to return to their beach vacations once again.

Scotland eventually stopped paying for the islands when Norway became embroiled in a civil war, but Orkney and Shetland were to remain in Norwegian hands for another 200 years.

NATURE NOTES
THE SCOTTISH THISTLE

SAM

The Scottish thistle is the national emblem of Scotland.

Legend has it that when the army of King Haakon of Norway was trying to conquer the coast of Largs in 1263, they removed their footwear to surprise the sleeping Scots. However, their feet were pricked by the Scottish thistles, making them hop around saying, 'Ooh' and 'Ahh' (in Norwegian accents). They all had to sit down on the grass, trying to pull out the spiny bits (we've all done it), which was when the game was up and the Scottish cavalry arrived.

I like this version best – the idea of the Vikings sitting around examining their bare feet, when the Scots on ride up on horseback, saying, 'Ah-ha! Naughty Vikings! Got you!' It's very Pythonesque.

The Scottish thistle – a purple spear thistle with the Latin name *Cirsium vulgare* – is a powerful emblem and is found throughout the Highlands, Islands and Lowlands. It grows proudly to five feet (about Tom Cruise size) and has no enemies because of its spines, though I've seen the odd hardy Highland cow chewing on one. The thistle dates back long ago in Scottish history and was used as a heraldic symbol, but it had become recognised as a true Scottish emblem by 1503.

In 1687, King James II created a Scottish order of knighthood called the Order of the Thistle, which still exists today. However, I'm not a member. Yet. Hint, hint. I see there are a few Scottish academics who have been ennobled and made prickly knights, so armed with my two doctorates, it's only a matter of time! Sir Heughan of the Thistle.

In October, November and December, few plants flowers except hardy varieties, including dead nettles, sow thistles and the spear thistle, which are in bloom from July to October, producing nectar for summer and autumn pollinators and, later on, seeds for goldfinches.

Claire Fraser uses the thistle as a febrifuge (to reduce fever) in *Cross Stitch* (Chapter 19).

Scottish Saying
Cut thistles in May, they'll grow in a day.
Cut them in June, that is too soon.
Cut them in July, then they will die.

We Scots do love poetry, especially about death!

REGION OF THE MONTH
ROSS & CROMARTY, SUTHERLAND, CAITHNESS, AND THE NORTHERN ISLANDS (SHETLAND AND ORKNEY)

SAM

I toured Outlying Islands, the fringe play from the Traverse Theatre, all through the Highlands and Islands of Scotland. One of my favourite experiences was in Shetland. We took a ferry from INSERT which I recall took around seven hours [It's over 12 hours by ferry from the mainland}. I remember standing outside on deck, my back to the page engine for warmth, listening to music on my CD player (showing my age!) and watching the vast ocean pass by. It was in the summer months and the sun never really set below the horizon. Shetland was bathed in glorious light, which made the days long but rather hard to sleep at night (if indeed you can call it night). Before each performance in the small community hall, I'd run the dirt track along the coast. I specifically remember skinny dipping in the blue water and sitting on the beach. What a way to get into character before a performance. Luckily I remembered my clothes!

Graham: Which makes a change.

SAM

I'm fascinated by Shetland's history and connection to Scandinavia. The locals have a wild and strong nature, as many consider themselves and the island not part of Great Britain at all. It does feel remote and disconnected there. I'm sure during winter it's really tough.

DRAM OF THE MONTH
14-YEAR-OLD CLYNELISH

SAM

Known by the locals as 'Electric City', Brora in Sutherland is the home of the Clynelish distillery. It is famous for its coastal landscape, salmon and herring fishing, and was the first town to receive electricity many years ago, hence its nickname. Though I wouldn't quite call it the Vegas of the North! It produces a unique 'waxy' whisky, with honeyed, butter notes and a bit of the coastal influence to make it more complex. It's like diving into the North Sea on a summer's day, with a flock of highland sheep for company. Or perhaps I've had one too many . . .

For a short time the distillery made Brora whisky, a strongly peated dram. It became one of the most rare and expensive bottles to acquire, costing around £1,500 per bottle. Thankfully, the Clynelish 14 Year Old is not as expensive and is just as silky and smoky.

ADVENTURE OF THE MONTH
BEN HOPE

SAM

The most northerly of the Munros, Ben Hope is a solitary and seldom-visited monolith of a mountain. I feel sorry for it, isolated, looking out over Loch Hope, Durness and the North Sea beyond. There is no higher point nearer than Ben Klibreck far to the south-east, so it offers a terrific vantage point. The view is a vast desolate wilderness dotted with lochans (small lochs) and the occasional distant peak on the horizon, whilst the sea beyond stretches away towards the Arctic, and on a clear day, you may just spot the Orkney Islands in the distance.

GRAHAM

Before I donned the tartan of the War Chief of Clan Mackenzie in *Outlander*, I knew very little of this clan. I think I'd been to school with a Mackenzie (his dad drove a Jaguar – very, very flash where I came from!), but that was about it.

One of my favourite castle visits during *Men in Kilts* was to Castle Leod, the seat of the Mackenzies in Kintail country, near Inverness. It's such a beautiful spot with three trees planted by Mary de Guise (Mary Queen of Scots' mother), near to the castle itself. It's when you hear about things like that, you know this place is packed to the rafters with HISTORY.

We speak about that visit at greater length in *Clanlands*, but I've since taken an interest in the clan itself.

Well, it seems rude not to.

It appears that the clan began its life in the eleventh century with the great Celtic Chief Gilleoin na h'Airde, a direct descendant of the High Kings of Ireland. (The connections with Ireland that the Scottish clans have are fascinating, but that will have to wait for another book.)

The name comes from *MacCoinneach*, meaning 'Son of Kenneth', which translates as 'Son of the Fair Bright One', as opposed perhaps to a clan whose name translates to 'Son of the Ugly Stupid One'. (I'm sure one exists.)

The first recorded Clan Chief was Alexander Mackenzie, 6th Baron of Kintail, who rose to prominence in the fifteenth century for his support of the King against that mega-clan, the MacDonalds. Their power grew to encompass the lands of Kintail, all the way over to Ross-shire and the Isle of Lewis.

There was a time when the name Mackenzie was synonymous with serious tartan power, and they got much of that power by being the King's enforcers in the North. When the Highlanders would get a wee bit uppity, it was the Mackenzies that the King would call on to whip them into line. The sort of Scottish equivalent of Luca Brasi from *The Godfather*. They were certainly never shy of a fight. At Bannockburn, five hundred of them turned up for the Bruce to batter Edward II's army to pieces.

The MacDonalds were a constant source of violent attention from the Mackenzies. In 1491, they pummelled the MacDonalds at the Battle of Blar Na Pairce. Then they decided to attack several clans at once during their raid on Ross (the area, not some unfortunate bloke called 'Ross'), where they crossed swords with the clans MacDonald of Lochalsh and MacDonald of Clanranald, and, for good measure, that other clan who were never far from a punch-up, the Camerons!

When Clan MacDonald invaded Ross-shire in 1497, guess who it was that drove them out. Yup, those good old 'Fair Bright Ones', the Mackenzies.

Jump to the sixteenth century and they were busy fighting the English at Flodden, (where they got comprehensively defeated). And in case you thought their feuding days were slowing down, they then turned their malevolent eye towards Clan Munro as well. They were also on the side of Mary Queen of Scots when she fought her half-brother James Stewart at the Battle of Langside. Maybe that's why her mum planted those trees . . .

By the start of the seventeenth century, the Mackenzies were everywhere and, probably because they had nothing to do that weekend, decided to invade Lewis with 700 men and kick seven bells out of the MacLeods. By the eighteenth century, the clan was divided in its loyalties between the Jacobites, with George Mackenzie, and the government with Kenneth Mackenzie, his cousin and chief of the clan, which no doubt made for some interesting family gatherings.

It must have been exhausting being a Mackenzie. Sometimes it was almost like, 'If it's Tuesday, we must be fighting the Munros!'

One wonders how much time your average Mackenzie spent at home with his legs warming by the fire, watching his children grow, and eating his porridge.

'Ah, Jock, yer back!!! It's been months!!!'

'Yes, Morag, but I can't stay. I'm just doing a quick clothes wash, and I'll have to get going again.'

'But why, Jock????'

'Got to fight the MacDonalds.'

'But you fought them a few months back!'

"Noooooo! THAT was the Camerons.'

'Well, just before the Camerons then.'

'That was the bastard MacLeods, woman!!! Have you not been paying attention? We haven't had time to fit in a return match with the MacDonalds, so that's scheduled for next week. Keep UP, MORAG!!!!!!'

Yes, it was never easy being a Mackenzie.

Or as Dougal was wont to shout at any given opportunity: 'Tulach Ard'!!!

BATTLE OF THE MONTH
THE BATTLE OF CHAMPIONS

GRAHAM

It's October and it's time for me to thumb through my Thesaurus to find new superlatives and adjectives to describe the gigantic feud between Clan Gunn and Clan Keith.

I love this one. These guys never forgot ANYTHING. This feud was a biggie!!

It all seemed to kick off when Helen of Braemore decided to marry Alexander Gunn.

Helen was of Clan Gunn too, being the daughter of Lachlan Gunn.

Now, it would seem to a reasonable person that if two people wish to marry, they should be allowed to do so.

Helen was known locally as 'The Beauty of Braemore'. Not the 'passably okay-looking' Helen of Braemore, or 'on a dark night at a distance of thirty yards she won't scare the sheep' Helen of Braemore. No, she was famous in the surrounding land for being an absolute stunner.

She had known Alexander since they were wee children and had been betrothed, probably since they first played kiss chase when they were six years old.

Enter Dugald Keith of Ackergill.

The story goes that he was out riding one day (probably passing a succession of hideous crones that populated the landscape), when he happened to see Helen.

Not so much 'love at first sight', more 'lust at first sight', Dugald decided that they should definitely get to know each other.

Rather than pop over for a chat, maybe invite her out for a drink and dazzle her with his wit and sensitivity, Dugald decided instead to attack the Gunns on the eve of Helen's wedding. He and his men burst in, killing any Gunn they could (including Helen's childhood sweetheart, Alexander) and dragging her off to Ackergill Tower.

If Dugald thought this forthright approach would win Helen over, he was to be sadly disappointed. Having taken her to the castle, Helen became victim to what one chronicler described as Dugald's 'crude and licentious behaviour'. (No poetry and lute playing then, I presume.)

Helen took the only course available to her and asked her keeper to let her go to the top of the tower to 'take in the view'. Helen decided that the best way of taking in the said view was by throwing herself off the top of the said tower.

As one can imagine, the Gunns were not pleased.

So began this most massive of feuds.

Jump to the so-called Battle of Champions. It took place in either 1464 or 1478. (Given how violent and lengthy this feud was, it's not surprising there is such confusion over the date! Basically, any date up to yesterday is probably safe!)

It took place at the Chapel of St Tears, near Wick in Caithness, on the north coast of Scotland.

It was decided that in order to settle the feud, riders on twelve horses each side would meet and slug it out. You wonder how the riders were chosen. Was there a competition? Did they draw lots? Was it seen as a great honour?

The twelve Gunns arrived first and decided to have a wee prayer at the church while they were waiting to start the bloodletting.

The Keiths then turned up. Were they late? Were they delayed? Who knows, but if they were slower getting there, it might've had something to do with the fact that the Keiths decided to put two men on each horse.

Yes, that's right. 24 Keiths against 12 Gunns.

Well, you can guess how well that went for the Gunns.

I wonder when they noticed that the Keiths had double the men? From a distance? Or was it when they came to dismount and they noticed that there was another guy sitting behind the first one?

You can almost hear the Gunn cries of, 'Now hold on just a second!!!', before they were cut down.

Incredibly the Gunns managed to slay a good number of the Keiths, but eventually the Keiths succeeded in decorating the walls of the chapel with the blood of several Clan Gunn members.

You can still see the bloodstains on the walls to this day.

The Keiths then stole the sword from the Gunn Chief, George the Crowner, also known as *Am Braisdeach Mor* (the great broach-wearer). Not content with the sword, they also took the big broach and other adornments. These were never found again.

Without the sword, a new chief could not be named. Hence why, to this day, Clan Gunn has no named chief.

The surviving Gunns could not bear the thought of the big broach and sword being in the possession of the dastardly Keiths. (Clearly this broach was something special. Perhaps it was the envy of other clans. 'Would you look at the broach on him!!!' 'I wish I had a broach that big!!!!' That sort of thing.)

They found the Keiths celebrating their victory and set about them in true Highland fashion, firing an arrow into the throat of the Chief of Clan Keith.

Fifty years later, William Hamish, the grandson of 'the great broach wearer', along with several of his kinsmen, fell upon a party of Keiths travelling through the Helmsdale area. They killed all fourteen of them and topped off their day's fun by cutting off the head of George Keith, the leader, and dividing it into two pieces.

I'm not sure why they did this. Presumably after cutting off his head, they needed to do something even more barbaric!

'Let's cut it in two, William!!!!'

The two clans finally buried the hatchet by signing a treaty. In 1978.

Yes, 1978.

The feud had only lasted for 500 years.

SAMHAIN, HALLOWEEN

SAM

We Scots love our Fire Festivals and there are four, placed throughout the year: at Imbolc (February), Beltane (May), Lughnasadh (August) and Samhain (October). The Celtic folk divided the year into two parts – darkness and light. Samhain represents the beginning of darkness and the fire ceremonies would have been an appeal to the good spirits for a mild winter, to ward off the evil spirits, and probably a big thanksgiving for the element that would create light, warmth and food during an incredibly difficult period of the year. In the spring, fire represents the sun and the cleansing dark spirits to make way for regrowth and later bless the harvest.

In the TV version of *Outlander*, Claire falls through the stones at Samhain, because of the filming schedule, but in Diana Gabaldon's book, she crosses at Beltane. Both are the ending of seasons in the wheel of the year, but there is so much superstition, ghostly tales and connection to our ancestors at Samhain – pagans believe the veil between the spirit world and our world is at its thinnest, so it proved a great time for Claire to fall into Jamie's world.

On *Men in Kilts*, we visited Wormiston House to discover

more about paganism and witches from expert Leonard Law. Leonard's hobby was collecting pieces of torture equipment. Let's think about that for a moment – that is his real life HOBBY – torture equipment. And he was REALLY enthusiastic about it. Although I was instantly wary, especially as Leonard was sporting a charming T-shirt with depictions of skeletons and devils being burnt alive, I immediately saw an opportunity to have some . . . fun.

At. Graham's. Expense.

In the dungeon, I'd set up a witch to be in there to grab Graham's hand through a small hole in the wall, when he opened the door and he look gingerly inside, no one was there. Magic!

Standing inside the dungeon together, Leonard took us through his implements of torture and I had the great idea to try everything on Graham. The Grey Dog seemed happy with the thumbscrews (I really should have tightened them further), but as soon as the witch's branks (a sort of iron head muzzle) was placed over his well-polished head, his inner panic and turmoil was palpable. I could hear his voice rise and awaited the classic phrase, 'I'm a celebrity, get me out of here!!'

Graham asked to be let out of the branks. I'm not sure why, but he insisted.

'I want this thing off now! Like Right Now. Quickly – I *mean* it, Sam!!'

He was finally released and took a number of minutes, quietly huffing and puffing, one hand against the wall for support, all the time eyeballing me with simmering ire. As Graham's heart rate returned to normal and his beard debristled, Leonard recounted the tale of one of his ancestors – Besse Mason – who had been put to death by the descendants of the Lindsay family that owned Wormiston House. Sensing some excellent evening entertainment, I was keen to invite Leonard for dinner with the current laird of Wormiston, but Graham suggested otherwise, his face inches from mine, his finger stabbing me in the chest.

'That's not a good idea, Sam.'

GRAHAM

And speaking of shocks n' horrors it was only when I moved to Canada when I was seven years old that I discovered the joys of Halloween.

[*Sam: Wait! What? You're a lumberjack?!*]

Up to that point, it had passed without incident. Simply another day in the calendar that coincided with the clocks going back and plunging us into darkness for another six months.

Trick or treating was like a revelation to my seven-year-old self.

When it was explained to me what it involved, I couldn't actually believe it:

'So, I go out – in costume – with an empty pillow case and knock on people's doors. They then fill my pillow case with sweets (candy). I then go home and stuff myself until I vomit?'

I clearly remember that first time I went out. In those days, there was no question of being accompanied by an adult. This was kids only. Gangs of small children in search of a sugar rush, roaming the neighbourhood with sacks.

My first costume was a skeleton outfit. I recall feeling so excited.

Even though I obviously went out alone during the day at that age, it was perhaps the first time I'd been out at night without an adult.

But no one gave it a second thought. Children had no fear then, and if adults feared for them – well, they never showed it! My parents wished me a good evening and I set off in the neighbourhood in Vancouver where I lived (near Dunbar), and returned home probably ninety minutes later with a sack bulging with treats like some diabetic smorgasbord.

It has turned into one of my favourite days of the year. With children of my own, I love watching them roam the streets in search of treats. In New Zealand, where I live, all the children go, as one, and go to every house.

We did Halloween when my eldest was growing up in Santa Monica, and the effort some people put into their decorations was truly astonishing. Huge, elaborate structures, sound effects, jump-scares, gardens turned into makeshift graveyards. Amazing!

When I finally left Canada as a child after two years of joy, to return home to a non-trick-or-treat Britain, I looked sadly out of the window as the plane banked across the night sky, affording me a last view of the lights twinkling in my neighbourhood below.

The date I left? 31 October.

NATURE NOTES
AURORA BOREALIS (THE NORTHERN LIGHTS)

SAM

I've seen the Northern Lights in Galloway and when I was in the Arctic Circle. Utterly amazing to see and definitely one for the bucket list, autumn is the best time to see the Aurora Borealis in Scotland, because it's on the same latitude as Stavanger in Norway and Nunivak Island, Alaska.

These green and other worldly polar lights are not an organic firework show or 1990s disco, but instead are caused by solar winds disrupting the earth's magnetosphere and charging atmospheric particles within it to emit light of varying colour and complexity.

Top spots include: Shetland, Orkney, Caithness, North West Highlands, the Moray Coast, Outer Hebrides and the Isle of Skye.

GRAHAM

My one and only experience of seeing the Northern Lights was with my father. Dad had been a Second World War pilot and then joined civil aviation after the war. In 1968, he got a job with a Canadian airline and we emigrated to Canada to be all together. Living in Vancouver for the next couple of years was truly some of my happiest childhood memories.

When we emigrated, it was my dad who flew the plane. A 707, which at the time was the largest four-engine plane in the world.

In those days, flying was so exciting. No airport security, no X-rays , just glamorous people sitting in comfort (even in economy), being served actual food and drink. Back then, people always dressed up to go on a plane. I still do, which is a throwback to an earlier time (like me I suppose), while I am surrounded by people in shorts and flip flops.

During that flight I was invited up to the cockpit. (Again, in those days children were always invited to the cockpit.) I knew my dad was a pilot, of course, but it's only now, as an adult, that I truly appreciate how incredibly cool that was. My dad was FLYING the plane!

I stepped into the cockpit and saw the inky black sky surrounding the plane as it flew into the Arctic night. He invited me to look out to the right – and there was a truly unforgettable sight. The Aurora Borealis. The Northern Lights.

Like a veil of dancing light shimmering and shifting across the horizon, a dazzling otherworldly display of something so fantastical, it literally took my breath away.

I shall never forget it, and I'm so glad I got to share that moment with my dad at 37,000 feet as he flew us to our new home.

One day I want to see them again with my own children.

GREAT SCOT!

NOTABLE BIRTHDAYS, DEATHS AND SIGNIFICANT EVENTS

4 October 1821 – John Rennie died. Not the inventor of the indigestion preparation, but one of the best civil engineers of his era. He designed bridges, canals, docks and lighthouses.

5 October 1849 – The Ardnamurchan Lighthouse was illuminated for the first time. Designed by Alan Stevenson, uncle of Robert Louis Stevenson. Bit talented those Stevensons!

15 October 1902 – Edinburgh's Balmoral Hotel opened.

19 October 1954 – Actor Kenneth 'Ken' Campbell Stott born in Edinburgh.

GRAHAM

I worked with Ken Stott on *The Hobbit*. He played my elder brother Balin. Ken and I already knew each other from a pub in London that we both frequented in the late 1990s / early 2000s, called The Pineapple, on Leverton Street, in Kentish town. A great pub in those days.

Little did we know we'd end up playing brothers in Middle Earth.

One of the earliest scenes we shot was when we met in Bilbo's hobbit hole, Bag End. We wanted there to be an unusual greeting.

I went for it, picking Ken up off the ground and swinging him around like a toddler (I was particularly strong during *The Hobbit*). For some reason Ken didn't appreciate being swung around like a seven-year-old, so we ended up 'headbutting' each other instead. Much better!

Ken was amazing in the films, such a great actor, but he hated wearing prosthetics. Each day on wrap, Ken would immediately tear off his prosthetic nose.

After a while I followed suit and decided to hold on to my nose after filming. This led to an obsessive collecting of every

Dwarf nose on the movie (sometimes we got a bit bored, OK!?).

By the end I had every dwarf nose, plus Gandalf's nose and Bilbo's ears.

Weta Workshop very kindly mounted them all, like some macabre butterfly collection in a glass cabinet, which I have proudly displayed in my home in New Zealand.

28 October 1854 – The death in Dunkeld of Charles Edward Stuart, Count Roehenstart, the illegitimate son of the legitimised daughter of Charles Edward Stuart, better known as Bonnie Prince Charlie.

30 October 1822 – Caledonian Canal opened, linking Inverness to Fort William.

31 October 1765 – The Duke of Cumberland, aka Butcher Cumberland, died aged forty-four in London.

31 October 1745 – The Bonnie Prince and Jacobite army marched south from Edinburgh, disregarding advice to stay put in Scotland and wait for French support.

31 October 1888 – John Boyd Dunlop from Ayrshire patented pneumatic bicycle tyres for McTavish's comfort.

NOVEMBER

Clan Mackintosh
Motto: Touch not the cat bot a glove
[*Sam: Er, don't touch the cat's bottom but, if
you do, wear a glove? Makes sense.*]
Lands: Inverness-shire

KEY DATES

1	Samhain (end of harvest/beginning of winter)
11	Remembrance Sunday
25	Thanksgiving
30	St Andrew's Day – an excuse for a good cèilidh!

COMPETITION CORNER
CÈILIDH DANCING

SAM

As our journey through the seasons draws to a close, with Samhain marking the beginning of winter, so too must our rivalry cease. (For now.) I think there needs to be an acceptance that we are both good at different things and that's why we get on.

[*Graham: Absolutely. You can lift heavy things, I can quote Nietzsche (and hit a golf ball, kick a rugby ball and swing a hammer). But let's let bygones be bygones and draw a gentlemanly truce.*]

[*Sam: Yes, let's. And not mention again your gargantuan appetite, pointy toes, little blue shoes, and all the things you couldn't do, like abseil, surf and drink.*]

Except I think a few cliff-hangers for Graham would be hilarious in *Men in Kilts 2*, don't you? Shhh, don't tell him, but I'm thinking Graham skydiving in a kilt, or wing-walking across Shetland dressed as a sheep? A lion keeper for a day at Edinburgh Zoo, or a warder for a week at HM Prison Barlinnie (aka the Big Hoose!).

But one thing we both do well is dance. Well, I can dance. He thrusts a lot. It's very unsettling. Like a Gollum in pointy shoes! Cèilidh dancing is very different to formal Scottish reeling, (which is Highland dancing formalised by the Victorians), and is something we all grew up with and love. It's the community-based impromptu party, fuelled by whisky, with music, song, dancing and storytelling.

Only for *Men in Kilts* we had no whisky (for once) and I was complaining bitterly about it. But the music lifted our sober spirits and we were soon having fun and sweating tons. I lost my shoe, dancing partner and sense of direction, and Graham's shoes were coming undone, but he didn't care because he was captivated by Sophie-of-the-Green-Dress, the lead dancer of the Stockbridge Reelers attired in a beautiful gown, who was tall, elegant and exactly Graham's cup of Lady Grey tea.

Even as we were being taught the 'Dashing White Sergeant', which is a dance I know extremely well, Graham insisted on showing off his hip action by freestyling. Poor Sophie, subjected to the now infamous hip sway and thrust, right in front of her. We were all speechless, but maybe he thought she was impressed. He became a lot more animated and chatty, and his hips loosened up, which was impressive for a sexagenarian.

We both had to dance with Sophie at the same time, like some strange love triangle. I have to admit she had on a beautiful dress and looked very attractive, so we were both vying for her attention, with me not wanting to be outdone by ol' Snake Hips.

Her boyfriend was there (one of the other dancers) and he was far from happy. I felt bad for him. The whole time he never broke a smile, refusing to look us in the eye, and was quite rightly rather sulky. Sophie, however, was wonderfully sultry, playing up to us and watching us compete for her attention.

I had been taught the traditional Scottish dances at school, part of the school curriculum. As a teenager, I disliked the whole affair and was mortified by this organised 'fun', however, as an adult I love going to cèilidhs and they are the best part of any celebration, be it a wedding, New Year party, or impromptu knees-up. My uncle, he of the wicker variety, also has a cèilidh band called Two Left Feet, and they play all over Scotland.

It is fast, sweaty and breathless stuff, as the music swells and gets faster, the dancers are flung around the dance floor, and it can (and always will) be very chaotic. It's also the best way to sweat out some whisky. My favourite dance is 'Strip the Willow', which ends up like a group of whirling dervishes, spinning around each other, or is rather reminiscent of scenes from Robert Burns' Tam o' Shanter, with the devil leading the dance on the bagpipes.

GRAHAM

I'm beginning to get the feeling that Samwise is running out of things to feel competitive about. Competitive cèilidh dancing? Really?

My feelings about cèilidhs have always been that the goal is to have fun and enjoy oneself, rather than beat the other dancers. Perhaps I've been misguided all along. There was I, going to a cèilidh to swing myself and others around with joyful abandon, stomping and clapping and whooping in the spirit of collective delight – while all the time what I really should've been doing was following Sam's lead and crushing the other dancers with my competitive kilt swinging, in an effort to 'beat' them!

In essence, I feel that Sam is clutching at the proverbial straw. Having been beaten at so many things that actually fall within the realm of competition, he is now trying desperately to create competition out of anything at all. Things like weaving baskets and cèilidhs. Perhaps we should explore competitive brow-furrowing . . .

But in the spirit of competition, I am happy to agree that Sam is, indeed, cèilidh champion, if that restores some of his injured pride.

[*Sam: It's a win!*]

I can't remember my first cèilidh. (In fact, it is in the nature of cèilidhs NOT to remember them, simply because of the sheer amount of whisky consumed.)

One does stand out, though. It was on the Isle of Mull and

was the New Year's dance at Dervaig Town Hall in around 1992. We had arrived on the island on the boat that delivered the newspapers, early in the morning the day before. The skipper of the boat made the crossing at 7 a.m., already drunk, swigging from a bottle of single malt.

I should've known what Mull would deliver the next day. And it wasn't the papers!

I remember we had decided to get there early to get a seat and a quiet drink before things really kicked off.

We arrived at 7 p.m. (yes, five hours before midnight).

They were already five deep at the bar. There were no seats left. Just a scrum of booze-laden men and women milling around like a herd shortly before the stampede begins.

Men, and women, weren't even bothering with glasses; they were guzzling whisky straight from the bottle.

It was going to get messy.

The local farmers were there in force and proceeded to dance the various cèilidh reels with a passion and strength that beggared belief.

If this was a competition I was definitely losing.

I saw women thrown into the drum kit by the sheer power of the farmers' dance-style. Women with their ear rings torn from their ear lobes.

When I expressed concern to one woman, who was standing bleeding in front of me, she merely laughed, saying, 'Och, it's great!!!'

As Dougal MacKenzie's cocktail reviews would say, 'I have no recollection after 9 p.m. that evening.'

Another memorable cèilidh was in New Zealand during the filming of *The Hobbit*.

In one location where we were filming, there was a severe shortage of women so the local community chartered coaches from the nearest big town (Invercargill) to bus women into the cèilidh, in the hope of finding some willing brides for the priapic farming community of Central Otago.

The evening was like a repeat of Mull all over again, but with the added sexual tension of a bunch of lonely sheep farmers encountering women, as if they were some exotic lost tribe, in a dance hall with access to copious amounts of booze and ceaseless energy.

I tried to sit out most of the dances (after all, I had spent the day running all over the surrounding countryside wearing a 70lb costume being chased by imaginary Wargs).

The ladies of Invercargill were having none of it, however. One lovely woman strode over to me, uttering the fabulous line, 'Why aren't ya dancing? Are ya some kind of homo?!!!'

So I staggered to my feet and joined the fray.

Another evening that is blank from 9 p.m. onwards.

Suffice to say, the next morning Dwalin the Dwarf stumbled around the hillsides vainly contributing to a 750 million dollar trilogy of films feeling like an elephant had taken a gigantic dump in his head.

In comparison, the cèilidh at Borthwick Castle was a very mild affair. I do remember, however, that Sam and I both did most of the dancing with our laces undone!

Competitive shoe-tying anyone?

REGION OF THE MONTH
LOCHABER, FORT WILLIAN
AND THE GREAT GLEN

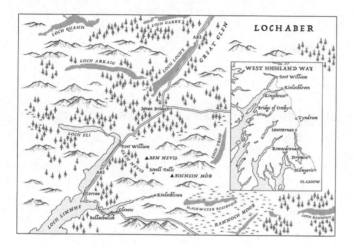

SAM

I've always been fascinated by Fort William. To be honest, despite being a bit of a mecca for tourists, the gateway to the North at the foot of Ben Nevis, and the end of the West Highland Way, it's rather a grey and dare I say, uninspired wee town. Translated from Gaelic as the 'Black Garrison', you begin to realise the town was taken over or developed by the British to have a strong and oppressive hold over the Highlands. It does, however, sit on the shores of Loch Linnhe and the Glen Nevis valley, home to Steall Falls. The nearby Nevis Range Mountain Resort has ski runs and a bunch of forest trails.

Loch Linnhe leads north-east into Loch Lochy and Loch Ness, following a geological fault known as the Great Glen Fault, creating a natural border that bisects the Scottish Highlands into the Grampian Mountains to the south-east and the Northwest Highlands to the north-west. The Great Glen or *An Glenn Mor* runs sixty-two miles across Scotland like a diagonal scar that separates Scotland into two sections. It's iconic and it felt like the appropriate name for my production company, The Great Glen Company, as we celebrate the heritage and pride of Scottish produce: from whisky, tartan and tweed products, to *Men in Kilts* and TV production. Graham: And there was me thinking all this time it was named after your cousin Glen whom you thought was great.

ADVENTURE OF THE MONTH
BEN NEVIS

GRAHAM

I have climbed Ben Nevis. Twice. It is the highest mountain in Britain. 4413 feet, or 1345 metres. So it is a comfort to me that despite the fact that Sam has climbed many more mountains than me in Scotland, whenever he has stood at the summit of one of them, I have always been standing that little bit higher up.

The first time I climbed Ben Nevis was in my twenties (and, no, Sam, I wasn't wearing a tweed suit and hobnail boots). I do remember, however, seeing a few people on that climb wearing flip flops, which even to an inexperienced climber such as myself seemed a tad rash.

I went with some friends, and it was a spur of the moment thing. We might've taken some food (probably jam sandwiches wrapped in tin foil), but we might not have. I do have a reputation for being woefully under-prepared for this sort of thing. I almost certainly didn't have a proper backpack, or wet weather gear. I was probably wearing only shorts, a T-shirt, and plimsolls. Such is the ridiculous optimism of youth (that and a cavalier disregard for common sense). In those days I don't think Gore-Tex existed. I remember the backpack I owned was more like a small, dismantled iron gate with canvas stretched over it.

I imagine the 'climbing section' of Sam's wardrobe covers several cubic metres: crampons, gaiters, various fleece-lined coats, a waterproof jacket that reduces to the size of a teaspoon, plus a teaspoon that probably reduces to something at sub-atomic size. I can see it now, colour-coded garments for every conceivable weather encounter. Merino clothing layers that amount to the shearing of an entire flock of sheep, various walking/climbing boots tailored to the terrain, head torches, ice axes, signal flares, emergency freeze-dried rations, and perhaps his own team of huskies. (In short, everything that was missing from Scott of the Antarctic's expedition to the South Pole.)

It was a hot day during that first ascent, and I remember not feeling at all tired. (Well, I was only about twenty-five.) Considering it was in the 1980s, it's highly likely that everyone else doing the climb that day was smoking like a chimney and guzzling cans of cheap lager for hydration.

While 'Ben' is from the Gaelic for 'mountain', the origin of 'Nevis' is unclear. It could mean 'Heaven', 'Venomous', 'Cloudy', or even 'God'. Take your pick.

Weather-wise, Ben Nevis can be a bit tricky. It has around 261 gales a year with 4350 mm of rain (or 171 inches). Compare that to London, which gets 23 inches a year, or even Fort William, which is right next to the mountain (81 inches), and you can see that Ben Nevis is very wet and very, very windy.

Like any moody companion, Ben Nevis can change in a matter of moments from warm sun and T-shirt weather to freezing cold, lashing rain, and dense fog.

The second time I went was as part of a series of hikes for a company called iFit. They asked me to do fifteen hikes around Scotland, where I would be followed by a POV camera and a skeleton crew. It was my job to talk to the camera about anything and everything that came into my head on the hikes, in order to provide an immersive experience for the user, who would be accompanying me on the walk from their very sophisticated treadmill. By the end, I think I was talking about my favourite colour or the last time I'd cut my toenails, as I had exhausted every topic I could think of.

When we left the hotel, the weather did not look good. The forecast was almost zero visibility accompanied by horizontal rain.

But once we began the climb, the fickle weather gods decided to shine. We ascended the mountain in gorgeous sunshine with very little wind, affording us sweeping views all over the Grampian region. It really was magical. I even managed to do it in a kilt.

The descent was, in some ways, harder than the climb up, as my 58-year-old knees took a pounding with every downward step. Our cameraman and stills photographer, along with Nicky Holender, my trainer and companion for the day, decided to RUN down the mountain.

The cameraman and photographer were both ultra-marathon runners, and set off like mountain goats down the steep slope that I was picking my way down as if I was in high heels.

But, for that moment at the top, when you're standing on a rocky plateau of 100 acres seeing for 120 miles in any direction, the climb was definitely worth every creaky step. As I contemplated the fact that I was at the highest point of land for 459 miles in any direction, I realised childishly that wherever Sam Heughan was in Britain . . . I was looking down upon him.

CLAN CAMERON

SAM

One of the most ancient of the Highland clans, the Camerons are thought to descend from the Danish king, Camchron. Well, that's one theory. Another is that there was an ancestor with a crooked nose (an early rugby player?), who kicked the whole surname off. *Cam* is Gaelic for crooked (like the Shinty stick name 'caman'), which is how the Campbells allegedly got their name – being seen as untrustworthy from playing politics. So Campbell translates loosely as crooked mouth in Gaelic, as *beul* is mouth.

Legend has it that the first Cameron wasn't a Celt but British (or maybe Scandinavian) and came from Dunbartonshire, to the west of Glasgow. He was a bit of a lad and a 'bonnie fechter', and as a result had his nose bent out of shape in one too many dust-ups. Having been demoted to 'the second hardest man in Dunbartonshire', old crooked nose moved to Lochaber and, after a wee while, pretty much owned the joint, amassing vast swathes of land over generations. The Cameron estate at Achnacarry is 60,000 acres in size, even today!

Like all clans there are plenty of other theories of Cameron family origins, the real genesis most likely lost in the mists of the Lochaber landscape and the murky waters of time. A clan described as 'fiercer than fierceness itself', we met the current Cameron Chief and 27th Lochiel, Donald Angus Cameron, on our *Clanlands* adventures. A mild and spritely man – who was not remotely fearsome – he hosted us at Achnacarry Castle and invited us to look round the Clan Cameron Museum which, if you ever find yourself travelling down the Great Glen, is well worth a visit.

CRACKING CASTLE OF THE MONTH
ACHNACARRY CASTLE

SAM

On the banks of the Loch and River Arkaig is the ancestral seat of the Camerons – Achnacarry Castle. It was burned down by government forces in the aftermath of the Battle of

Culloden, the Gentle Lochiel having pledged his allegiance to the Bonnie Prince. Many years later, the castle was rebuilt and eventually played a pivotal role in the Second World War, becoming the first ever British Commando Basic Training Centre for four years (1942–46). About 25,000 commandos (the bravest and best of fighting men – think Special Forces level) and personnel completed their training here, including Sir Simon Fraser, 15th Lord Lovat, the military legend who instructed Bill Millins to play the bagpipes during the Allied Invasion of Normandy in 1944 (see JUNE).

With Ben Nevis only eighteen miles away, the Lochaber landscape proved the perfect perilous terrain on which to train these men to defeat the German foe. A few miles from the castle, just above the village of Spean Bridge, is the Commando Memorial, overlooking some of the treacherous training grounds, the Nevis range looming down ominously. The memorial is a reminder of their endeavours because, like the Highlander warriors before them, these men were a breed apart.

One Second World War veteran who had a great impact on me (and whom I portrayed in the film *First Light*) was Geoffrey Wellum. Not a commando, Geoffrey was a Battle of Britain legend and the youngest Spitfire pilot in the Second World War. He was energetic and incredibly humble, never thinking of himself as a hero, which of course he was. He hid the internal stress and loss of his friends with great dignity and was very supportive during my time studying him for my role.

One of the high points in *First Light* was learning how to fly a Spitfire. I was shown how to take off, land and perform evasive manoeuvres, just as Geoffrey had during his time with 92 Squadron, with only the use of a basic manual! I was proud when shooting the start-up sequence, after having studied the manual myself, to actually fire up the Rolls-Royce Merlin engine. It stuttered then . . . yes . . . exploded into life – exhilarating stuff.

Like a high-end performance car with wings and machine guns, these planes were a major part of aiding the British to victory in the Battle of Britain, along with the selfless and dedicated young men who piloted them. They were left to figure it out for themselves and if they came back alive, they'd graduate to pilot. Their sense of duty and sacrifice is hard to comprehend and it truly was an honour to portray Geoffrey.

My grandpa Ginge was a soldier in the Second World War, but was medically discharged during a training exercise that caused him to break his leg. However, I believe he was sent to Africa along with some other family members to serve for a time. They never really spoke about their experiences, though one relation of mine was so horribly burnt by the African sun that he still bears the scars on his head today, at the age of ninety-four.

My understanding of the Second World War was enhanced by my role in *Island at War*, my first TV job after leaving drama school, for the ITV channel in 2003. It was a poignant story about the German occupation of the Channel Islands told through various families and their relationships with the occupying forces. I played Philip Dorr, an undercover Special Forces operative, sent back to the islands to do reconnaissance. Whilst back on the island, he unwittingly forged a wary friendship or respect for the German commander, played by the excellent Philip Glenister.

Despite filming in the Isle of Man, it was harrowing and striking to see the small fishing villages and towns converted into German-occupied Britain. The production had organised large swastikas to be hanging from the town hall and a procession of hobnailed German soldiers marching through the town. It must have been terrifying for the locals, so close to the shores of the mainland, to see the might of the German army present on their small islands. Even more fascinating to witness were the relationships, and in some cases, respect that developed from both sides for each other. It was my first TV job and I learnt a lot, working with a remarkable group of actors. And, speaking of actors . . .

Graham, what did you do in the war? Were you in the Home Guard like Captain Mainwaring in *Dad's Army*? You must have been in the armoured pram division at least . . .!

15 November 1915 - David Stirling, founder
of the SAS, born in Perthshire.

SAM

Lieutenant Colonel Sir Archibald David Stirling, DSO,
OBE, British Army Officer, mountaineer and founder of
the Special Air Service (SAS), was born in Lecropt,
Perthshire, in 1915. He established the SAS in July 1941,
around the same time the Commando Training centre was
set up at Achnacarry. This was by no means a coincidence,
because a range of special units were created at that time,
by order of Prime Minister Winston Churchill, to
undertake daring operations against enemy forces. Men
like David Stirling and Roger Courtney, who established
the Special Boat Service (SBS), wanted to find a new way of
waging war.

By selecting like-minded and extraordinary individuals,
they could train for, plan and carry out their own operations.
And their key supporter, Winston Churchill, wilfully
overruled the army top brass to give these Special Forces the
funding and autonomy they required.

These small raiding units proved deadly and effective,
sabotaging communications and attacking enemy airfields
and ports in the dead of night. During their Second World
War operations in North Africa, they destroyed over 300
enemy aircraft and were a snip of the price of running a
battalion. The former Irish Lions rugby player, Lieutenant
Colonel 'Jock' Lewes, who embodied the SAS training and
ethos, personally destroyed more enemy planes than a single
Royal Air Force (RAF) fighter pilot.

The SAS and other Special Forces units are still in
operation today and only a very few service personnel
succeed in passing the gruelling selection process, including a
test called 'Endurance', which is a forty-mile march up and
over Pen y Fan in the Brecon Beacons in under twenty hours,
carrying a 75lb pack.

Successful candidates receive a sandy beret with a winged
dagger badge and SAS parachute wings to become a member

of one of the world's elite fighting forces, a blueprint for other Special Forces units such as Delta Force and US Navy Seals.

David Stirling died on 4 November 1990.

Strangely, I have a very tenuous connection to David Stirling – not only via my Andy McNab film *SAS Red Notice*, but also through his great-niece Rachael Stirling, an actor with whom I shared a manager (and a few glasses of wine). Part of acting royalty, her mother was Dame Diana Rigg and her father was Archie Stirling, a Scottish theatrical producer and Laird of the Keir estate at Lecropt, where his uncle David Stirling was born. There is also a statue to Sir David Stirling that we pass by on most days shooting *Outlander*, as it stands on a promontory overlooking the rolling hills of Stirling and the secret location of Fraser's Ridge and the Big House.

As I said, I made a film in 2020 called *SAS Red Notice*, released on 12 March 2021 worldwide, based on Andy McNab's bestselling novel of the same name. I immediately loved the script, which was written by Andy McNab and Laurence (Larry) Malkin. They both invited me to dinner at a Michelin-starred restaurant (of which Graham would have approved), and we spent the evening discussing the British military and the nature of psychopaths. Andy is a self-confessed psychopath – he even wrote a book called *The Good Psychopath's Guide to Success* – and my character, Tom Buckingham, is built in his mould.

Essentially he is a good psychopath, who has to pretend to exhibit emotions such as love. It was so layered – I was an actor pretending to play a guy who has to pretend to feel something, psychopaths being devoid of emotions – which is quite a challenge!

The story begins when Tom takes his girlfriend to Paris to propose, and the train is taken over by criminals in the Channel Tunnel. With hundreds of hostages' lives at stake, Tom is their only hope, but he's unarmed and cut off from his Special Forces team. The set was amazing, the action incredible and so much fun. Andy was there every day overseeing the combat training. It was every boy's dream to be moving around in a tactical unit, clearing out the bad guys. And my cast mates of Ruby Rose, Tom Hopper and Hannah John Karmen made it a truly great experience. Who doesn't want to blow up a train and fight baddies?

DRAM OF THE MONTH
DRUNKFAST

GRAHAM

Bit of a gear change, but I have chosen this book to announce my own drink. Sam has inspired me in so many ways, but none more so than his ruthless and fanatical devotion to flogging his own whisky (and SAS films). So I thought it was about time I did something similar.

I considered Rum (too piratey), vodka (too Russian), crème de menthe (too disgusting), so I have finally settled on the following.

Its main ingredient is 'Buckfast'. For those who have not had the pleasure, Buckfast is a version of red wine mixed with caffeine. As we mentioned earlier, it was invented by Benedictine monks in the 1880s and until recently was made by the monks of Buckfast Abbey, where a Saturday night was no doubt a memorable experience.

It's not exactly a wine, instead it is unfermented grape juice fortified with ethanol (which is an industrial chemical used as a solvent and added to gasoline). Caffeine is then added.

Buckfast or 'Buckie' is credited with multiple acts of epic self-destruction, inducing complete memory loss coupled with unbridled debauchery.

It has my name written all over it.

But to make it uniquely mine, I'm adding my 'secret' ingredients of lighter fluid and deck sealant to give it a distinctive 'nose'.

To borrow from Sam's glowing description of 'Sasquatch', or whatever his whisky is called, I would describe it as follows:

> I mature it in oil drums so the underlying industrial character is at the forefront. The nose is packed with creosote, cough medicine and the aromas of a construction yard, the mouthfeel of cotton wool, galvanised steel, rotting fruit and the unmistakable fragrance of a cornered wolverine, it repeatedly slaps the tongue and then crescendos and surrenders to a follow-through of amnesia and the symptoms of a massive stroke.

I'm calling it 'DRUNKFAST'.

[*Sam: I like it.*]

I haven't settled on a label yet, but any suggestions are very welcome. I'm considering a tasteful silhouette of a man crouched over a toilet bowl? Or a portrait of Lacroix? Which, come to think of it, amounts to the same thing.

I've had a few test runs with friends and I've had some glowing reviews, see below:

'I have no clue about anything after eight o'clock yesterday, Graham. Thanks, mate.' *S. W., Liverpool.*

'Woke up with my head down the toilet, sweating uncontrollably, with a house full of dead plants. What a drink!!!' *G. O'R., Edinburgh.*

'I went to the family Christmas and woke up in a Turkish prison with a full beard and an enormous number of Russian mafia tattoos all over my body. I would recommend "Drunkfast" to anyone.' *S. H., Glasgow.*

'I am now working as a goatherd in Libya, having no memory of the previous six months, and I live with about two dozen cats and a pot-bellied pig. I can't thank you enough, Graham, for bringing "Drunkfast" into my life.' *T. M., Libya.*

'Drinking "Drunkfast" was a near-death experience. All my hair has fallen out and my body has erupted in boils. I cannot remember my own name. Wow!!! Thank you!!'
Anonymous.

[*Sam: Coming soon to a store near you . . . Er, sounds delicious, but stick with the white wine spritzer, please!*]

BATTLE OF THE MONTH
THE THIRD BATTLE OF YPRES (AKA THE BATTLE OF PASSCHENDAELE) 31 JULY–10 NOVEMBER 1917

GRAHAM

It may appear that I am obsessed with the fighting prowess of the Highlander. I confess that I am. There is a strong thread that runs through the history of the Highlander that connects him to the mad-dog savagery of William Wallace, right through to the First and Second World Wars and then everything in-between.

One such example is the third battle of Ypres in 1917.

Basically after Culloden, the Highlander became the go-to choice of the British Army when it came to kicking the enemy repeatedly in the balls.

Seringapatam, Assaye, the Plains of Abraham, Waterloo, Ypres, Lucknow, the list goes on and on and on.

At Ypres, two Highlanders won the Victoria Cross on the same day in July.

Alexander Edwards was twenty-nine when he joined up in 1914, practically an old man!

He survived the Somme, becoming a sergeant, but then he was sent home on leave with a raw throat infection! Which no doubt was a gigantic, mega source of embarrassment to such a monumental warrior as Alexander. Meanwhile two other members of his family, brother John and cousin George, won the Military Medal and also the Distinguished Service Order, the latter for capturing 200 Germans single-handedly.

Dinner at the Edwards' home must've been a lively affair.

'Two hundred?!!! I dinnae get out of bed unless I'm slaughtering five hundred in a day!!!'

'What sent you home, Alexander?'

'Throat infection.'

'Bwaaaaaa!!!!!!!!! Pass the salt, you complete Jessie!!!'

But Edwards returned in time for Ypres. On 31 July, he attacked along with his regiment the Seaforth Highlanders, and was ordered to take out enemy positions on the banks of a stream.

The weather was horrendous. Torrential rain and boggy mud hampered the advance. To a fella like Alexander, this was probably a typical balmy summer's day on the Moray Firth.

Seeing that they were getting nowhere, he crept forwards and found a particularly irritating German machine-gun emplacement.

Armed with only two revolvers and a massive dose of bad-assery, Alexander walked into the gun emplacement and immediately shot dead the German on the machine gun, and then used the rest of his bullets to kill the rest of the crew inside. When they were finished, he probably used the revolvers as clubs.

It was then that he realised he'd been injured by a sniper's bullet.

At this point, most normal individuals would call it a day. But not Alexander Edwards!

He decided this sniper had to go.

Ignoring his wound, in the words of his medal citation, he 'crawled out to stalk him'.

If only the poor German had realised what manner of man was stalking him. A man for whom creeping up on his enemy and silently murdering him was woven deep into his

DNA. It was possibly a Sunday afternoon pastime around the Moray Firth. Perhaps straight after church?

Alexander hunted the doomed sniper across open ground and in his line of fire, until he got close enough to finish him off.

A bit like Grandmother's Footsteps, except in this case, grandmother gets bayoneted to death and chokes on her own blood.

While Edwards was laying waste to Deutschland single-handedly, another Highlander, Private George McIntosh, was getting busy.

He was in the 1/6th Battalion of the Gordon Highlanders (as you will have deduced, the Highlanders could never get enough of stacking up the corpses).

He and his comrades came under withering machine-gun fire on the morning of 31 July. To put it in context, the German Maxim machine gun could fire between 450–500 rounds per minute.

Rather than shelter with his comrades from this hail of lead, McIntosh ran towards the guns.

The sight of a single figure sprinting towards them in a kilt armed with only a revolver and a single grenade must have flabbergasted the Germans. But not enough to stop them shooting at him.

Probably while bellowing the McIntosh war cry, 'Loch Moigh!', bullets ripped through his backpack and tattered his kilt.

Undeterred, McIntosh leapt from crater to crater until he reached the machine gun. The terrified Germans threw up their hands in despairing surrender, but George was in no mood for mercy. He tossed in the grenade, killing two of them, while he watched the rest flee in terror from his mythic presence.

He then picked up the two machine guns (each weighing 60 pounds), and put one on his shoulder and one under this arm and walked calmly back to his own men.

(I think we should challenge Sam to do this next season, but only after I've been repeatedly shoot at him for ten minutes.)

When asked why he took it upon himself single-handedly to attack two machine guns, his response was typical in its Highland brevity: 'Somebody had to gae forrit.' He also knew he could throw a grenade further than anyone else (probably while bench-pressing a horse with his spare arm).

Meanwhile back with Alexander Edwards, we find him opposite several enemy strong points. When he found out that a major from his cavalry unit was lying badly wounded in no-man's-land, he ran out to get him and carry him back.

At this point, Edwards was soaked in his own blood, and received another piece of red hot shrapnel in his knee.

Swathed in blood, barely able to walk, Edwards simply explained his motivation to the other men: 'If I had not gone on, it would not have given the boys much encouragement . . . the wound on my arm was worse, the sleeve was torn from my tunic, my hose tops were down over my boots, and I was covered with mud. Oh, what a game . . .'

Oh what a game!???

Just remember, if you are of Highland descent, the blood of people like George McIntosh and Alexander Edwards flows through your veins.

Alba gu bràth!! Scotland forever indeed.

NATURE NOTES
THE POPPY

SAM

The common poppy (*Papaver rhoeas*), also called the field poppy or corn poppy, flowers all year round in Scotland and across Britain, and is used as a symbol of remembrance to honour those who fell in the First and Second World Wars and other conflicts. It also signifies hope for a peaceful future.

In the First World War, owing to extensive ground disturbance, the soil churned by a myriad of explosions, poppies bloomed in no-man's-land and between the trench lines of the Western Front in France. A Canadian doctor of Scottish descent, Lieutenant Colonel John McCrae, was moved by these humble, scarlet flowers flourishing amidst the carnage of war, and in 1915, after losing a friend at the battle of Ypres, he wrote 'In Flanders Fields'.

In Flanders Fields
In Flanders fields the poppies blow
Between the crosses, row on row,
That mark our place: and in the sky
The larks, still bravely singing, fly
Scarce heard amid the guns below.

We are the dead. Short days ago
We lived, felt dawn, saw sunset glow,
Loved and were loved, and now we lie
In Flanders fields.

Take up our quarrel with the foe;
To you from failing hands we throw
The torch; be yours to hold it high,
If ye break faith with us who die
We shall not sleep, though poppies grow
In Flanders fields.
John McCrae, 1915

GREAT SCOT!

NOTABLE BIRTHDAYS, DEATHS AND SIGNIFICANT EVENTS

11 November 1918 – Armistice Day: the First World War ended on the 11th hour of the 11th day of the 11th month.

12 November 1869 – Edinburgh University became the first academic institution to permit women to study medicine.

SAM

Women were permitted to study medicine at Edinburgh University, but not to graduate. However, one intrepid woman gained a medical degree from Edinburgh in 1812 under the name of Dr James Barry, and went on to become an army surgeon!

I'm sad that I don't have an honorary degree from Edinburgh, I'm afraid Glasgow and Stirling Universities got there first, but I'm always open to another doctorate. Perhaps Edinburgh would be so kind? Even if it is only to wind up Graham, who is deeply offended that he has to call me Doctor, Doctor Heughan.

[*Graham: I'm curious what the 'honorary degrees' are in honour of . . . an intensive three-year degree in deadlifts? Services to the Ginger Community? In recognition of his contribution to body waxing?*]

[*Sam: Film and charitable work. My body has never been waxed. Well, once.*]

13 November 1850 – Novelist and poet Robert Louis Stevenson born in Edinburgh.

13 November 1939 – The first bombs dropped on British soil in the Second World War fell on the Shetland Islands.

GRAHAM

I honestly did not know that the first bombs dropped on British soil landed on the Shetland Islands. [*Sam: They must have had something against sheep? Thankfully they did zero damage, apart from one unsuspecting, poor wee rabbit.*]

The Luftwaffe certainly spent a great deal of time after that dropping them all over Britain, with the London blitz lasting between May and September 1940. France had just fallen and Britain was alone in Europe to face the Nazi threat. Looking back, it is truly incredible that Britain survived.

It came down to a combination of hubris on the part of the Luftwaffe and Hermann Goering, the decision by Hitler to invade Russia in 1941 (very big mistake), and perhaps most importantly, the galvanising leadership of Winston Churchill and the sheer grit of the British people.

My mother joined the WAAF (the Women's Auxiliary Air Force) in 1941, where she became an engine fitter on aircraft, and helped to deploy the huge barrage balloons all over the skies of London. She chose the Air Force because, as she put it, 'they had the best uniform'. It seems as good a reason as any.

Before she was in the Air Force, she worked at an umbrella factory in Wood Street in the City of London. She told me that one day she got the two trams and a bus from her parents' house in Lewisham into the City. When she got there, the entire street had been destroyed in a bombing raid the night before. It was now an enormous pile of rubble. The umbrella factory had been levelled.

When she told me, I imagined the trauma, the tears of an eighteen-year-old seeing this devastation. I gently asked her what she did.

'Well, there was nothing TO do. I just got back on the bus and went home.' Such a remark epitomises the attitude of that generation, I think. They simply got on with life.

On another occasion, she was with her family crammed in the air raid shelter in their garden, when a bomb landed so close by that it blew the air raid warden through the door and onto her lap.

He survived intact, but again, when I asked whether she was scared, she said, 'I was more worried that a strange man was on my lap.'

My Uncle Tommy, her brother, was in the Royal Navy and piloted a landing craft on to Sword Beach during D-Day under fire. He survived that day with only a broken nose for an injury.

My Aunt May, my father's sister, was also in the WAAF. My dad joined the RAF in May 1942 at the age of twenty, having suspended his apprenticeship as a printer. Starting out as an engineer in the Air Force, as the demand for pilots grew, my father volunteered to train. He learned to fly on Stearman biplanes in Pensacola Florida with the US Marine Corps, having sailed to America on the *Queen Mary* when it was commandeered as a troop ship. When you consider the dangers of the North Atlantic at the time, even the crossing must have been terrifying.

He returned to fly Lancaster bombers as the war drew to a close. He never spoke about the war (like so many men and women). At the end of the conflict he was sent to RAF Valley in Anglesey, Wales, where he met my mother at a dance.

He saw her on the dance floor and asked his sergeant who she was.

'Oh, that's Ellen Alexander. But don't bother, she's engaged,' came the reply.

'I'm still going to ask her to dance.'

Six months later, they were married. I still have the letter she wrote to him on the eve of their wedding, framed and hanging on my wall at home. It's one of the most romantic things I've ever read.

They stayed together for the next fifty-seven years, until he passed away in 2003. During this time he re-joined the RAF, flew coastal patrols during the Cold War, and then joined the fledgling civil aviation business and flew all over the world. After his retirement, he taught London bus drivers how to fly. Truly, a full life!

My mother's last words to him, when we went to view his body at the funeral home, were, 'You promised me an adventure, Alec, and you gave me one.'

15 November 1873 - A statue to Greyfriars Bobby was unveiled at Greyfriars Kirkyard.

SAM

Ah, the poor wee 'dug'. Outside Greyfriars Kirk, an ancient graveyard and church in Edinburgh city centre, stands a bronze statue of a diminutive Skye terrier. 'Bobby' was the faithful dog to a local policeman, who in the 1850s would patrol the streets with his master. They trudged through the snow and dirt of Edinburgh, season after season, year after year. Unfortunately, John the policeman died of tuberculosis and was duly buried in the Kirkyard.

Heartbroken and missing his owner, the wee dog kept watch, laying on his master's grave every day, only leaving for a wee spot for lunch at one o'clock (he was a very punctual dog). The whole of Edinburgh got to know him and Bobby became a personality, remaining loyal to his master for fourteen years, never leaving his grave. Even now, his statue keeps watch over the graveyard, his wee nose golden, where the locals and tourists have rubbed it for good luck. I'm tearing up . . .

24 November 1942 – Comedian and actor Billy Connolly was born. The Big Yin!

30 November – St Andrew's Day, the patron saint of Scotland. Another excuse for a party.

30 November 1957 – Actor Gary Lewis (Stevenson) born in Glasgow. 'My man, gies a hug!'

DECEMBER

KEY DIARY DATES

METEOROLOGICAL START OF WINTER: 1 December–28 February

1   Start of Winter

11   National Christmas Jumper Day

21   Yule/Winter Solstice (astronomical start of winter)

      Release of Text for You, my rom com with Priyanka Chopra and Celine Dion.

25   Christmas Day

28   Duncan Lacroix's Birthday (born in 1971)

31   Hogmanay (New Year's Eve)

REGION OF THE MONTH

GLASGOW

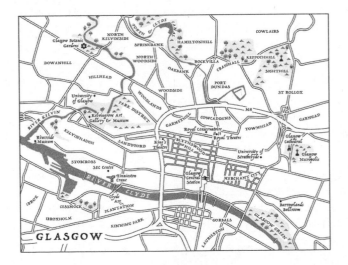

SAM

Glasgow, a city of 800,000 people (300,000 more than the
capital Edinburgh), which has forged many a hot-headed
Scot, including my sidekick Graham. It's a city I have lived in
for the past ten years, ever since I landed the role of Jamie
Fraser, in fact. I first visited 'Glasgee' as a teenager to attend
my first concert, to see the Silencers playing at the
Barrowlands, a famous dance hall, made from wood with
incredible acoustics. I distinctly remember a pre-show libation
in a Weegie Bar that had sawdust on the floor, to soak up the
spilled booze. And blood. Or perhaps my memory is fading, a
bit like McTavish's around the time the bill is brought over.

I attended the Royal Scottish Academy of Music and
Drama (now the Royal Conservatoire) for a three-year degree
in Classical Acting. Shakespeare, Stanislavsky, Meisner,
Chekhov, etc. Graham: 'Cough'. As you can see, I've used all
these techniques in *Men in Kilts*, although Graham still holds
the Medal of Merit for Mime. It's a great city, despite my
being originally from Edinburgh, which is perhaps more
dramatic and beautiful. It's the people that make Glasgow the
place I currently call home.

The River Clyde and the Kelvin cut through the city, with
the bohemian West End being a wonderful place to find a
good coffee shop or art gallery. It does, however, rain literally
every day, being on the west coast, but that doesn't dampen
the locals' spirits. The taxi drivers are the most chatty, so be
prepared to tell them your life story and opinions on Scottish
Independence or the football scores, whilst travelling down
Sauchiehall Street. I love the Kelvingrove Art Gallery and
Museum (where we held our first MPC Gala, next to the
stuffed animals and ancient artifacts) and the park, a
wonderful place during the rare summers days to relax on the
grass and people watch. Glasgow also happens to be only a
45-minute drive to Loch Lomond and the Arrochar Alps, the
first of the lowland Munros, so it's an ideal location for a
weekend adventure.

GRAHAM

Now that our sporting competitions have come to a close for now (though God knows what that ginger madman has up his sleeve for next year), I thought it would be good fun to compare our Christmas pantomime experiences in the month of December. Pantomime is a singularly British experience with elaborate, crude, garish and OTT entertainment aimed at . . . children! I'm not sure where pantomime was invented, perhaps England, maybe Italy, but whoever did invent it never imagined it being performed in the Gorbals district of Glasgow (a tough, impoverished area), at the Citizens Theatre in front of 600 feral school kids.

For those unfamiliar with 'panto' as it is known, it is the traditional theatre performed at Christmas and New Year. It's often a family occasion. For some it is their first exposure to live theatre, for many it is often their last.

[*Sam: He's BEHIND you!!!!*]

The really traditional style involves the re-telling of favourite fairy tales, 'Cinderella', 'Sleeping Beauty', 'Babes in the Wood', 'Aladdin', and so on.

One of the many things that distinguish traditional panto from regular theatre is that the lead 'hero' (Aladdin, Peter Pan, Robin Hood) is played by a woman, known as a 'principal boy'. At the same time, the villainous female roles (the Ugly Sisters, or any 'Dame' character) are played by, you guessed it . . . men. Very forward thinking.

Before you ask, no – I have never played Dame, although Ian McKellen fulfilled a lifelong ambition to play Dame at the Old Vic in London not so long ago. I hear he was very good.

Panto has always been particularly popular in Scotland. There are many true panto stars, not reality-show wannabes like in England, but professional actors who make an incredible living every year playing in these eagerly anticipated productions.

I'm not sure why Scotland holds panto so dear to its heart, but it certainly does.

The other thing that distinguishes panto from regular theatre is that it is truly interactive. It positively encourages the audience to shout out, sing along, boo, cheer and generally make as much noise as possible. In that sense, it really harkens back to the origins of theatre, when audiences often called out advice to the actors, or let their views be known on what was happening in front of them. (This happened to me performing in a women's prison and an institution for the criminally insane – but more of that another time!)

Which brings me neatly back to Glasgow. Not that I'm comparing the panto at the Citizens Theatre to a lunatic asylum but . . . you get the idea.

At the time I performed there in 1992, the Citizens Theatre (or the Citz as it was fondly known), was run by a wonderful triumvirate of Giles Havergal, Philip Prowse and Robert David MacDonald. Giles did the panto, among much else. He loved panto. He saw in it the purity of theatre, and as a way of bringing young people in to enjoy live performance.

[*Sam: I performed in Giles's last Panto/Christmas show. I do hope it wasn't my performance that put him off.*]

The Citz was a theatre of major European significance. These three openly gay men transformed a run-down building from the 1970s onwards and turned it into an award-winning theatre of excellence known all over the world. And they did it in one of THE most deprived neighbourhoods in Scotland – the Gorbals.

The area was well-known for violence, razor gangs, chronic unemployment and deprivation.

But Giles, Philip and David gave the community something to be proud of and to love.

I was once stopped at night, walking through a literal wasteland on the way to perform there, by a gang of decidedly unfriendly youths. Basically, I was about to be mugged.

They asked me where I thought I was going. They may also have called me a 'wanker' and/or 'a bastard'. When I told them I was on my way to do a play at the Citz, their attitude changed completely.

They insisted on escorting me safely to the stage door. They asked me what play I was doing, and generally enthused about the building, calling out 'Good luck!' as we parted. It fair brings a tear to your eye . . .

All of this is by way of background, to give you a sense of the place this theatre held in the community and the importance of panto.

I went on to perform in a number of productions at the Citz in regular plays, *Romeo and Juliet* and *Don Juan*, as well as my own play about Vincent Van Gogh, but my first experience of treading those hallowed boards was in *Pinocchio*, directed by Giles himself.

I was chosen to play the villain, Bragonzi – the evil puppeteer (no surprise there). I knew a good friend who had played the same role at the Citz many years earlier.

'Any advice?' I asked him.

'Wear a cricket box around your balls.'

That should have told me a lot.

It was an amazing baptism of panto fire. We rehearsed for two and a half weeks, then opened to full houses every night. There was a live band and they would play the introduction (to get the audience worked up) while the curtain was down. Behind the curtain stood Pinocchio himself. I shall call him Colin, to preserve his anonymity. He would stand, every performance, dressed as Pinocchio behind the curtain, shouting abuse at the audience and giving them the finger. Obviously they couldn't see him or hear him (over the band), but as soon as the curtain flew up, he WAS Pinocchio! All jerky wooden arms and legs. The kids loved him. It just so happened that he HATED them!

My role as the evil puppeteer required the audience to hate ME. Which they did.

I would have coins thrown at me, when I wasn't being called a bastard by five-year-olds.

During the show there is what is called 'the run around'. At this point the 'hero' and 'villain' run into the audience themselves. I chase Pinocchio and the kids go crazy. Lots of fun!!

Except . . . no.

Because there are three levels to the audience (stalls, circle and upper circle), there had to be three sets of heroes and villains. I ran around the stalls, while my 'doubles' entertained the other two levels.

As I ran into the audience that first time, I finally understood my friend's advice, as my balls were subjected to repeated punching by the small curled fists of seven- and eight-year-olds, shouting, 'Take that, Bragonzi, ya fuckin bastard!'

The poor guy who doubled me in the upper circle had it even worse. These were the cheap seats, where he was frequently dragged to the ground and subjected to a savage beating, until the usherettes hauled the primary-school children off him.

Whenever I ran into those audiences, for some reason I found myself thinking of landing craft at D-Day. All that was missing were the machine guns (which I have no doubt the kids would've brought in, if they possibly could).

[*Sam: I used to go every year as a boy scout to watch the Citz Pantos and have a vague recollection of a campy actor, running away from our group of boisterous juvenile delinquents.*]

We were equipped with radio mikes (to ensure we could be heard above the screaming abuse), which were controlled from the lighting booth. They were supposed to be turned off the moment you left the stage.

On one memorable show, I was ushering Pinocchio off stage to 'join me on Pleasure Island' (the kind of remark sure to get one arrested these days). As I passed the proscenium arch, off stage, my mike was supposed to be turned off.

It wasn't.

Instead, the audience were treated to Bragonzi telling Pinocchio, 'Get off the stage, ya little wooden bastard!'

Ah, the joys.

As you can imagine, doing this sometimes three shows a day (2 p.m., 5 p.m. and 8 p.m.), took its mental toll.

We became a cast of raging booze hounds. Every night a dressing room would take turns in becoming an impromptu cocktail bar, where we mixed the kind of drink only Lacroix could love, and stayed until we were kicked out. At which point we would go to the pub over the bridge (open till 2–3 a.m.).

By the end of the run of performances, I was reduced to a ball of aching genitalia and an enlarged liver.

I remember waiting during one performance in the vestibule behind the audience to make one of my grand entrances. I was dressed in a huge top hat and a floor-length red coat with zebra-stripe lapels. Inconspicuous – not!

I found myself with three young kids, whom I presumed had gone out to the toilet and were now on their way back in.

I smiled at them, and realising it was probably a big deal to be standing so close to one of the 'actors', I tried to put them at their ease as they stared slack-jawed at this prancing peacock.

'Hey, lads, enjoying the show?'

What followed was their succinct critical appraisal of my work.

'It's shite.'

SAM

My first introduction to panto was at the Citizen's Theatre, when as a very young boy I watched a middle-aged Graham playing a polar bear, or a man dressed as a penguin, being chased down the aisle by another creature, but little did I think, one day I'm going to work with *him*.

[*Graham: I have always drawn the line at playing animals.*]

[*Sam: Grrrrrrrr.*]

I love pantos and used to watch them and other plays at the Citz all the time, driving up from Cub Scouts in New Galloway. I was a sixer or a niner, I forget what they are, but I did have an impressive sleeve of worthless badges. Top toilet-roll maker, fastest tea handler, etc. I loved the badges and accessories. One of my first roles in panto was in a version of the Twits at the Citz, in which I played one of the birds.

The Citz was known for its very extravagant, rather camp shows, and my costume was a pair of high platform shoes, skin-tight sequin flares cut at the pubic bone – so barely enough to cover my crown jewels – a corset and a carnival headdress. Not panto as such, it was more a Christmas show. I tend to get the classier offers like *A Christmas Carol*, whereas Graham generally does more 'It's behind you!' Krankie-style pantos.

I think he'd make an excellent Captain Hook and I would love to play that part too – there are some amazing speeches – but sadly I'm just not old enough. Perhaps I could be Peter Pan to his Captain Hook. Then he could get his revenge. Finally. Graham: I've ALREADY played Captain Hook you ginger tufted bag of offal! You seriously have never read ANY of my contributions to this book!

Although come to think of it . . . Graham would also make an excellent Tinkerbell.

His Highland coo voice would make it hilarious.

21 December - Yule, Winter Solstice.

SAM

We've all heard of Yule logs (right?), Yule fires and Yule feasts, but what exactly was Yule? Well, it was an observance of the winter solstice that is still marked by Germanic (probably of Anglo-Saxon descent) and Norse cultures today. Central to the Vikings' Yule feast was a boar head decorated with laurel and rosemary, which would make a nice starter for the Grey Dog, but fill the rest of the guests up until Hogmanay. He'd be dabbing his whiskers with a napkin saying, 'Yes, yes, that was very good indeed. What's next?'

The Yule log tradition was started by the druids (Celtic priests), who lit a log to conquer the darkness of winter and ward off evil spirits, during a time when they believed the sun stood still for twelve days until it was reborn again on the shortest day known as Yule. Yules fires were lit for a similar reason and a way of marking the middle of winter.

Many Christmas traditions we have today are rooted in Celtic history (holly and ivy, mistletoe, gift-giving and making merry all played their part), but what is remarkable is that Christmas was actually BANNED in Scotland for 400 years. In fact, Christmas Day was only declared a public holiday in Scotland in 1958.

Before the Reformation in 1560 (when Henry VIII went around dissolving and ransacking the monasteries, seizing churches and executing his wives – come to think of it, he'd be a great case study for Andy McNab), Christmas in Scotland was merely another religious feast day. However, after the Reformation, the powerful Protestant Kirk frowned on anything that had even the faintest whiff of incense and passed a law in 1640 making Christmas festivities illegal. People still celebrated the feast day, but it didn't become an ingrained part of our culture until the mid-twentieth century.

CRACKING CASTLE OF THE MONTH
BLACKNESS CASTLE

GRAHAM

To fans of *Outlander*, Blackness Castle, on the south shore of the Firth of Forth, is forever the place where Jamie Fraser had the longest flogging scene in history. The whipping of Jamie went on for so long that if you look closely, you can see that Dougal's beard has grown by the end of it.

Tobias Menzies probably developed a hugely muscled right arm from all the thrashing he did. I'm not sure how many lashes Jamie received, but I think I stopped counting after the first 750.

[*Sam: A hundred. Twice.*]

Jamie survived, however. His back, now resembling a large, well-cooked piece of brisket, a permanent reminder to us all of the first of a number of painful encounters our friend has had at the hands of dear old Black Jack.

In fact, I had already spent a long time at the

fifteenth-century fortress many years before. I filmed *Macbeth* there in 1996. I played Banquo (my second time as the side-kick to Macbeth). It was a really great experience, filled with Scottish actor friends who filled out the roles of Macduff and Ross (Kenny Bryans and Iain Stuart Robertson), as well as working with Jason Connery as Macbeth.

In many ways it was like a precursor to my *Outlander* experience. Lots of guys, thrown together in a quintessentially Scottish setting, having a great time. I think I've said before that *Macbeth* is probably my favourite of Shakespeare's tragedies. Its pace, the action, the characters, are all tremendous. Looking back at the photos, it was also during the period where I was in complete denial about my hair loss.

Hair loss is a difficult subject for men. The first time I shaved my head was for a play at the Citizens Theatre in 1993. Prior to then, I'd spent the previous three years trying to pretend to myself that I wasn't going bald.

Mainly by refusing to look too closely at the top of my head.

The shaven-headed look for the Citizens plays worked well, but for some reason best known to myself, I decided to grow my hair again in time for *Macbeth*.

Looking at those photos now, my hair resembles a field of wavy corn that has been blighted in several places. I used to spend far too long combing it into place, in the hope that hair would miraculously start sprouting all over my scalp.

In the early days, I tried special shampoos, treatments, even visiting a 'trichology' clinic. I was being hopelessly ripped off, but it made me feel like I was doing SOMETHING!

If the hair transplants of today had been available then, I would probably have tried it.

But fortunately they weren't.

Now I can't imagine not having a shaved head. I would be horrified if I suddenly had a thick mane of hair. In many ways it helped my career, at a time when it was becoming fashionable to have a shaved head (prior to that you just looked like a criminal – mind you, perhaps I still do!).

But I digress.

Blackness Castle will always hold a special place for me. Not only because of *Macbeth*, but because it has become forever associated with two wonderful working experiences, and it stands as the swan song for my hair. After 1996 it was forever shaved. I feel like Black Jack would approve.

SAM

Blackness also holds some strong memories for me. Rather chilly, uncomfortable ones. When I filmed there, it was freezing! It wasn't quite Christmas but close enough, especially when I had to take my top off for the hundredth time and be whipped for being a ginger.

It was towards the beginning of Season One of *Outlander*, whilst the last wisps of Graham's hair were being blown away on the easterly breeze. The scene required me to take off my top and I had been training for months to look as butch as possible. For several hours that morning, my long-suffering but ceaselessly energetic make-up artist Wendy had been applying two prosthetic back pieces with vast amounts of glue. The 'cuts and subsequent scars' of the repeated whipping.

'Go'an, big man, yer looking braw,' she said, slapping me on the prosthetic back, as the last piece was then 'sprackled' with paint and fake blood (a painstaking process that can take hours and made me almost wish I was actually whipped instead). Tobias Menzies, playing the psychotic redcoat 'Black Jack Randall', was to go into a fury of whipping, leaving Jamie's back in tatters but yet, Jamie Alexander Malcolm MacKenzie Fraser, 'King of Men', lover of Claire, etc., would NOT scream or utter a word in defiance. It became a battle of wills, Black Jack trying to force Jamie into submission.

Tobias began the punishment, relishing the brutal treatment. He cracked the cat o' nine tails hard, a cruel whip with nine flails, used by the British military to mete out punishment. It was to hit the prosthetic, not TOO hard, as my back would be protected by the thick latex. I also had some padding shoved down the waistband on my kilt, to protect my arse (Black Jack would attack that later). However, the cat had different ideas and the strands whipped round the sides of the latex and caught my body on both sides.

As the camera was running, I didn't want to say anything and stayed in the moment. The crowd looked on. I held my breath as it whipped the sides of my back and stung like hell! Jamie's father was directed to faint and subsequently have a heart attack at watching his son being treated so badly. A really rough day for the Fraser family.

Being the consummate professional, I stayed silent and hung on to the iron cuffs tying me to the whipping post, the pain of the metal digging into my wrists helping me forget the pain in my back. It was a gruesome scene. Bits of the bloody back prosthetic would fly off as the whip slashed and cut. I'm glad to say I didn't lose my hair at Blackness, but I did leave with some rather spectacular red whip marks on either side of my back.

CLAN MACKINTOSH

GRAHAM

A few incidents have already been mentioned regarding the savagery of the Mackintosh clan, (their battle on the North Inch, the battle with the Farquharsons, their being one of the first clans to charge at Culloden – for more on these see *Clanlands*), but I think it is worth taking the time to look at their other great feud, with Clan Comyn.

The sheer number of feuds going on in Scotland at any one time was truly breath taking. It makes you wonder if there was some clan feud competition going on with a medieval version of Sam Heughan competitively trying to run the best, and most gob-smackingly violent feud!

The Mackintosh feud with the Clan Comyn (now known as Cumming) was a very bitter one indeed, as it involved the English (it was always guaranteed to add an extra helping of eye-watering bloodletting if the English were involved).

Before Robert the Bruce (he of the small horse and war axe), Clan Comyn was probably the most powerful clan in all of Scotland, claiming its lineage from not one but two Scottish kings.

In his quest for freedom and independence for Scotland, Bobby the B decided that the Comyns were most definitely 'in the way'.

Robert's elegant and straightforward solution to this obstacle was simply to murder the Chief of the Comyns in a churchyard, Greyfriars churchyard to be exact.

As usual in these situations, this caused a bit of a rift between the Bruce and the Comyn gang. So much so that the Comyns decided to fight for the English at Bannockburn (see JUNE).

This is where the Mackintoshes entered the story. They decided to stand against the Comyns and alongside the Bruce, thereby sealing an already bitter hatred between these two clans.

Jump forward just over a hundred years (a mere blink of an eye in the world of clan feuds) and the Comyns decided to steal a lot of Mackintosh land along with Castle Rait, which the Mackintoshes had called home since 1238.

As part of the seizure of land and castles, the Comyns hanged four boys on a nearby hill (to this day known as *Knocknagillean*, which translates as 'Hill of the Lads').

Guess what happened next? Yes, the Mackintoshes retaliated.

Cue the slaughter of a lot of people with the surname Comyn.

Then it was the turn of the Comyns to invade the Mackintosh lands of Moy and try to drown the Mackintoshes on the Isle of Moy, where 500 Mackintosh types were minding their own business. Along came the Comyns, who proceeded to build a dam downstream, like a gang of homicidal beavers, causing the loch to rise.

Seeing this imminent threat to the entire village, the clan chief had the very clever idea to ask who was the strongest swimmer there.

Rather foolishly, someone put up their hand.

He was then sent to swim and break the dam, thus drowning all of the Comyn warriors who were settling down to watch the fun. Unfortunately for our Mackintosh swimmer, he lost his life in the process.

No doubt he had a great song written about him though.

Probably exhausted by hundreds of years of slaughter, and no doubt running out of people to name Comyn, the Chief of the Clan decided to call a truce and sensibly invited the Mackintoshes to a celebratory feast at Castle Rait.

Always keen on a good meal, the Mackintoshes accepted the invitation.

I think you can sense where this might be going, can't you?

The Comyn Chief had plans that didn't involve relaxing over the cheese plate at the end of the meal.

Swearing his men to secrecy, he told them to ensure a Mackintosh was sat between them at dinner. This was seemingly done to reassure the Mackintoshes, but in fact it was to ensure that when a boar's head was brought into the banquet, each Comyn had a Mackintosh right next to him that he could stab in the heart.

Sneaky, I hear you say.

But love always finds a way to balls things up.

And so it was that the Comyn Chief's daughter was secretly in love with a Mackintosh warrior.

She met him at their usual spot. (A large stone – well, addresses were tricky in those days. They couldn't say, 'I'll meet you at the pub.' It had to be, 'I'll meet you at the usual enormous stone.') Before they got down to any saucy houghmagandy, the Comyn girl told her lover of the plot to kill them all.

Thus alerted, the Mackintoshes accepted the invitation, but took the precaution of carrying a dirk concealed in their plaids.

After what was probably an exceptionally long and boring speech by the Comyn Chief, the boar's head was brought in on a silver platter.

That was enough for the Mackintoshes. They leapt to their

feet while bellowing their war cry, 'Loch Moy!!!!', and proceeded to butcher the Comyns where they sat.

A few of them escaped death. Among them was the Chief of the Comyns, who was no fool. He knew that his daughter was spending a lot of time hanging around a big stone with one of the Mackintosh lads.

Before you could say *Fhad's a bhios maide sa choill, cha bhi foill an Cuimeineach* (this war cry translates as 'As long as there is wood in the forest, there won't be deceit from Clan Comyn' – ironic to say the least – and quite a mouthful when you're running into battle!!), big Chief Comyn had flown up the stairs chasing his deceitful daughter to give her a taste of his broadsword.

Seeing that Dad was in no mood for a quiet family sit-down to iron out the problems, she leapt out of the window, grabbing a curtain so she could swing out and drop into the arms of her waiting lover, who was clearly a strapping lad if he was able to catch a falling woman from a castle window!

But before she could do so, or because she had second thoughts about dropping thirty feet into the arms of her Mackintosh stud, she swung backwards towards her waiting father, who duly cut off both her hands with his gigantic sword.

Without the benefit of hands, the poor girl fell to her death.

Overcome with grief, the clan chief decided to abandon Castle Rait forever. It has not had a tenant to this day.

So, handily (if you'll forgive the pun), that finally put an end to the feud between the Comyns and the Mackintoshes.

NATURE NOTES
MISTLETOE (*VISCUM ALBUM*)

SAM

Kissing under the mistletoe probably goes back to the druids. Although Graham, who looks like a druid, may know more . . .

We don't really see people sporting mistletoe these days, it's all PlayStations and Xboxes. I don't even know where to find some, unless it's in the fruit and veg section of the local grocery store. Perhaps next to the mint and coriander.

For many cultures, the Romans included, mistletoe was a highly prized plant with medicinal and magical qualities. My first introduction to the plant was in the Asterix books as a boy, reading about Getafix the druid, who was always up an oak tree gathering the hemiparasitic plant.

Mistletoe signified fertility and there was even a Starz *Outlander* promo video for Season Three, which had clips of memorable snogs in the show happening under cartoon mistletoe with Christmas music playing. It was pretty cheesy, but very festive.

The plant was also a symbol of peace. If enemies met in woodland under mistletoe, they would drop their weapons and form a truce. I would like to do this with Graham one day, when we finally decide to stop giving each other grief, but I draw the line at kissing him.

GRAHAM

It's the time for festive fun, and who better to guide us through this most party-max of times than our very own resident hedonist, Duncan Lacroix.

I caught up with him on a rare night of complete sobriety and he imparted the following words of wisdom:

Duncan Lacroix's Christmas

1. First off, no point in coming to 'the party' that IS December without good preparation. Start training early. I recommend September at the latest (every other weekend, go balls out). Some start in January. Fair play to 'em.
2. Always have a Santa hat in your pocket. Santa is always welcome.
3. Crank up the volume mid-October so you hit your stride in time to gate-crash those early Christmas parties.
4. Whenever you feel like you may have drunk too much, get up and dance (full on, not any of that mincy, shuffling pish!). Sweating helps.
5. Learn how to make a great Christmas cocktail. I like the ones that you don't know are coming until your mouth goes numb.
6. Buy a sleigh. [*Sam: Or steal one.*]
7. Learn the lyrics to Slade's 'Merry Christmas Everybody!' and belt it out at every opportunity whilst posting on social media.
8. Cultivate a collection of chunky knit sweaters. [*Sam: Or just steal Graham's collection.*]
9. Run naked at least once in a built-up neighbourhood, but DON'T go local.
10. Take up pipe smoking.
11. Always carry a supply of airline sick-bags and a ball of string.

Happy Christmas!

28 December 1971/1970/1969 – The birth of Duncan Lacroix.

GRAHAM

28 December 1971 is reputedly the date of Duncan's birth, but it is hard to pin down the year exactly. It could've been 1969, '70 or '71. The doubt over his exact year points to the mystery surrounding his birth. Not so much 'born' as 'delivered to the Earth' by forces beyond our understanding.

[*Sam: I believe there was a seismic shift.*]

It is rumoured that the infant Duncan downed his first pint of Guinness at six months old, when reputedly he grabbed it from a relative and necked it in one. There are certainly photos of the baby Lacroix's crib filled with empty Tennent's lager cans, but so much of Duncan's arrival among us is shrouded in myth and portents.

While it is no doubt true that he had a considerable amount of chest hair on his tiny infant body (the photos exist), it is harder to prove the rumour that he punched the midwife.

Duncan has always lived an independent life, on the edge. He dabbled with the life of a hermit as a toddler, then burst onto the music scene at fifteen years of age as the inventor of hip-hop. He 'retired' at seventeen years of age citing emotional and nervous exhaustion, only to re-emerge two years later as Steve Jobs' mentor (something he rarely talks about). In his biography, Steve Jobs states, 'When I met Duncan Lacroix, I knew that I was in the presence of a revolutionary mind. I owe everything to those booze-soaked nights in Galway with the man I came to call "Father".'

Acting came late to Lacroix. Bored with being the trailblazer of technological innovation, and already on his third marriage, Lacroix headed to the Himalayas to become the first man to summit Everest while drinking a bottle of whisky. It was at the top of the world where he realised that theatre was calling him.

By the time he had gone back to Ireland, Lacroix had already played most of the major roles in Shakespeare along the way. His Lady Macbeth in Kathmandu is still spoken of to this day by those lucky enough to have seen it.

Leaving behind computer invention, theatre and a string of broken hearts, Lacroix was forced to make a difficult choice in 2013 – join forces with Elon Musk, who had begged him to help with developing rocket technology, or play Murtagh in *Outlander*.

Outlander was simply too big an opportunity to miss for a man who has conquered everything in his path. The rest is history.

ADVENTURE OF THE MONTH
HOGMANAY
31 DECEMBER & 1 JANUARY

SAM

If you have a party bucket list, put Hogmanay straight at number one, because there's honestly nothing like it – in Edinburgh there are four days and nights of events, street performers, concerts, cèilidhs, torchlit processions and the big Hogmanay party itself. It's the greatest New Year's Eve party in the world. In other parts of the world, New Year's Eve can be a big anti-climax (we've all had those nights), but never ever has a Hogmanay disappointed.

Now being 3.7 per cent Norwegian myself, I didn't know this Scandi DNA was responsible for my party genes. It's thought Hogmanay was brought over in the eighth and ninth centuries by the Vikings, who wanted to get fully on it and celebrate the arrival of the winter solstice or shortest day (now 21 December). In Shetland, the New Year is still called Yules, derived from the Scandinavian midwinter festival of Yule. Before Christmas became a public holiday in Scotland, most people worked over that period and only gathered for a party and exchange of presents at New Year.

The word Hogmanay comes from the seventeenth-century Norman French *hoguinané*, a form of the Old French *aguillanneuf*, meaning 'last day of the year, new year's gift'.

Impressed? I am!

Hogmanay Traditions
- Redding the House – clear your debts, clean the house, take the ashes out before the bell strikes midnight. Scots don't spring clean; they new year's clean, ready for a fresh start.

- Saining – I do this every year without fail. It's important to bless your house and livestock by flicking magical water everywhere from a river crossed by the living and the dead, then burn juniper branches before letting the fresh air in (because you've set all the smoke alarms off!).
- Fire Ceremonies – the fire processions ward off evil spirits, apparently.
- Hospitality – an important word in Scotland, especially at Hogmanay, when you should welcome as many friends and family as you can into your home and break bread and make merry.
- Cèilidh Dancing – pop a kilt on and do some traditional dancing.
- First-footing – the 'first foot' in the house after midnight should be a dark-haired male to ensure good luck. This probably goes back to Viking times, when a blonde stranger banging on your door wielding an axe left you on the 'back foot', rather than the 'right foot' to start a new year! The dark-haired male should bring pieces of coal (to keep the hearth warm), shortbread, salt, a black bun and a wee (make it a large!) dram of whisky.
- Singing – and shouting and slurring – Robert Burns 'Auld Lang Syne' immediately after midnight.
- Loony Dook – a new tradition that started in Edinburgh in 1986 as a Hogmanay hangover cure. Now up to a thousand people in crazy costumes throw themselves into the freezing water of the Firth of Forth.
- The Kirkwall Ba' Game – every Hogmanay, Orkney shopkeepers barricade their doors and windows in preparation for a chaotic mass football game, played with a cork-filled leather ball on the streets of Kirkwall between the Uppies and Doonies (the Doonies live north of the cathedral, and the Uppies, south).

I used to love going first-footing – visiting friends, neighbours and random households after the stroke of midnight. Whoever's house you stumbled into would return the gift of 'first-footing' with a drink to keep you warm on your journey . . . to the next household! It was basically a domestic pub-crawl, receiving a drink in every household before you stumbled home on New Year's Day. I remember when I was growing up in rural Scotland, the locals would leave their doors open with a bottle of whisky and some food on the table. If they were also out first-footing, you were welcome to let yourself in and help yourself to some sustenance. People were very trusting!

As a teenager, on Edinburgh's Princes Street, I watched the impressive fireworks light up Edinburgh Castle. My second favourite part of the evening was a particular time when a waterfall of fireworks would be ignited, cascading down the granite rocks and high stone fortifications. It looked like a waterfall of fire or lava, falling into the gardens below.

Thousands of revellers would line the streets and, at midnight, count down from ten to zero before bursting into song. Everyone would join hands in a rowdy rendition of 'Auld Lang Syne'. My favourite part was after the song, wishing everyone that passed by a 'Happy Neeeew Yyyeeaarrr!'

Occasionally you'd get a kiss or a hug from someone, hidden in a variety of winter clothing to keep out the bitter cold. It was hard to tell if they were a friend, or some random drunk stranger that was exceedingly happy.

Auld Lang Syne
Should auld acquaintance be forgot and never brought to mind?
Should auld acquaintance be forgot and auld lang syne
For auld lang syne, my dear, for auld lang syne,
We'll take a cup o' kindness yet, for auld lang syne.
Robert Burns, 1788

DRAM OF THE MONTH
A HET PINT

SAM

Carried in a copper kettle, a hot pint was offered to warm revellers on their first-footing rounds over a century ago and sounds rather delicious!

Ingredients

4 pints of mild ale
1 tsp grated nutmeg
4 oz sugar
3 eggs
½ pint of Scotch whisky

Method

Put the mild ale into a saucepan with a heavy base, add the nutmeg and bring to a simmer. Do not boil.

Stir in the sugar, dissolving it.

Beat the eggs thoroughly and gradually add the mixture to the ale, stirring all the time.

Add the whisky and turn up the heat. Do not boil.

Pour into heated tankards (not glass) and back into the saucepan. Repeat this until the liquid is clear and sparkling and then serve with a smile and a steady hand.

A Het Pint can also be made with white wine and brandy instead of ale and whisky.

[*Sam: Er, Graham, this could be a novel way to enjoy your New Zealand Sauvignon Blanc!*]

GREAT SCOT!

NOTABLE BIRTHDAYS, DEATHS AND SIGNIFICANT EVENTS

1 December 1787 – built by Robert Stevenson and Thomas Smith, Scotland's first lighthouse was lit at Kinnaird Head, Fraserburgh.

6 December 1745 – Charles Edward Stuart retreated from Derby.

8 December 1542 – Mary, Queen of Scots, was born at Linlithgow Palace. One of Scotland's most famous women (and most tragic), she reigned from 14 December 1542 until her forced abdication on 24 July 1567. Imprisoned for nineteen years in various castles in England by Queen Elizabeth I, she was deemed guilty of plotting against her and beheaded on 8 February 1587.

11 December 1970 – Ewan Bremner born in Edinburgh

24 December 1724 – General George Wade was appointed Commander-in-Chief of the British army in Scotland after he had reported on the need for military roads in the country.

25 December 1954 – Singer Annie Lennox OBE was born in Aberdeen.

28 December 1734 – Rob Roy MacGregor died.

31 December 1720 – Charles Edward Stuart was born in Rome.

GRAHAM

It seems fitting to end this book with the birthday of Bonnie Prince Charlie. I wonder what he'd think of all that has been written about him, never mind the films, TV series and even this Almanac.

He was born in Rome on 31 December 1720, and was named Charles Edward Louis John Casimir Sylvester Severino Maria Stuart.

[*Sam: I often think Graham must have some similar middle names that he dare not impart to me, for fear of ridicule.*]

Charles, like his father and grandfather before him, grew up with a strong and unshakeable belief in the divine right of kings. I mean, when you're a king, why not go the whole hog and believe you are chosen by God himself?

In December 1743, his dad, James II, named him Prince Regent, which meant that he had the authority to speak and act AS the King himself. He didn't waste much time gathering a couple of French ships and sailing to Eriskay in Scotland, to begin his ill-fated rebellion against what he saw as those pesky German usurpers, the Hanoverians! Considering he himself was Italian, this seems a little bit like the divine pot calling the secular kettle black.

By now we all know what happened in the rebellion of 1745 and if we don't, it's about time you re-read *Clanlands* and watched *Men in Kilts* and *Outlander*!

[*Sam: Mark me!*]

After the ill-fated Battle of Culloden, he finally managed to hitch a ride on a French ship in September 1746. You can find a cairn on the shores of Loch nan Uamh in Lochaber that marks the spot where Bonnie Prince Charlie departed Scotland forever.

He settled in France, where he decided to devote himself to numerous love affairs, including living with Clementina Walkinshaw (with whom he had a daughter Charlotte). He had met Clementina during the rebellion, although many believe she was in fact a Hanoverian spy.

Charlie wasn't going to give up on being King, however. Even going to the lengths of visiting to London in secret and converting to Protestantism in the hope it might help his cause.

It didn't.

He re-converted to Catholicism a few years later.

Then, in 1759, during the Seven Years War, Charles was invited to meet with the French foreign minister, who was planning to invade England with a colossal force of 100,000 men. He wanted to bring Charlie along with as many Jacobites as he could. But one meeting with the prince was enough to change his mind about inviting him to that particular party.

As it was, the invasion was soundly beaten off in a series of naval battles while Charles languished on the continent, by all accounts boozing heavily and generally being a bit of a royal pain in the ass.

Even Pope Clement XIII was less than impressed, refusing to give him the same recognition of being King that he had given to his recently deceased father, James.

In 1772, Charlie wed Princess Louise of Stolberg-Gedern, a marriage that ended eight years later amid accusations of spousal abuse, but not before Louise of the extravagant German surname had been busy testing the royal mattress with another man.

Finally, the handsome prince came to the end of his life, a bloated, lonely alcoholic figure in Rome, dying on 30 January 1788, aged sixty-seven.

It was exactly 139 years TO THE DAY since his great-grandfather Charles I was beheaded on that wintery morning in London.

Now that's what I call bad timing.

[*Sam: And the rest is, as they say, history – with a great big dollop of romantic fiction.*]

EPILOGUE

SAM

Well, what a journey through Scotland. A year spent in the company of two friends that despite their constant bickering and thinly veiled competition, are currently in a loving embrace, sharing a large dram or twelve of Sassenach. It has been our pleasure to share with you some insights, anecdotes and useless wisdom about our bonnie wee country.

We hope you have enjoyed this epic adventure through the calendar year. I feel ready to do it all again! And we have so much to look forward to, Graham and I are working on a number of projects, together and apart, and we hope there will be another *Men in Kilts*, certainly more *Outlander*, and you can always count on us getting together for another escapade or two. Join us on the next one!!!

Until then . . . *Sláinte*!

Now pass the bottle, my friend!

ACKNOWLEDGEMENTS

Sam

This really is a unique wee book and it would never have come into existence without the foresight and creativity of the brilliant Briony Gowlett, the hard work and dedication of Charlotte Reather and the consistently charming, (many times) bloodthirsty ramblings of my bearded travel companion Graham McTavish. Thank you to them and to everyone in this book, too many to mention but I'll try: Wendy, Duncan, Caitriona, Marina, Sophie, Richard and all of my Outlander friends. Alex and the GGC team. My brilliant Agents Ruth, Theresa, Zoe, Thea. My family and of course my mother, Chrissie.

Graham

To everyone who has been there when I needed them (that list is long). You know who you are but here are some special mentions:

Garance, my daughters Honor and Hope. My comrades in arms, Dougy, Paul, Paddy, Chris and Mark.

All of those wonderful folk who have helped me put food on my table:

My manager, Cheri, Dawn, Caitlin and everyone at CAM, Glenn, Adrian, Adam and all at Artists Representatives, and, of course, Zoe at United Agents.

Once again my thanks go out to Briony Gowlett and the great people at Hodder & Stoughton, and the ever patient Charlotte Reather. Thank you both for guiding us on our second journey together, and reining in my more eccentric scribblings.

Thank you also to our wonderful *Men in Kilts* director Kevin Johnson, and all at Boardwalk, as well as our stellar crew who made our wee road trip into a joy and, most importantly, kept me alive. Next time you have to wear a kilt too, Kevin!

Last, but not least, my driver, companion, gentle tormentor, co-author, borderline lunatic, and dear friend, Sam Heughan: For making me laugh, face my fears, and learn new lessons about the joys of companionship, I can't imagine doing any of this with anyone else, mate.

Charlotte

I'd just like to thank my patient husband, Ed, and my children, Tallulah, 6, and Matilda, 4, who still talk about Sam and Graham like they're family. That is until they hatched a plan to 'get rid of them so they could have Mummy back!'

FURTHER READING

WEBSITES
electricscotland.com
highlandtitles.com
outlanderlists.weebly.com
rampartscotland.com
scotclans.com
scotlandinfo.eu
scotlandwelcomesyou.com
undiscoveredscotland.co.uk
visitscotland.com
wild-scotland.org.uk
scottishwildflowers.org

AUTHOR BIOGRAPHIES

Sam Heughan is an award-winning actor and philanthropist, best known for his starring role as Jamie Fraser in the hit TV show *Outlander*. From his early days at the Royal Court Theatre to his most recent role in the forthcoming *Text For You* movie, featuring Priyanka Chopra and Celine Dion, Sam has enjoyed a career in theatre, television and film spanning almost two decades. He has created a multi- award-winning whisky business (shamefully plugged in this book), created and produced his first, critically acclaimed TV show: *Men in Kilts* and become a *New York Times* bestseller with the former *Clanlands* book. With his growing success and fame, Sam has also lent his voice and platform to raise funds and awareness for many notable charities, including Marie Curie UK and Blood Cancer UK. In recent years he has raised over $5 million for blood cancer research, hospice care, food banks, the environmental defence fund and testicular cancer awareness education. Due to his outstanding contribution to charitable endeavours and artistic success he was bestowed by the University of Glasgow and the University of Stirling with an honorary doctorate in 2019. His next endeavour is to convince McTavish to jump out of an aeroplane, in a kilt.

Author photo © Dave Foster

Graham McTavish has always sought out danger while simultaneously overcoming life's challenges, since his early days as an explorer for the Royal Geographical Society. His work amongst the people of the Yuqui tribe in Bolivia was enough to have a small shrine erected to him by those shy, humble people. His collection of awards is small but deeply meaningful to him. Of special significance is his award for services to the little-known world of miniature reindeer husbandry.

He is the proud patron of the 'Miniature Reindeer Society of Saariselkä' in Finland. It was as a cycle courier, first in Delhi, then London, that Graham really caught the acting bug. After performing in amateur theatre he finally went professional and had to give up his on-and-off work as a trapeze artist. He has now been acting for over 35 years in theatre, film and television. On film and TV he is best known for his roles as Dougal MacKenzie in *Outlander*, the fierce Dwarf Dwalin in the *Hobbit* trilogy, Dracula in *Castlevania*, and Djikstrea in *The Witcher*, among many other characters beginning with the letter 'D'. He has performed in theatre all over the world from the Royal National Theatre in London with Ingmar Bergman, to the Metropolitan Museum of Art in New York with his own play co-written with the artist Nicholas Pace. He now finds himself as co-creator and producer of *Men in Kilts*, something that would definitely make his Father smile. He has, obviously, also sung opera at La Scala in Milan. He is doubly delighted that the dream of his 12-year-old self to be a published author has finally come true . . . again!!

Author photo © Dave Foster

Charlotte Reather is a leading country lifestyle journalist, columnist and comedy writer. She is also the co-writer of the bestselling *Clanlands* by Sam Heughan and Graham McTavish and *Extreme Fishing* by Robson Green (2013). She lives in West Sussex with her husband (a former Royal Marine) and two daughters, and is currently writing her first novel.

charlottereather.com / @charlottereather

Author photo © Matthew Davidson